MEMOIRS OF A MAGMAN:
P.I. & Crooked Cops

◊

Volume One

ALFRED J. HUDON

iUniverse LLC
Bloomington

Memoirs of a Magman: P.I. & Crooked Cops
Volume One

iUniverse books may be ordered through booksellers or by contacting:

iUniverse LLC
1663 Liberty Drive
Bloomington, IN 47403
www.iuniverse.com
1-800-Authors (1-800-288-4677)

Because of the dynamic nature of the Internet, any Web addresses or links contained in this book may have changed since publication and may no longer be valid. The views expressed in this work are solely those of the author and do not necessarily reflect the views of the publisher, and the publisher hereby disclaims any responsibility for them.

ISBN: 978-1-4502-5321-5 (sc)
ISBN: 978-1-4502-5322-2 (e)

Printed in the United States of America

iUniverse rev. date: 12/03/2013

To my friend Police Officer
Sgt, Bill Kelly. Without Your
Encouragement this book
Would not have been written.

CHAPTER 1
Memoirs of a Magman: P.I. and Crooked Cops

After clicking away on the computer keyboard for a few days, I read over the dozen or so pages I had written. I highlighted the pages and then hit the delete key, and they were gone. Again I began typing, as I had done many times before. After reading what I had written, I deleted the pages every time, because they didn't make much sense. I was attempting to write about my past experiences as a private investigator My friend Kelly had come up with the bright idea that I write about my experiences after he read some of the notes I had kept over the years about my work.

Before I began, I knew that I had a few major problems that Kelly wasn't aware of. I had a problem with spelling and with grammar; I felt that to be successful at writing; I would need those two main "ingredients." I compared writing without spelling and grammar to trying to cook up a great meal without using the right ingredients. I had no problem conversing with people in a proper manner or writing business letters and reports, but when it came time to try to write a lengthy story that could easily be understood by readers, I found it rather difficult. When I attempted to do so, I soon realized that writing wasn't for me. I sure didn't want to make an ass of myself; so after a lot of writing and deleting, I decided it would be in my best interest to forget about Kelly's wise suggestion.

A month or so later, my good friend Kelly, a sergeant with the Royal Canadian Mounted Police, stopped by the office and said that he was being transferred to Nova Scotia. Kelly had another few years to serve before retiring; as for me, after working in the private security industry for over forty-five years, I was contemplating retirement. When I mentioned that to Kelly, he replied, "Then you'll have plenty of time to work on your book."

One afternoon he came to the office to pick me up for lunch; at the time I was occupied with someone, so Kelly went to the rear office to wait till I was finished. After a few minutes, he hollered, "Fred! What are all those yellowish notes on the desk? They look like they have been here for years."

I replied, "They're just notes I've kept about my work that I'm going to shred."

"Mind if I read a few?" he asked.

"No, go ahead," I replied. "It's just a lot of crap, but you may find some of it amusing."

Later, while we were having lunch, Kelly said, "You know, Fred; I found those notes of yours interesting. If I were you, before disposing of them, I would enter them in the computer. Someday you should write about your experiences."

I asked, "What do you mean, write about them?"

"A book!" he replied.

I couldn't help but laugh. "Are you serious?"

"Yes, why not? You have good stuff, and it would make interesting reading. It could show businesspeople how to go about dealing with problems that they encounter within their businesses."

Kelly wasn't aware of the problem that I had with spelling, and I wasn't overly excited about his idea that I write a book, but I did say I'd think about it when I retired. A few months after Kelly made the suggestion, I looked over some of my notes and began typing away on the keyboard. Beside my grammar and spelling, I also had another problem—I am a two-finger typist. That in itself would make it very difficult for anyone to write a lengthy book. Even if I were successful, by the time I finished, I could be very old. If loss of memory crept in; I'd be asking myself, *What the hell is that all about?*

Kelly stopped by another time to say that he was going to Nova Scotia, and he and I went to a nearby restaurant. Kelly again brought up the subject of my notes, asking if I had thought of doing anything with them. I said, "Yes, and not only did I think about it, I also tried writing, and it just didn't work out."

"What's the problem?" he asked

I looked at him and said, "Well, Kelly, I'll tell you what the problem is; I have a few. Number one, I have a problem with spelling. The second is my grammar."

"I don't see anything wrong with your grammar; you're a well-spoken person."

I said, "Yeah! But it's different when I try to put things in writing."

"As for your spelling," said Kelly, "you're not the only one who has that problem. We have university graduates who can barely spell or read. I read a good number of your notes, and I found no problem with your spelling or your writing.

I said, "Yeah, but it's quite different when I try; besides the problems that I mentioned, when I read over what I wrote, it just didn't make any sense."

Kelly replied, "Just keep it simple. Today you don't need to be a genius to write a book. If you check the book stores, you'll find that some of the books don't interest a lot of people."

I smiled. "Yes, I agree with you, and I feel that's probably what will happen with my book."

"No!" said Kelly. "I don't believe so, because you'll be writing about issues that people will find interesting and could benefit from."

When Kelly said that, I thought back to a brief article that I had written that appeared in the newspaper shortly after I arrived in town; I called it "Taking care of business." It focused on store operators' rights and the laws that were in place for them to use whenever they encountered acts of theft by shoppers and staff. Shortly after the article was published, I received calls from a few business owners, saying that they appreciated what I had written because it outlined how they could go about dealing with certain issues. The article was all about store operators taking precautions to protect themselves. At the time, back in the 80s, the local police department didn't have the program now called "Crime Prevention," when a police officer pays a visit to businesses to talk about the issue of protection against theft. Months after I had written about the problem, one day, I noticed Officer John driving around town with a sign on his police vehicle doors that said Crime Prevention Officer. Frenchie later told me that after the police chief read my article, where I explained the difference between police officers' responsibilities and security officers' responsibilities; he decided to appoint an officer to go around town talking about the issue of crime prevention. I had written that police officers usually wait for a crime to happen and then they try and solve the crime, but most security officers are trained to prevent certain crimes. As far as I was concerned, the main part of our work as security officers was prevention. I ended the article by stating: "If a criminal act such as theft was prevented from happening, that would mean that police officers would have more time to deal with other important issues." Frenchie mentioned why the police chief had decided to have an officer go around to talk to people, saying, "Oh, yes. It bothered him, and he seemed pissed off when he read what you said about preventing crimes."

I thought about the article I had written and the reaction from business operators who had read it, and I said to Kelly, "You could be right. Maybe I'll give it another try later." A few months after Kelly left for Nova Scotia, he called and invited Wilma and me to go and spend a weekend with him and his lovely wife. I accepted, and we spent a couple of days in Halifax, which we enjoyed very much. I missed Kelly after he had left; he and I were close friends. He again brought up the subject of my writing a book. I hadn't said anything to Wilma about what Kelly had suggested, so she asked, "What is that all about his writing a book?"

I quickly answered, "Oh, it's nothing. Kelly suggested that I try my hand at writing a book about my work."

Kelly said, "Oh, yeah! I'm sure it would be interesting." He again mentioned that it could be useful for business operators or individuals contemplating going into business.

Wilma, after giving me a serious glance, laughed and said, "Kelly, have you ever seen Fred use a computer?"

"No," he replied, "not really, but he did mention that you had a lot of experience and were good at it; maybe you could give him a hand getting started."

Again she laughed. "Are you serious? Help him write a book? You don't know what he's like; I could end up in a mental institution or have a serious heart attack." Seeing the expression on her face, we laughed to change the topic.

I said, "Don't worry, Kelly, someday I may find a way to get it done."

Wilma joked, "Oh, yeah, I'm sure!"

For the next couple of years, I kept pretty busy and didn't think any more about writing, until one day when I was having a coffee with Yolanda, who, like Kelly, was a close friend; when I mentioned to her that I was going to retire and that I would be closing my office, she asked, "What are you going to do once you do?"

I replied, "Oh! I'll still do some work, but I will choose what I want to do."

Yolanda responded, "You'll be semi-retired?"

I said yeah, and just to see what she would say, I added, "And besides that, I was thinking of writing a book."

I expected her to laugh, but instead she gave me a serious look and said, "Fred, that would be a good idea. You'll have a lot to write about."

I grinned and said, "Yeah, maybe so, but you're aware of my problem."

She asked, "What's that?"

I replied, "Spelling, which you know I'm not too good at."

She answered, "That's really no problem! The computer will automatically correct any misspelled words. Before you begin, all you need to do is click on the spelling and grammar correction on the computer, and each time you misspell a word, the computer will correct it."

I was unaware of that. "Oh! Really?"

"Yes," she replied. "Whenever I'm typing fast, I make mistakes, and the computer indicates the corrections.

I knew that if I needed any advice, Yolanda was the right person to talk to, because before she opened her own secretarial business, for years she was the secretary for the Regional Industrial Commission that owned the building complex where I worked. My office was just down the hall from where she worked; I was doing security work for the Commission whenever I was needed. As time went on, she and I became good friends. One day after I had written up a report concerning work that I had completed for the Commission and brought it to her office, she came to see me and pointed out a word that I had misspelled. I said to her, "I need to be more careful, because when it comes to spelling, I'm not too hot."

She laughed it off, saying, "Don't worry about it. I'll correct it." As she was leaving, with a friendly smile she said, "By the way, if you care to, whenever you need a business letter typed, I'll be glad to do it for you. You handwrite it, and I'll rewrite it using my computer. That way, it will also look more business-like."

I replied, "That's nice of you."

She said, "Your handwriting is neat and easy to understand, but like I said, it would be more impressive to have it typed."

I replied, "Okay, whenever I have something lengthy that needs typing, as long as you don't charge too much, I'll bring it over for you to do."

She answered, "Don't worry about the charge."

That was the beginning of having Yolanda do my typing for me. While she was with the Industrial Commission, she continued to do so. Whenever I'd offer to pay, she shrugged it off, saying, "When you're out, bring me a coffee." After she left and started her own business, we continued being friends, and often I used her service. Yolanda was about ten years younger than I and very attractive, but our relationship never went beyond friends. At times, we'd go and have lunch or just a coffee together. Yolanda was a special type of friend who was always there and asked for little in return. I have found that dealing with people in today's society, it's mostly about "me" and "what can I get?" rather than "what can I give?" With Yolanda, it was reversed. She got pleasure from helping people, and it wasn't all about her, which I find is rare today.

After I mentioned the book to Yolanda and she said that I could use the computer to correct my spelling and grammar, I said to her, "Okay, I'm going to give it a try. How about when I have a certain number of pages done, you review my work or rewrite it if needed?"

She replied, "Sure, that's no problem."

When I returned to the office, the first thing I did was to boot up the computer. I went into Tools and clicked on spelling and grammar, and then I proceeded to type a few sentences, purposely misspelling a few words. As Yolanda promised, the misspelled words were instantly corrected or the computer indicated that the word wasn't spelled correctly; I could then look it up in the dictionary. Once I had a bit more confidence, the question was, how would I begin? What would I write about?

A few nights later, after reading over some of my many notes, I once again began typing away on the keyboard. After I had completed a few pages, I read them over and found that I was doing much better than my previous attempts, thanks to the spelling and grammar corrector, but I deleted those pages too. How should I begin? I thought of what Kelly said: "Keep it simple." I decided that was just what I would do. To do so, I needed to go back to when I first got into private security.

I directed my writing toward small business owners and operators. As Kelly mentioned, I felt they could benefit from my experiences as a private investigator and security consultant. Approximately 80 percent of my work consisted of acts of theft and fraud, and that was the subject I chose to write about. The remaining 20 percent would focus on people I dealt with and their personal problems, including my own.

CHAPTER 2
Interrelated Experiences and Advice

For ten years prior to getting into private security, I had done other types of work and was known as an easy-going person. I liked people and usually found a reason to have a smile on my face. That quickly changed soon after I began working as a private investigator; I found very little to smile about. Some issues that I dealt with were amusing at times; some were a bit sad, and others were downright disgusting.

Two major problems that business operators have to deal with in some form or other each day are theft in the workplace, an escalating problem, and theft committed by outsiders. For store operators, dealing with shoplifters is a continuous problem. Addressing issues of theft in the workplace involves first the rights of the business operator and second the rights of the workers.

I'll define a corrupt employee and suggest the correct approach for a business operator to deal with that problem. Bear in mind that a deceitful employee cannot only hurt business operators financially; they can also cause a good deal of stress and trouble among other, more honest employees who are there to do an honest day's work. Thieves, whether employees or outsiders, such as shoplifters, are much more educated today in both the act of committing theft and their rights. Yes, even thieves have rights, because of union and labour regulations. If employees are not unionized, labour boards fight for them. At one time, an employee could easily be dismissed, but today, it's a different story. So if a business operator doesn't want problems from either of these organizations, which go out of their way to protect corrupted workers, it would be wise for business operators to educate themselves about labour laws and regulations regarding employees. Otherwise, they could find themselves in a costly and stressful legal situation.

Regarding employees who continually steal from their employers: I have found that that type of theft isn't restricted to the ordinary employee; theft is also committed big time by people who hold positions of trust, such as managers, supervisors, and unscrupulous bookkeepers who are good with figures, especially when it comes to covering up their devious thefts.

Some of the complex problems that business operators have to deal with each day can become very costly and complicated, especially if an operator doesn't have the knowledge or know-how to deal with unpleasant issues. Over the years, I often said to business operators that being successful is all about taking care of business. Whether a personal or business problem, you'll find great relief once you have found the solution and know how to resolve issues; most importantly, having knowledge and know-how leads to solving problems. Deceitful employees and others who intend to rip you off can be very cunning. It could be a close member of your family.

The word *steal* is defined as "means to commit theft." Over the years, I have often used the phrase *ripped off,* as in "You've been ripped off." Theft comes in many forms, but it can be broken down into two main components: the actual *act* of committing theft and the *intent* to commit theft. There is a great deal of variance between the two; however, to commit theft, a person or persons must actually be in possession of the stolen property. In other words, anyone who leaves or even tries to leave their workplace with property they do not rightfully own commits an act of theft and can therefore be charged under the Criminal Code of Canada. The word *property* carries a wide definition and means most anything that one personally owns, from simple office supplies to more expensive merchandises. Stealing means taking such items and converting them to one's own use.

As for an intent to commit an act of theft, the law provides that even if a crime is not committed, everyone who has the intent to commit an offence or admits to doing anything for the purpose of carrying out his or her intention can be found guilty of an attempt to commit the offence. Whether or not it was possible under the circumstances to commit the actual offence is a question of law. In other words, the courts will look at the facts to determine if an act of intent to commit the crime was demonstrated. Evidence of similar acts done by the accused prior to or after the offence with which he or she is charged is admissible to establish a pattern of conduct. It appears that if the accused has perpetrated enough actual thefts so that his or her intention to steal could easily be ascertained from these acts, he or she could be guilty of at least a charge of attempted theft.

An important factor that a business owner should consider before bringing criminal charges against an employee or employees is the repercussions that may occur if criminal charges are indeed laid in court, whether the accused is found guilty or acquitted. If the accused is found guilty, there could be no repercussion, legal or otherwise, against the owner. But if the accused is acquitted by the court, giving him or her the benefit of the doubt; the way is open for the accused to institute legal proceedings in damages against the owner. His or her chances for success in such action will depend on the quality of evidence introduced at his or her original trial. Chances are very slim that he or she would succeed, unless of course the evidence presented in court was mere fabrication.

If the accused is found guilty of a charge of attempted theft, the possibility of legal action on behalf of the accused against the owner is very remote. If the accused is acquitted, his or her chances to succeed in an action against the owner will depend on the quality of evidence submitted at the original trial.

The owner who had the employee arrested could also be held responsible for damages on account of false arrest; however, such legal counteraction would only succeed if the accused-turned-plaintiff could convincingly demonstrate before the court that he or she was deliberately victimized by the owner or his representative.

Regarding repercussions that one may encounter in dealing with a corrupt employee or employees: repercussions could come in many forms. There is no getting around the fact that such situations place a great deal of stress on a person. With that in mind, I strongly recommend that unless an employee is caught in the actual act of committing a crime, it would be wise not to have the individual arrested. It's a simple rule of thumb—when in doubt, do not arrest. So, what options are then open to the business person who suspects an employee or employees of stealing? I'll outline the correct manner and the tools that can be used to assist in the apprehension of a dishonest employee in the act of committing a criminal offence.

To begin with, having firm, irrefutable evidence for the court—evidence that will lead to an actual conviction of theft—is so important that it cannot be stressed enough. One of the most serious mistakes I have encountered over the years is people hurrying to have criminal charges brought before the court without having solid evidence to back up their case usually because of an employer's general inexperience with dealing with employees who are ripping them off. Having some knowledge regarding how the police and the courts view someone charged with theft is an asset. If the courts are in doubt in regards to the evidence presented before them, a conviction will not be handed down—it's as straightforward as that. Therefore, I recommend not rushing when gathering evidence. When in doubt, an employer has time to wait, due to the simple fact that a dishonest employee keeps stealing.

I have found that employees who say they stole only once (that happens very rarely) usually share the same story when they are caught in the act: "This is the first time I ever did anything like that;" "I don't know why I did it, but I will never do it again," etc. When I hear an accused tell me that, I think back to an incident some years back when I was involved in retail security. One evening, a young woman was brought to the office after she had been caught shoplifting. Responding to questioning as to why she had stolen the merchandise, she tearfully pleaded it was the first time, and she really didn't know why she did it. After listening to a lecture on stealing and what could happen to her if she continued, she was put out of the store, with no charges laid against her. The following morning, I was in court on another security matter and suddenly noticed the same young woman seating directly in from of me. Imagine my surprise when she was called up in front of the judge while the prosecutor read off no less than four—count them, four—shoplifting charges against her. Three of them had been committed on the same day, meaning that she was caught at three different locations and charged with theft. So much for the story she told me about it being her first time and how she would never do something like that again!

In retail security, very seldom would I have criminal charges laid against a shoplifter, due to the fact that most of one's time could be spent in the courts. After seeing how leniently most shoplifters were treated by the courts, I felt it was a waste of time being there, because very little punishment would ever be handed down. Most would be given a lecture by the judge and sent home. It seemed that for the courts, for whatever reason, shoplifting was just not regarded as a very serious offence. And when one hears someone referred to as a shoplifter, it really does not sound that serious. However, if you hear someone refer to another person as a thief, that sounds far more serious, doesn't it? The word shoplifter is a mild word used to refer to someone who is caught stealing merchandise from a store. Personally, and I'm sure there are few merchants who would disagree, I believe a thief is a thief, and they should all be dealt with accordingly in the courts, no matter what label is given to them by society. A thief who steals from his or her employer or one who steals merchandise from a store is no different from a thief who steals someone's purse or wallet—an act of theft in any form is an act of theft.

As I see it, the only difference between the two is what was stolen and the actual cost of the items which were taken. A person could walk into a store and steal a pair of fifty dollar shoes and get away with it. The next day, the same individual goes to work and rips off his or her employer for a hundred dollars from the cash register. It could be a hundred dollars' worth of groceries that she or he passed over the counter to a family member or friend so the true cost of the items weren't entered into the cash register. (For example, if the merchandise cost $115 but the person working the cash only rang in items for the amount of $15, the store is out $100.) The only difference between the two acts committed is in the amount. The crimes are the very same—both incidents are theft, pure and simple, just carried out in different ways.

If the person who stole the shoes had been caught by the store's security personnel and charged, the person would be looked upon as a shoplifter. If the person was caught handing the groceries over the counter without charging the full amount, that person would be referred to as a thief if a criminal charge was laid. Personally, if I were a dishonest person, I would prefer that someone refer to me as a shoplifter rather than a thief. The word *thief* sounds harsh; it doesn't have that quiet ring to it like *shoplifter* does. But while *shoplifter* is a far milder word, no matter what other name or definition is used, a thief is a thief. People may have different techniques and reasons for stealing, but at the end of the day it all amounts to the same illegal act. If one person is involved in a small-time theft while another steals on a bigger scale, they have both stolen.

For example, let's say you have an employee who steals ten dollars a day from you, whether in cash or merchandise; a second employee who works out in the warehouse occasionally steals a couple of hundred dollars' worth of merchandise. Who would you say is the worst employee, the one who steals only ten dollars a day from your business on a regular basis or the bigger thief out in your warehouse who is ripping you off every so often for a couple of hundred dollars? Actually, the employee who's ripping you off on a daily basis could be your worst employee, because he or she does it every day and gets away with it. If the person is not dealt with, sooner or later that employee will not be satisfied with just stealing ten dollars. Such a worker will steal hundreds until someone catches them in the act, but by then the employer may have already been taken for thousands.

Do you realize if you are being ripped off by any employees? Perhaps you are one of the fortunate employers who doesn't have that problem. Perhaps you are just too busy to notice. As one business operator put it: "I knew I was being taken, but what could I do about it?" That line of thought brings to mind a story about a dentist I'll refer to as Mr. Conrad. Although he had a huge clientele and worked fifteen to sixteen hours a day, for years he drove around an old, broken-down car, because he felt he couldn't afford a new one. One day, parked outside a shopping mall waiting for his wife, he noticed one of his office staff driving up in a new car. He began to wonder how she could afford a new car on the salary he was paying her. He was well aware that she had a few school-age children and a husband who very seldom worked.

The more he thought about it, the more concerned he became, because part of her job was taking care of the books, which was something he very seldom bothered to review. Understandably suspicious, he decided one weekend to look over the office ledgers to see if anything that looked out of order in the numbers. Not surprisingly, Mr. Conrad soon discovered that the receptionist had been ripping him off big time. The more he searched, the more he found. Over the years, she had been fixing the books and pocketing a large amount of money.

After he got rid of his corrupt receptionist, he'd often laugh about it. "There I was, working my behind off and driving around in an old, battered car, while my receptionist was sporting around in a new vehicle, living high on the hog with my money." While the dentist had a good sense of humour, he had learned a very costly lesson in regard to honest bookkeeping and taking care of his business. And that's but one of thousands of stories concerning theft in the workplace. Theft comes in many forms; these criminal acts are committed on a regular basis by many employees—and, sad to say, even by family members.

It is not just the average Joe or Sue who's ripping off employers, either. People in high positions are more experienced at it than the average person; whenever they steal, the scale is big-time. Some of the most deceitful people I have encountered over the years were those who held highly respected jobs. One was actually the president of a large business. That individual, whom I shall refer to as Mr. Claude, operated a couple of franchised stores and restaurants and a few condominiums. I was hired by him to investigate a couple of young women employed as cashiers. He knew they were stealing money but wasn't sure how they were going about it.

After a week or so on the job, not only was I able to prove the two young women had a scam going, but I soon discovered Mr. Claude was not exactly a candidate for Business Person of the Year—he was dealing in stolen credit cards.

I'll start with the two dishonest cashiers. When customers paid for their merchandise and left the store without picking up their receipts from the counter; the pair would pick them up and cancel the sale that was previously entered and place the receipts in the cash register. Once the store was closed and the two cashiers were reconciling their cash drawers, they would pocket money equal to the cancelled receipts.

They also had a smooth way of obtaining the receipts from customers, especially elderly ones. At the end of the cash transaction, instead of handing the receipt over to the customer, the cashier would make it appear that she had placed the receipt into the shopping bag—instead, she would carefully drop the receipt on the floor. After the customer left, she picked it up to make use of later.

When the investigation was over and I had gathered sufficient evidence, the two were taken to the office and confronted with the theft. As expected, they denied any wrongdoing. After I went over the evidence with them, they were given the choice of either facing up or having the police called in and criminal charges laid. After the consequences of what they would have to endure if the police were summoned were explained, they quickly agreed it would be in their best interest if they dealt with us instead.

Reluctantly, they admitted to stealing a small amount of money, but before the interrogation was over, it was learned that between them, they had stolen more than—wait for it—$50,000 in a two-year period. A portion was used to buy a new car, which they both shared. Most of the stolen money was eventually paid back to the store by their parents, who were called to the store and shown the evidence that clearly implicated their daughters. The agreement was that the police would not be involved and no charges would be laid against the two as long as the stolen money was recovered.

As for Mr. Claude—some of the most deceitful people I have met have been among society's upper ranks, and that fellow was a high-class thief who dined with bankers and shareholders. One day during my investigation of the two young women, I was approaching a doorway when I overheard Mr. Claude speaking to another man. Through the crack of the doorway, I saw Mr. Claude with a credit card in his hand. As he spoke, he cleaned off the credit card with a tissue, as if removing his fingerprints, and then he handed the card to the other man. "Here, take that card. Tomorrow, come to the store and spend a few hundred dollars. Later, return again and do the same"; those were his instructions.

Sure enough, the owner had his own scam going; involving stolen credit cards or cards obtained from the store. A number of the cards had been left on the counter by customers. Whenever a card was found, it would be dutifully turned in to the office. If the unfortunate soul who had left the card didn't return to retrieve it, the owner would take the credit card and give it to a certain person to use for shopping in his store. The card would be used to buy six or seven hundred dollars' worth of merchandise. The following day, the man who was involved in Mr. Claude's scam would then return all the merchandise and give the card directly to Mr. Claude. He in turn would pay the man for his services and then have all the items placed back on the store shelves to be resold. The credit card used in the scam would then be destroyed.

As you can see, Mr. Claude was profiting from his dishonesty; not only would he be paid for the merchandise by the credit card company, but he also had the merchandise back to sell all over again. So while two cashiers were ripping him off, he was blatantly ripping off the credit card companies and the card holders.

Some years later, I learned that Mr. Claude lost almost everything he owned because of his crooked ways, including his two franchised stores. In the end, he was just like any other small-time crook who didn't know when to stop. His greed led to his downfall, like many other people who deal in dishonest schemes to achieve their goals. Once they begin, they usually can't stop. For some, the end comes when they are caught and brought before the courts to face the consequences of breaking the law.

However, when it comes to so-called "white-collar" thieves, their fear of being caught and charged is generally nil, because in one way or another, it seems their hidden crimes are often kept out of the public eye. In my opinion, if every white-collar crook was charged to the full extent of the law for their criminal acts and misdemeanours, there wouldn't be enough room in all the jails and prisons in the country to hold them. I make no distinctions when talking about white-collar crime, including lawyers, judges, police officers, and others within the justice system—no one should be above the law. Today, it is a regrettable fact of life that we are surrounded by corruption. At every level of society, one can find examples of some form of corruption, even in our churches.

Of course, one can argue that even fifty years or more ago, there was corruption within the churches; but it's only during the past ten years or so that we have begun to hear about it, because the criminal activities were kept well hidden. Take, for instance, the person or persons responsible for keeping track of money collected within the church. Is the true amount always accounted for? Or could it be that some part of that money is diverted to a dishonest church member's pocket before it reaches the bank?

Let's say I am the one who has the responsibility for accounting for church collections, and part of my duties is going from one church to another, gathering up the collections and counting the offerings. Let's suppose, for one reason or another there comes a day when I'm personally in need of a few extra dollars, and some of the loose change finds its way into my pockets. Obviously, I might have to change a few figures here and there to cover up for the money I pocketed from each church collection. Of course, in my mind the amount I actually stole was small—no big deal—and who's going to miss a few bucks in change or question me about it? After all, I'm known in the church to be a spiritually minded person—that was one of the reasons I was chosen to be responsible for accounting for the church collections. I was also known to be good with figures. Subsequently, I would have no problem adjusting a few figures here and there to account for my small acts of theft. Even if another member got suspicious of my wrongdoings, it wouldn't be any big deal, because the churches are very forgiving. The question is, if I'm capable of ripping off my own church, would I do so to others? The answer to that question is yes. If my morals were so weak that I would manipulate figures to my advantage so I could pocket a bit of extra money from my own church, then I'd have no problem doing the same at my place of work. In other words, I'd steal from any place or any one, as long as I knew I'd get away with it.

The most difficult person to deal with is a manipulative person who's skilful and spends a great deal of time conjuring up ways to deprive others of their money. This type of person should be closely observed. The problem is we never know for sure who they are, but there are some clues. I am usually careful when dealing with someone who typically has a quick and ready answer to everything—the type who, when questioned regarding an illegal activity, will give you that innocent look and say "Who, me?"

Chapter 3
Unquenchable Habits

Often when workers conjure up ways to rip off an employer, their scheme is so simple that an employer just wouldn't think of it. While having a coffee at Tim Horton's, I happen to be seated near the service counter. I was admiring a beautiful young woman who was being served, and I noticed one of the workers move the money the young woman had placed on the counter over among the tips. Sensing that that wasn't right, I continued to observe every time that worker served a customer. Within a period of about ten minutes, she served roughly a dozen customers. A few times, I saw her move money that was placed on the counter over among the tips. Back then, no cameras were being used as there are today. I thought to myself, "Well, well, isn't that little bitch smart?" I wouldn't call anyone a bitch when speaking to them, but I was thinking it. In my mind, just thinking the words doesn't cause any harm.

I recall one time when I was young, I went to confession, and the priest asked if I had any bad thoughts. I asked if thinking of people in a bad way was a sin. He said "Oh, yes, and if you swear and use bad words, it's a sin"; he then asked, "How many times have you done that?"

"A few," I answered.

"Okay," he replied, "say a few Hail Marys and you'll be forgiven." If I had been honest and truthful on that day, I believe that I would have been in the confession box for most of the day, maybe repeating the forgiveness prayer for a few days more.

Getting back to the worker—what she was doing was ringing in the money from customers who handed it to her. When customers put their money on the counter, sometimes she'd pick the money up and place it in the cash drawer, but sometimes she wouldn't.

Later that afternoon, I decided to call the owner to let him know what I had observed. When I explained what I had seen, he asked if I could identify the worker. I said yes, if I saw her again. He asked if I'd be returning to the coffee shop; I said yes because I often stopped by. He then asked if I'd give him a call before I went. I agreed. When he thanked me for calling, he said, "I wish that other customers would do the same when they see something like that going on."

I replied, "Being a private investigator, I notice such incidents. When I do, I don't usually get involved, because it isn't really my business, but because I noticed her doing that so freely, I did decide to let you know."

He replied, "So you're a PI. That is interesting. I am looking forward to meeting you."

The following morning, I called him and said that I was in the area and would be stopping by for a coffee. He replied that he was at another location, but he would meet me there shortly. He then asked what I looked like, so he'd know when he got there. I said, "I'll be easy to find. Just look for a man who's wearing a hat with the brim turned down a bit."

I arrived and got my coffee and sat farther down, away from the service counter. When the manager entered, he came directly to me and introduced himself. He smiled and said, "Yes, with that type of hat you're easy to find." He then asked if I had noticed the worker at the counter.

I replied, "Yes, she's standing next to the cash register."

He looked over and said, "Yes, she's who I thought of when you called. It's too bad—she's a good worker and has been here for a few years."

I said, "I could be wrong, but after what I saw, I am quite sure she's ripping you off."

He replied, "You say you're a private investigator? Well, how about if I retain your services for a week, so I'd be sure about what she's doing before I let her go?" He said that he felt that he was being taken by some workers, because frequently at the end of the day when the tally was made up, they were usually short a few dollars. "I don't really mind, but when it comes to thirty or forty dollars that can't be accounted for, that bothers me, but so far there isn't much I can do." He said it also happened at his other three locations.

I said, "Okay, I'll work on it for a week and see what I can come up with; then I'll give you a call." I asked him which shift that worker was on, and he said she usually worked during the day but sometimes filled in some nights.

When he mentioned being short of money on different occasions, I would later learn that that occurred quite frequently in such places; a generous amount of money wasn't finding its way into the cash register.

This was my first experience investigating coffee shop workers. It wouldn't be my last. I nicknamed places like Tim Horton's "little gold mines" because of the amount of money raked in each day. Aware of that, I charged a fair price for my services. Once I caught on about how some of the workers were ripping off their employers with simple gimmicks, I found the work was a good experience. I had investigated much more complicated crimes of theft in the workplace, but that was completely different, and I would soon learn why.

While conducting my investigation, I found that it wasn't difficult for workers to get away with what they were doing. At that location, I discovered that there was more than one employee involved; each used different strategies to steal. I quickly found that the worker whom I had noticed earlier had an accomplice; between the two of them, they had a nice little scam going to pocket extra money. There were other workers involved who didn't personally benefit from those deceitful acts that cost the operator a good deal of money. After learning what was taking place at the front counter, I turned my attention to the activities going on at the drive-thru. I refer to that type of thievery as the "counter sweep," and it's done in the following manner.

While one employee served the customer, another would just move the money over to the section of the counter where their tips were kept. Meanwhile, the employee who had served the customer wouldn't punch the cash amount into the cash register. Between them, they had one smooth operation going. It was very simple. When their work shift ended, they'd share the tips (which, of course, included the money that was supposed to have gone into the till). In the run of a week, what they stole between them could amount up to a good sum of money.

Other workers had another scam on the go; they would pass food over the counter to family members without charging. They'd prepare food package and then a member of the family would walk in, go up to the counter, and order a coffee to go. Along with the coffee, the family member would walk out with the stolen package of food. This, it turned out, was being done by a considerable number of employees.

It's easy to see that was costing the owner lots over the course of a week, especially when taking into account the counter sweeps. On top of all that, I observed another employee who worked at the drive-thru window serve forty-eight customers. Out of these forty-eight transactions, only sixteen were entered into the cash register; thirty-two were not. The same employee would remove money from the register and put it among her tips. The evidence I gathered concerning that employee was given to the police, and criminal charges were laid. Convicted of theft, she admitted to stealing under $5,000, but she knew she had stolen much more. The now ex-employee paid pack $4,500 because she thought that by making restitution the charges would be dropped. Naturally, she was quite wrong.

The problems I found in coffee shops and convenience stores are often similar. The difference is that dishonest employees in convenience stores have a bigger variety of items to choose from for their devious purposes.

For small business owners and operators, theft in the workplace has drastically increased in the past few years. This is even though employees at many place of business now are not permitted to have pockets in their work uniforms. Deceitful employees simply find other ways to steal, like the previously mentioned counter sweep.

Understandably, theft in the workplace can create a great deal of stress and dissatisfaction among employees. However, the manner in which employees are treated by their employers also contributes stressful situations they must endure while trying to carry out their duties. In some situations, the owners or managers take their personal problems to work with them—something that is never a good management practice. This results in a lot of their frustrations being unfairly taken out on the employees, who have to accept that form of harassment in order to keep their jobs. Obviously, that kind of atmosphere is hardly conducive to a productive work environment.

When management wants to get rid of an employee, certain tactics are used to bring hardship upon that employee, to try and make them quit and go home. With today's labour codes and worker protection laws to prevent wrongful dismissal, the employers are aware that they just can't fire an employee. They must have justifiable reasons to terminate an employee from his or her job. If they do not, they could find themselves in front of a labour arbitration board—and sooner than they think.

Therefore, the employer must abide by certain guidelines and rules. One fast food operator who was brought before the labour board after he had fired a young worker quickly learned a costly lesson. When it was found by the arbitrator that he had no justifiable reasons for terminating the young man's employment, the employer had to pay the young man two years' back pay. Plus he was ordered by the arbitration board to reinstate the worker's job, which he was forced to do.

That wasn't the end of that tale of workplace woe—after only a few days back on the job, the worker was once again told to hit the road. This time around, the operator believed he had just cause for the dismissal, as he had discovered the young man had lied on his work application. In his résumé, he stated he had previously done similar work, which he hadn't. The worker knew he had lied on his résumé, so no further complaint was filed by him.

Most honest workers are aware of who is stealing but say nothing about it. As one worker put it, "Why should I get involved? If others want to steal, let them steal. As long as I do my work and get my pay, I don't care. Even if I was to report it, what am I going to get out of it? The only thing I'll get is trouble from the other employees, so I will keep my mouth shut and do my work."

Most employees don't want to get involved, and some can't afford to, because if they did, it would mean losing their job. That problem arises when it is the boss or manager and not the employees who steals. In one incident when I was conducting an investigation in a pharmacy, it was the manager and her assistant who were ripping off the store. Before I began with the investigation, there had been a dispute between the two owners. One felt there was no reason to have an investigation done, because he felt there was no theft being committed among the employees. This dispute was settled when the other co-owner, Mr. Barry, agreed that he would pay for the investigation out of his own pocket, which is how I entered the picture.

Late one night, after store hours, I placed a small surveillance camera up in the ceiling where it wouldn't be detected. It covered the counter and the two cash registers. Every second night, I returned and removed the tape, which showed that many acts of theft were being committed. Toward the end of my investigation, I received a phone call from Mr. Barry's partner, the one who had felt no investigation was needed. He said he was leaving on holidays and wondered if I had found anything. When I told him yes, he asked if he could come over and see the tapes. In reviewing one tape with him, it was plain to see that one employee who had been serving a customer never entered any transaction in the cash register. She just placed the items in a bag and handed it to the customer, and the person walked out of the store without paying anything.

He saw another incident involving the same employee, when a man entered the store, walked over to the counter, and, after a short conversation with the employee, just reached over the counter, picked up a couple of packs of cigarettes, and shoved them into his pocket. The employee made no attempt to stop him. Next, he again reached over the counter and took a handful of lotto scratch tickets.

As I was about to rewind the tape so he could have another look, he asked me to turn it off. He sat for a few moments and became emotional, and he said, "That's my supervisor." When I asked why would she just stand there and let the man take things without paying, he replied, disgusted, "That's her husband."

I later learned from Mr. Barry, who had hired me, that the supervisor in question and her husband were always looked upon very highly by his partner, who treated them as though they were part of his family.

Besides the supervisor, three other employees used the same tactics to steal from the pharmacy. Out of six employees, the investigation and evidence proved that four were thieves. No criminal charges were brought against them, nor was anyone fired, including the main culprit, the supervisor. The reason given: "Hard-working employees are hard to find." Unbelievable!

The same result occurred when an investigation involving a couple of government employees was completed; one had a position in management. A videotape showed him committing twelve acts of theft at different times. That person was laid off with pay until a decision was handed down by his superiors with the government. Not only was he not criminally charged, he was allowed to return to work, because, as they put it, "It was his first time stealing." Even though they had videotapes of him stealing a dozen times, it didn't matter—he still got his job back.

The other person also caught stealing was fired; his acts of theft were not as serious as the ones committed by the manager, yet he lost his job. Was that justice? In my opinion, the average person doesn't go around stealing just for kicks or the thrill they may get from it. Today, people steal just to feed their families. A number of them are employed and getting paid very little, so they turn to shoplifting and ripping off their employers. When I asked one thief why she had stolen from her employer, the simple answer was "to survive." In most cases, however, a person doesn't steal to meet needs; people steal for their wants. Take for example, the husband who was stealing cigarettes and lotto tickets from the pharmacy. He didn't steal because he needed to; he stole because he wanted to. I see a great difference between a person's needs and wants.

Greed plays a huge role in why certain people steal. If people stole only for their needs and not from want and greed, I'm quite certain the problem of theft in the workplace and by shoplifters would be cut in half. That in itself could help to save consumers millions, if not eventually billions, of dollars.

Quite often when I'm walking through a shopping mall, I look around and think, "Who's ripping off who today?" I am quite sure that some shoppers are there to rip off a store or two by seeing what they can pocket. Or perhaps some merchants are ripping off unsuspecting customers with price gouging. How about the store employees—are a few trying to think up a way to get merchandise out at closing time without being detected? Workers have three ways of doing that: through the rear door or front door or passing an item or two to a family member or friend who's pretending to do some shopping. This form of theft is simple. Someone comes in and chooses a few items and then they go to the register where a friend or family member is working. One of the cheaper items is charged for and the two more expensive ones aren't, but all three are placed in the shopping bag by the clerk. The customer walks out very satisfied. Why not, when he got three for the price of one?

Over the years, I found that a large number of business operators weren't taking precautions to prevent such acts of theft from taking place. Large corporate-owned businesses have some form of security in place, which helps reduce theft by the consumers or workers. These huge corporate-run stores can recover their losses somewhat in the form of tax credits at the end of the year, but for small business operators, it's a different story. It doesn't really matter what type of business you're operating. You could be in the wholesale or the retail business, maybe operating a corner store or restaurant or coffee shop. Chances are that without security measures in place to help protect you, you're being stolen from in some form.

Let's use the operator of a small business as an example. Say you have a dozen employees; one of your workers found a way to rip you off each week for just a couple of hundred dollars, either in merchandise or money; at the end of the year that amounts to $10,400. Two hundred a week sounds rather small, but when you multiply that amount by fifty-two, it adds up to a good deal of money. Now, let's say not only one worker is stealing from you, but a couple; your losses are much greater—$20,800. If allowed to continue, in five years your loss of profit amounts to $104,000. This doesn't take into account what is being lost through other forms of theft, such as from shoplifters. When you combine the two, you're losing big money.

The problem with employees ripping off their employers is that it multiplies. It may began with one worker, but once a dishonest worker sees another employee getting away with theft, then he or she begins doing the same. The more employees you have, the greater the number of workers who may be stealing from you. Dishonest employees are one of the quickest ways you could find yourself with money problems, a closed store, and often bankruptcy. So it's wise for the business operator to take precautions and put certain security measures in place. If you, the owner, don't protect your business, who will? I have seen business operators take certain measures to protect themselves, but as time went on, they seemed to let their guard down and forget about security measures, and that was when the problem appeared, because someone was waiting for the opportunity to rip them off. I found some workers were very cunning and could think up many ways to outdo their employers.

The two main concerns business operators have are consumers who shoplift and corrupt workers, who, like vultures, are just waiting to seize the opportunity to steal. And once you let your guard down, that is precisely what will occur. Personally, I feel no matter what security measures are taken, businesses will continue to be ripped off, either by the deceitful employees or by the dishonest shoppers, but having certain security measures in place decreases the amount of lost profit. For small business operators to achieve success and stay in business, safety precautions must be taken. Otherwise, you can be assured that, somehow, some of your profits are finding their way into someone else's pockets.

Often when I'd investigate an act of theft by an employee, my first question to the owner was, "Who are you suspicious of?" In many cases, if family members were working in the business, they'd be the workers the owner was least suspicious of, even if there was good reason to be, because they were "family." Big mistake on the part of the owner. If I were operating a business where a good deal of money was changing hands and an act of theft had taken place, with my experience, no one would be excluded, especially family members, until the investigation was concluded and the culprit found. I have seen some hardened business operators break down and cry when it was proved that a trusted family member had committed the theft.

In one such incident, the owner and I were reviewing the videotape recording showing the actual theft as it took place. A woman was caught on tape removing money from the office safe; she lifted her dress and stuffed the money down the front of her panties. When he saw that, he said, "The bitch—that's my sister-in-law! I can't believe that! I pay her a good wage, and each year, I send her and my brother and their children away on a paid vacation for two weeks."

For some, it's hard to accept the fact that a family member is stealing. One of the problems I found with the incident involving the sister-in-law was the fact that the owner let too many workers have access to the office safe. If not for the video recording, we would have had no way of knowing who stole the money, because four people had access to the safe. I recommended that he changed the combination of the safe and only allow his office manager and assistant to have the new combination. Letting too many employees have access to a safe is a bit like letting too many people access your cash register. When money goes missing, who do you blame? It becomes harder to single out any one person.

It's all about taking precautions, especially if you're a businessperson who's not always around. If you're away a good part of the time, then your chances of being ripped off by workers increases. I believe in the saying when the cat is away, the mice will play. The cat is the business owner and the mice the employee who loves to get at your money whenever you're away.

One businessman who operated a few convenience stores hired me to do an investigation at one of his locations because of missing merchandise, which he felt was caused by employees, mainly on the late night shift. It wasn't long after beginning the investigation that I found that his merchandise was going out the rear door. Two night clerks were involved. They'd fill a box with items and place the box at the rear of the store near the door, which they would prop slightly open with a stick. Later, someone would drive around the back, open the door, take the box, and drive away. After the employees were fired, I met with the owner and discussed his operation methods for the three stores. He said that each morning, he began working at seven o'clock and finished at five. I asked him whether at night he ever went to any of the stores to make a casual check. He said no; when five o'clock came, he was finished till the next morning. I told him he'd be wise to stop by on different nights and spend a few minutes at each store. The workers wouldn't feel as free to steal merchandise, because they'd never know when he was liable to show up. He agreed that it was a good idea.

The problem of theft will always be with us; people will forever find or feel they have reasons to steal. Some steal for their needs, and others steal for greed, especially within a larger corporation. The only difference I have found between a large corporation that rips off consumers and employees who steal is in the amount and how they go about accomplishing their thievery. When workers commit the act of theft in the workplace in large corporations, it could run into millions; it's much less for smaller business operators, but in the end, it's all about theft. There's only one way to deal with that problem, and that is to take precautions, no matter what type of business you are in.

Another major problem that I have sometimes run into is business owners who co-sign a bank loan for a trusted employee. If for some reason the worker ceased to be employed with the firm and was unable to repay the loan, the business operator who co-signed would need to come up with the money to repay the bank. In one such case, after paying the bank, the businessman sued his ex-employee to try and recover his loss, which amounted to twenty thousand dollars. As in many court cases involving lawsuits of that sort, the businessman won his lawsuit. But in the end, he didn't get any of his money, for the simple reason that the person whom he had won a judgment against had no way of repaying him because he was unemployed, and so he owned nothing. My advice to anyone who's asked to co-sign a bank loan is to simply say, "No." Otherwise you may be stuck with repaying the loan, with no way to recover your money.

CHAPTER 4
Tracking an Unscrupulous Character

In another court incident, a trusted employee had embezzled forty-five thousand dollars from his employer and close friend. After pleading guilty and telling the court that he had used the money for gambling, he was ordered by the judge to make restitution for the money he had stole. He agreed to repay the money in instalments. Because he had no previous police record, the judge didn't sentence him to jail, on the condition that he repaid the money. Within a few weeks after the trial, the employer received five hundred dollars—that was the last time he heard from his ex-employee and friend. Later, when he tried to locate him, he learned that he had left the city and couldn't be found. Three years later, when I happened to speak with the business operator, he asked if I had any way of finding that person. I told him that I would try. I hadn't much to go on, other than his last known address and the name and phone number of a close relative. I called and told him that I was an old friend who had gone to high school with his cousin and had just arrived in the city. I was told that he had moved to Ottawa, Ontario; his cousin hadn't heard from him for a couple of years. The last time he had heard from him, he worked as a manager for an oil company.

I found that he wasn't listed in the Ottawa phone directory, so I phoned a private investigator in Ottawa whom I had previously worked with. I gave him the little information I had and asked him to check with the oil companies in the area. Within a week, I received a call from the investigator saying that he had located him; he was employed with an oil company as manager. The investigator also said that he was a home owner and had recently remarried. This was good news; he had a good job, and he was a home owner. To try and retrieve money from a deadbeat who isn't working or owns nothing is useless, but when a person has a good job and owns his own home, it's a completely different story.

Before I went any further, I had a problem. As a private investigator; in accordance with regulations, I wasn't allowed to collect money from people. If I did and the private investigator's licensing commission got wind of it, my security license could be revoked. When we had first spoken, the business owner said that because he had no way of finding his ex-employee; as far as he was concerned, he'd never get to see any of his money. But if I located the man and got some of his money back, he said, I could keep fifty percent of the amount I collected. At the time, I told him that I wasn't in the collection business, but I would see what I could do.

Once I had located the person, I had two options: one was to give the information I had to the business owner and let him go after him for his money, or I could try to collect the money myself. If I gave him the information and let him take are of it, that would mean very little beside the finder's fee for me. But if I took care of it, I'd get much more money.

Because I had some experience in collection, I decided to give the ex-employee a phone call at his work and see how he reacted. When I got him on the phone, I told him that my name was Bruno and that I wanted to set up a meeting with him to discuss how he wanted to go about repaying the money he had stolen from his past employer in Montreal. When I mentioned stolen money, he paused for a moment before asking who I was.

I answered, "Like I said, my name is Bruno, and if you don't care to meet and discuss the money that you owe, I will contact your head office and have a seizure placed on your salary. As you are aware, if we do that, your employer will learn about your theft conviction. Keep in mind that when you pleaded guilty a few years ago, you were handed a sentence on the condition you agreed to repay the stolen money, which you didn't; instead you left Montreal."

He quickly said, "No, no, I don't want you to do that; I need a bit of time to think things over."

I told him, "There isn't anything to think over; the money needs to be repaid."

"But I don't have the money."

I told him, "Sell or mortgage your home. Maybe your new wife can help you."   When he heard me mention his new wife, he quickly asked, "Did you call her?"   "No, not yet," I answered, "but we will, if we need to."

In a concerned voice, he said, "Please don't call her. She knows nothing about that."

"We'll have no reason to contact her if you repay the money. I'll give you a call in a few days; in the meantime, you come up with some money."

"I'll try," he answered.

I said, "I don't care how you get the money, but I want to remind you that if you don't, we'll be in touch with not only your employer, but also your wife.

I could sense the fear in his voice, especially when I mentioned contacting his wife and employer; for that reason I believed that I would get some money. How much, I didn't know. Instead of using my name I used Bruno, a good, solid Italian name, and instead of using "I," I said, "We'll be in touch"—giving him the impression that there were more people involved than just me.

After three days, I called him and asked if he had the money. He said, "No. There's no way I can come up with all the money." I asked how much he could come up with. After a long pause, he answered, "I don't really know."

Making a quick decision, I said, "Look, we're not going to fool around with that. Here's what I am willing to do: You come up with twenty-five thousand, and the rest of the money, the fifteen thousand plus the interest, we'll forget about. And believe me, you're getting off easy."

After some hesitation, he asked how much time he had to raise that money. "You'll have one week, and if you don't come up with the money, I'll be finished talking with you. I'll be talking to your employer next."

He had no way of knowing that if he had offered me any amount, even a few thousand, I would have accepted it, and that would have been the end of it. As far as I was concerned, if he had refused to repay any of the money, there was nothing I could have done. I believe the only reason he said that he'd try to come up with the money was that he was in fear of his employer and wife learning that he had been convicted of theft. As far as what I told him about contacting his employer and having his salary seized, as a private investigator, I couldn't have done that. It would have to be done by the person to whom he owed the money or a collection agency. Because he had already been ordered by the court to make restitution, I didn't feel they would have any problem putting a seizure on part of his salary. If they went that route, they might not recover any money, because I was quite sure that once the oil company learned that he had been previously convicted of theft, they would fire him. I was surprised that the oil company hadn't learned of his conviction when he first applied for the position as manager; perhaps they didn't bother to check to see if he had a police record.

When I had learned of his whereabouts, that information should have been passed on to the businessman so he could take any action he felt like taking to recover his money; that should have been the end of my involvement. But after talking with the man and giving him a week to come up with the twenty-five thousand, I figured out that someone else would go meet with him to pick up the money. I thought of getting a collection agency that I knew to do so, but I decided against that, because they'd ask for at least 35 percent, which would leave me with only 15 percent. Instead, I called a friend with whom I had previously done some work I could trust. At one time, he was a bill collector and was now involved in the trucking business. After explaining my situation, he agreed to drive to Ottawa and pick up the money. Once I was sure that the man had the money, for his service, he'd be paid a thousand.

On the seventh day of the week I'd given him to come up with the money, I called. He told me that he couldn't get the twenty-five thousand, but he did manage to get eighteen. He said that he'd need a month or so to come up with the balance. I told him that wasn't a problem, as long as he paid. He asked that I not go to his place of work or his home to get the money. He gave me a time and the name of a restaurant where we'd meet the next day, in the parking lot. I told him that I wouldn't personally be meeting with him; it would be someone else. After giving him the description of the person who was going, I told him that I'd be touch with him in a month's time for the remaining seven thousand still owed. Then I called my friend and told him that the money was ready to be picked up.

The following evening, he returned with the eighteen thousand in cash, and after getting his thousand, he left. I called the businessman and told him that I had found his friend, the ex-employee, and had managed to get eighteen thousand from him. When he came to the office to get his share of the money, I said that it cost me a thousand to have someone go to Ontario to pick up that money, so instead of giving him nine thousand, I gave him eight thousand, because he had agreed that besides my 50 percent he would pay for other expenses. I told him about the agreement I had made with his friend and about the balance which I would get in a month. When I handed him the money, he said, "I find it hard to believe that, finally, I'm getting some of it back." He left, very content with his share. As for me, it was the easiest and quickest nine thousand I had ever made, especially from just making a few phone calls. A month later, the ex-employee paid the remaining seven thousand. I was sure that if I hadn't gone after him in the manner which I did, threatening to expose his past with his employer and wife, he would have gotten away without repaying any of the money.

CHAPTER 5
Fine-tuning Schemes

Over the years, I have maintained that when an employee steals, employers should try and get the money back, or at least part of it. Whenever I questioned an employee or employees who committed the act of theft, I gave them a simple choice; they could either cooperate with me or they could deal directly with the police. They usually chose to deal with me, rather than the police.

The first thing I concentrate on is retrieving the money or merchandise that was stolen; after achieving that, I then decide if charges should be laid. In most cases, that would depend on what was stolen and the attitude of the person or persons I was dealing with; in most cases, if the person wasn't arrogant, no charges were laid. To me, it's all about getting back what was stolen. Whether money or merchandise, it really didn't matter as long as I managed to recover what was taken.

In many cases, I found that it wasn't only the workers who were stealing, but people who held positions of trust, such as managers and supervisors. Their deceitful acts don't happen only in the private sector but big time in our own government agencies. Take, for instance, our Supply and Services department. Each year; they're being ripped off for hundreds of thousands, if not millions, by some of their own corrupt employees, including people in management. One cannot compare what is stolen by individual workers within our government to what is stolen by trusted employees in management.

One superintendent carried out his acts of theft in a very devious manner by using phoney invoices, which we refer to as *padded* invoices, charging for work not done and ordering merchandise for his own use. One private contractor had gotten the job to supply and install alarm systems within the government. When the work was done, he handed his invoice to the superintendent. He was told to write up another invoice and add eighteen hundred to it for work that he wanted the contractor to do later. The contractor did what he was asked and later received a cheque from the government. Some months later, the contractor received a call from the superintendent. He was asked to go to his residence and install a security system in the superintendent's new home. The extra eighteen hundred that he had invoiced the government was payment for the security system. The superintendent did the same with an electrical contractor who had previously done work for him within the government; he also had the contractor invoice the government for extra work, which he later completed at the superintendent's new home, which had nothing to do with the government, but the government paid for it.

Such deceitful acts by persons of trust within our government will continue for the simple reason that whenever an invoice is approved to be paid by someone in management, there're very seldom any questions asked. If there happens to be a question regarding the invoice, we can be sure the unscrupulous government employee will have a suitable answer ready. The same can be said when a contractor is hired to perform some work and is paid an hourly rate. A contractor was charging $55 per hour; he was told when he wrote up his invoice to instead charge $80 per hour; the extra $25 per hour that he received would go toward other work he'd be asked to do later. In that incident, the extra work was done at the government supervisor's cottage and had nothing to do with the government, except the government paid for the work. A lot of the material that was used came from the government stockroom; in other words, it was stolen.

This just touches the surface of what's going on within our government when it comes to acts of theft committed by employees who hold positions of trust, such as managers, superintendents, and supervisors. And how about some of our ministers? Often we hear about devious acts that they and their business cronies are accused of through the news media. Usually these scandals arise when a new party takes power and forms a new government. They discover that millions of dollars of government money can't be accounted for; when questions are asked about where the money went, no one knows, sometimes not even the finance minister. Over the years, it seems that no matter what political party was in power, there's always the question, "Where have all those millions gone?" sung to the tune of that old song, "Where have all the flowers gone?"

As for large corporations and government agencies—investigations are more time-consuming and difficult to carry out than for smaller, privately operated businesses. When dealing with corporations and government agencies, there's much more work involved. For a privately owned business, you investigate certain employees up to the management level, but it can be a bit more complicated when investigating larger businesses, because there are many more people to deal with. It's similar to climbing a ladder; you start at the bottom and work your way up. You begin with individual workers, supervisors, and managers. Sometimes the investigation could lead all the way up to the CEO. People in management, I found, were very shrewd about covering up their deceitful acts, especially in large corporations; even if a supervisor or manager wasn't actually involved in the theft, they found a way to cover up the theft by workers, rather than report it to higher management. Their reason was mostly to show that they were in control and doing a good job as managers, although I found that some proved they were incompetent by doing so.

CHAPTER 6
The Reality of a Private Investigator

Back in the mid-60s when I first began working as a private investigator, I found the work very intriguing, but it wasn't comparable to the private detective series shows I saw on TV, with the fancy cars and beautiful women. As for having a gun strapped to my chest; in accordance to the regulations that govern private investigators, it wasn't permitted. I did carry a gun at times, but if the licensing commission had learned of it, my private investigator's licence would have been revoked.

For eight years when I first got into private security, I was employed by privately owned security agencies and was involved in all aspects of investigations, including gathering evidence for divorce cases. That type of work, I wasn't too fond of. It could get messy and a bit dangerous After eight years of experience as a private investigator, I applied for and received a licence from the Quebec Justice Department to operate my own security agency. When I got my permit, I concentrated mainly on cases that involved acts of thefts and fraud.

As mentioned, theft can be done in many ways. If a person or persons take something that doesn't rightfully belong to them; they are committing an act of theft. If a person fraudulently obtains money in any manner, including auto- or work-related accident claims; that also is theft through fraud. Insurance companies and workmen's compensation are paying out billions of dollars each year to phonies, and in the end; it's the taxpayers who pay. With other types of theft, especially in the workplace, small business operators have to bear these losses; for some, it can be drastic.

When I first began doing investigations in work-related claims, most of the fraudulent claims investigations were lengthy and, at times, very boring. I had previously worked for a number of years in the retail business investigating employee thefts, which was a good experience, because deceitful employees could think up many ways to rip off their employers. I also gained quite a bit of knowledge about how certain large corporate-owned stores went about ripping off consumers. Retailers are losing billions of dollars a year through thefts by shoppers and deceitful employees. As for large chains of corporate-owned store ripping off consumers, it could be said that such store operators weren't actually stealing, but in my opinion they were. If that happens at each of their stores, how many millions are they raking in each year through devious pricing?

An act of theft can be carried out in many ways. For instance, I'm doing some shopping in one of the large corporate chain stores and pick up an item that is advertised in the flyer as on sale. Not only is the sale price shown in the flyer, but there is a large sign next to the item in the store, plainly shown the reduced price. Thinking I'm getting a good deal, I put one in my shopping cart among other items. After paying for my merchandise, I get home and check my receipt, and I find that I was charged the full price for the item that was on sale. That happens over and over again, and I found the problem wasn't with the smaller, privately owned stores that try to survive by competing with larger corporate stores—it was the large corporations that have stores all over the country that continually rip off consumers with that gimmick. As with many other shoppers, my mistake was not paying attention to the price of the items that were scanned while I was at the checkout counter.

When I first noticed the problem, I returned to the store with the item and my receipt and was refunded the difference. After it occurred a few times, I returned and asked to speak with the store manager. I asked him why I was being charged the regular price for the item that was supposed to be on sale. His answer was that they hadn't had time to change the prices in the computer. I said to him, "I see they had time to place a sale price next to the items. "You mean to say that no one had time to enter the sale price in the computer?" His response was, "Yeah. At times that happens."

Over the years, I have learned to be more careful when I shop at the large stores, and I pay more attention to items as they are being scanned. Are price scanners 100 percent accurate? They might be most of the time, but maybe not all of the time. So it's wise for consumers to pay attention when their merchandise is being scanned at the checkout counter. The same can be said regarding large grocery outlets, especially if the cashier who is scanning your items is carrying on a conversation with someone, which often happens. Could it be because he or she isn't paying attention to their work that an item was scanned twice? Yes, that could happen.

Whenever I'm overcharged for an item, I don't bother questioning a cashier, because it wasn't her fault; she went by the prices that were showing on the register. Instead, I speak with the manager. It's always the usual story—they didn't have time to change the prices. As far as I'm concerned, stores that charge full price for merchandise that is supposed to be on sale are stealing. Could I or other consumers accuse the store of stealing? No, because as far as they are concerned, they weren't purposely trying to rip off anyone; they only forgot or didn't have time to enter the sale prices in the computer.

Theft is committed in many ways. In a significant number of incidents, such as with the large stores, it's hard to prove that their intent was to rip off the consumers, but when the manager doesn't see to it that sale prices are entered in the computer, that's a smooth way to get extra cash from shoppers who believe they are being charged the sale price on merchandise. To me, that is a form of theft, but as consumers, there's nothing we can do other than take precautions and keep a keen eye on what we're being charged whenever we're at the checkout counter. We don't usually encounter that problem with smaller, privately run stores; it's always with the chains of corporate-owned stores.

Each year retailers are ripped off for billions of dollars by thieves, and a good number of these act of thefts are carried out by inside workers. No matter who does the stealing, we as consumers end up paying for their thievery when the retailers hike up their prices to cover their losses, perhaps including phoney sale prices.

Some of the worst types of thieves work for small business operators—corrupt employees who cook up many ways of ripping off their employers. Each year, because of employee theft, many small business owners are forced out of business and into bankruptcy. I feel that could be prevented if the owners weren't so trusting. Many incidents involve not only unscrupulous employees but family members, people who owners wouldn't think could steal from them.

Going back forty or fifty years, a person who operated a business didn't have the problems in the workplace we have today and many of the reasons people now steal didn't exist. Back then, if anyone stole from their employer, it was either groceries to feed the family or items they could sell to get extra money. Today, the problem is much greater and much more serious; people have more reasons to steal, including to feed their drug, alcohol, and gambling habits. If an employer has an employee with any of those problems, he should beware and take precautions, especially if the employee is in a position of trust, such as handling money. No exception should be made, especially with close family members. I have a simple saying—if in doubt, check it out.

One of the most serious problems we have today is employees who steal from their employer to feed their gambling addiction. Since our government got into the gambling business and allowed gambling machines to be placed where they are easily accessible to anyone, the theft has greatly increased. This problem isn't going away soon. And if the small business employer has one such a person on the payroll; precautions need to be taken. If not, there's a good possibility that some of the business's money could be fed into these gambling machines.

In one incident, a wife was responsible for taking care of the books for the business that she and her husband ran; in a period of two years she managed to doctor the books and hide over seventy thousand dollars that she lost gambling. The husband began to get a bit suspicious when his wife would leave the office and often not return for hours. When she did return, he found her to be nervous; she would jump at him for no reason, especially if he asked where she had been. For a while, he began to think that she was having an affair with another man. I got involved after receiving a call from a friend who knew the husband; when I spoke with the husband, his main concern was that she was seeing another man. He said that she left the office for her lunch hour, and mostly she'd return around one, but a couple of times a week she would return a few hours later. When he questioned her as to where she was, she would tell him that she had lunch with a friend, and then they walked around the mall doing a bit of shopping.

One afternoon, after she had returned late and said that she had been out shopping, he went out and checked her car and saw she had bought nothing. Later, he noticed her at her desk eating a sandwich. He thought to himself, *Why is she eating a sandwich when she told me that she already had lunch?* And he wondered why there were no items in her car. That Friday, around 11:30, I parked across the street from their business and waited for her to leave the parking area. When I saw her drive out half an hour later, I followed her. When we reached a shopping mall, I expected her to drive in; instead, she continued on. Fifteen minutes later, she reached the outskirts of town, and she pulled into a restaurant and bar. Instead of going in the front entrance of the restaurant, she used a side entrance. I parked. Ten minutes later, I walked in through the front entrance and ordered a sandwich and coffee. I didn't see her seated anywhere in the restaurant area, so I said to the waitress, "I was supposed to meet a friend here, and I don't see him. Maybe he used the side entrance, and he's waiting for me at the bar."

"No," she answered, "the bar isn't open at this hour of the day." Pointing to a door at the rear, she added, "Maybe he could be in there, playing the gambling machines." After finishing my coffee and sandwich, I walked into the rear room. There she was, along with a bunch of other people, playing the slot machines. I left and called the husband; I told him that she hadn't met another man. Instead, she had driven to a restaurant and bar, and she was in there gambling. When I mentioned gambling, he said, "She can't be, because she doesn't gamble." I told him to go see for himself and gave him the location.

I later learned that he did drive out to the restaurant, and she was still at the gambling machine when he walked in. The mutual friend who had introduced us said that the husband was relieved to know that she wasn't seeing another man. As for the seventy thousand that she later admitted taking from the business; the husband just shrugged it off as a learning experience. Because the husband was operating a very successful business, he could afford to take the seventy thousand loss, but if he had been in a smaller business, the outcome from the wife stealing to feed her gambling addiction could have lead to the business's demise.

CHAPTER 7
Sophisticated Security Systems

When educating business operators in the early 80s, I pointed out that certain tools were available to them, such as video cameras and recorders, which at the time they weren't aware of, because such cameras were very seldom seen anywhere then, especially in stores or the workplace. As a private investigator who had previously used spy cameras, I was aware that cameras and other electronic gadgets would soon become available to anyone.

As for deceitful employees—business operators must bear in mind that in any business where a large cash flow changes hands without some sort of security in place, they may find that a good part of their money finds its way into one, or a few, employee pockets. Whether money or merchandise, in the end, it all amounts to theft.

The actual act of theft can be simply defined. If I take *anything* that doesn't rightfully belong to me without the consent of the owner; I'm committing theft and could be charged with a criminal act. Even if I wasn't successful in carrying out the actual act of theft but had tried, I could still be charged with intent to commit theft. It's wise for business operators to know what laws are in place to protect them.

One day, while having lunch with a business owner who was having problems with employee theft, I told him that once he caught an employee, the police should be called, and he should have the person in question charged. Doing so would send a message to other employees that theft wouldn't be tolerated. That was precisely what happened. The culprit went to court and was found guilty of theft. The business operator placed a notice on the bulletin board that if anyone was caught stealing, the police would be summoned, and the thief would be charged.

You achieve results by setting examples, and that is what that business operator did. If I were an employee and knew that if I stole from my employer I would go to court, I would think twice before I'd take a chance. That's the way to cut down on theft in the workplace. If workers are caught stealing, have them charged, depending somewhat on what was stolen; if the item is inexpensive or the amount of money is small, you wouldn't want the police involved. A serious lecture on theft may help, if you intend to keep the worker. A sure way to prevent any future problems is to fire the person or persons who have committed the act of theft.

Regarding money—theft typically occurs when a great deal of money is changing hands. If you operate a business where workers are steadily handling money, you can be assured that certain employees will be strongly tempted to pocket a bit of your cash. A deceitful employee can think up many ways to get some of your money in his pockets. It seems that his mind is always at work, coming up with new gimmicks to rip his employer off.

In the society that we now live in, we're surrounded by corruption and thievery. People are filling their pockets and bank accounts with money acquired by illegal means. Anytime we read a newspaper or watch the news on TV, we hear about large corporations and government officials ripping off the taxpayers for hundred of millions of dollars. When that is made public, the government then appoints a committee and spends another hundred million to have the allegations investigated. When it's over, the thieves within our government, along with their business friends, walk away practically scot-free.

Take Enron in the United States. The heads of that corporation pocketed billions before filing for bankruptcy and putting about sixty thousand employees out of work. I refer to that type of people as big-time thieves. Within our own government, we have the same problem; it never seems to stop, no matter who's in power. As for our government officials, I could describe a good number of them in one word: *disgusting*. It's all about greed, and the rich get richer and the poor get poorer.

I often use the word *greed* when I refer to people who hold positions of trust and earn good money. They really have no reason to steal, but if they live above their means, eventually they end up in debt, as happens within many families and those who live the high-society life, which they can't really afford. As the saying goes: "We must keep up with the Joneses down the street"; the difference is that the Joneses can afford to live in luxury, with their high-priced vehicles and their high-society homes, surrounded with lots of other goodies that come with being successful. The person who lives up the street really can't afford to live in the same style and manner the Joneses do; so sometimes to compete, they turn to committing acts of theft.

Regarding employees who steal: those employed by large corporations often commit big-time acts of theft. At smaller businesses, the opportunities for workers to steal huge amounts aren't common, but if the theft isn't detected and is allowed to continue, it could eventually add up to a great deal of money. Keep in mind that many workers who first begin to steal at smaller businesses often do so after seeing others get away with it. Soon instead of having only one or two thieves as employees, you have a few more. As far as I am concerned, thieves are similar to rats; if you don't rid yourself of them, they will quickly multiply, and then you'll have a major problem. Personally, I feel that the main cause of theft in the workplace is poor management. If theft is allowed to continue, it could eventually put a small business into bankruptcy, which happens each day throughout the country. If smaller businesses ends up in bankruptcy courts, there's a good chance everything will be lost, including the owner's home.

But the out come is different when theft is being committed within large corporations, such as government agencies due to the fact that they can write off their lost from tax credits. Getting back to the issue of the two, one way the one supervisor was ripping off his employer was via a sneaky little trick that started with showing up at work an hour or so before everyone else. He'd take one of the school buses parked in the yard, drive over to his van, remove five or six five-gallon cans from his van and place them in the school bus. Then, he would drive over to the government gas pumps, fill the cans, and return to his van to unload them. With the theft of the gas complete, he'd drive the school bus back to where it was supposed to be and then head home to stash the gas before returning to his workplace. By the time he got back, other employees were reporting for work, all unaware he had already been there earlier for criminal purposes. All in all, it was a very simple scheme with a built-in safeguard: he used one of the school buses to pull off his scam. If another employee had shown up early for work and saw him at the gas pumps with the school bus, they would have thought nothing of it, because part of their work involved fuelling the buses. If he had been seen at the gas pumps with his own van, other employees may have become suspicious.

The videotape showed the same supervisor going to the plant on weekends when no other employees were around. On those occasions, he was much more brazen: instead of using a school bus, he'd place the cans in the rear of the company truck, drive over to the pumps, fill the cans in the rear of a company truck, and then drive the truck home to get rid of the gas. He would then drive the company truck back to the yard. Again, if someone had seen him at the pumps with a company truck, they'd think nothing of it. It would seem that he was just putting gas in the truck, but instead of the gas being pumped into the gas tank of the truck, he was filling up the hidden gas cans he had placed at the rear of the truck.

The videotapes showed the same supervisor committing the same act of theft over and over again. So what was his punishment when he was finally caught? As a matter of fact—nothing much; he sat home for two weeks getting paid by the government until it was decided to let him return to work.

Each year the government published certain statistics, stating the amount of money the government had lost that year in theft. That particular year, it was around one hundred thousand dollars, accounting for all government agencies. As far as I am concerned, according to some of the facts that I'm aware of, that hundred thousand could easily account for just one of the agencies within the government. Personally, I feel that if certain figures and facts were shown clearly to the public (meaning the taxpayers), it would soon become utterly apparent that a hundred thousand was a mere drop in the bucket. Sad but true.

One of the problems I have encountered over the years is that certain persons in management hide the facts as to what is actually taking place within their departments. Some section heads and managers in large corporations and government agencies have ways and means of keeping the actual numbers and what's really going on from reaching their superiors. To simplify, I will explain it in the following manner.

Let's say I'm the owner of a small business like a coffee shop or convenience store. I have a manager whose responsibilities include reporting any wrong doing he or she may encounter, such as employees who continuously are short of money when doing up their daily cash and can't account for it, to me. The manager found no way to correct that problem and hides it from me by covering up for these losses, because she doesn't want me to know she's not fully in control. To do so may show she is not the right person to be in management.

Well, the same thing can be said regarding large corporations and government agencies whose managers are incompetent. They also hide the true facts to keep their positions within the company. I see very little difference between a manager who's in charge of a small coffee shop or convenience store being dishonest than one who's in management for a large corporation. It amounts to the same thing: deceit. The only difference between the two managers is their responsibilities. The large corporation manager may have bigger problems to deal with than the coffee shop manager, but as I see it, an incompetent person is just that—incompetent.

So how does one take steps to correct a problem of incompetence? The answer is that one must learn how to resolve problems instead of unwittingly contribute to them. More effort should be placed on influencing and controlling the behaviours of workers who are responsible for creating the problems.

There are many feasible solutions for dealing with problems in the workplace. First, you must pinpoint the problems, and then find the person or persons who are responsible for creating the problems. Once you've got those matters nailed down, you can concentrate on effectively applying workable solutions.

And don't rush. The normal reaction, understandably, is to hurry to get the situation taken care of, but it's best in the long run to think the matter over very carefully. It's essential to make sure that before approaching the instigators that you have the correct solutions and the skills to apply them. I have found in dealing with particular problems, especially if they involve a good employee I wouldn't want to lose, that a soft approach is best when trying to resolve the matter. If you want to get rid of the employee, by all means use a stronger approach, but do it legally. (Remember, as discussed earlier, it's important to protect yourself when firing someone.)

CHAPTER 8
Unscrupulous Employees

Here's yet another incident from my files involving a government agency and the ever-popular problem of shrinkage. At year end, government agencies (and private companies) try to account for whatever goods and items they have on hand, but when it comes to unscrupulous employees, it appears there is no shortage of ways and means to hide thievery. My case in point deals with a supervisor in the New Brunswick Services who ripped off the government by having certain materials and services supplied to his residence without him having to pay a penny.

His scam was with security systems. He would have the supplier and installer who looked after the alarm systems add a few hundred dollars here and there to each invoice to cover the cost for the security systems that would sometime later be installed—you guessed correctly—at his home or cottage.

As for the installer, it didn't bother him, as long as he got paid, and he was always sure to be paid, because he was invoicing the government. A good number of government officials are doing the same today, and it's never the rank and file but a person of authority. This scam is being used in the government over and over again, and they just keep paying with the taxpayers' money. Believe me, if I had the money for which governments were being ripped off on an annual basis, I could retire a wealthy person. Again, it's all about dealing with figures and knowing how to manipulate the system.

As for small business operators, if they don't want to end up in bankruptcy court with closed doors, they must acquire the necessary knowledge to handle the problem of theft in the workplace. Referring to methods and techniques that are greatly needed today in the workplace; one must strive to learn and understand that these simple techniques can lead to a much better relationship in the workplace between employees and management.

As previously mentioned, those in management who take their personal problems to work each morning are looking for trouble—that in itself is not a good way to begin a productive day. For instance, let's say that you are a manager in sales. It could be in real estate or automobiles, or maybe you supervise a crew of door-to-door vacuum cleaner salesmen. Those sales people must be motivated, and good leadership means it's the responsibility of the person in charge to get them motivated. This cannot be achieved by leaders who show up each morning in a foul mood, grumbling about this or that problem at home. Most employees don't fancy having to deal with a grouchy boss, which in itself can cause some employees to be less productive. (Remember, they've got their own problems too.)

I have found that contented employees tend to be productive employees, which is a simple enough concept. Effective management creates motivation; less experienced and skilful supervisors and managers are basic de-motivators. There are people who are self-motivated and begin their work each morning with a positive attitude, while others need to be motivated. Good communication between management and employees is a must; if that isn't achieved, there will always be some sort of friction between the two. To achieve one's goal (which, presumably, is to operate a thriving and profitable business), one must break down these barriers, and that means eliminating corruption and stress in the workplace.

As for learning new problem-solving skills and techniques, one must first acknowledge the importance of developing these new skills and techniques. Then and only then will someone acquire sufficient knowledge to deal with the growing situations they may confront in the workplace. Personally, I would begin by taking inventory of my present skills and how I've been applying these skills to correct and reduce problems. Situations differ from one another; as a leader, one need to be able to cope with different situations effectively.

Some small business operators may feel they have to put up with corruption and theft because they can't afford to hire a private investigator with knowledge in dealing with such problems. Here's my advice as an investigator. First, list the problems you have encountered in your business. List them in order of priority: place the most serious one, which I feel should be theft, at the top, and then concentrate on the most pressing one. If you hire a capable private investigator to solve the theft problem and he catches the culprit, once you rid yourself of said culprit, you may find that some of the lesser problems are greatly reduced.

Keep in mind that theft in the workplace causes other situations among employees that place a great deal of stress on them. To repeat an earlier statement, stressed workers are not fully productive workers. Once you rid yourself of problems such as theft in the workplace, you may soon notice a better working atmosphere and that other employees' performance has greatly improved.

Today, we have very effective methods and techniques for dealing with problems and situations, but you need the right knowledge to make use of them. I'll explain the manner in which you, as a business operator, can go about taking care of certain problems in the workplace, such as theft. It's all part of taking care of business. If you believe that you need to hire a private investigator, be sure to get all the details about the investigator's costs ironed out once you have explained the nature of your problem. If she or he mentions an hourly rate, request a total cost for the investigation instead of an hourly rate, which could run into a good deal of money.

Also, before the investigator begins, ask for a few references, including some cases he worked on and personally check the references. Make a phone call, ask questions, and see if other clients were satisfied with the work before giving him the go-ahead. As with other professions, investigators do at times rip clients off by overcharging for the amount of time they actually spend on a case. Remember, though, that private investigators can charge a client any amount they choose. It's their prerogative.

As is the case with some police officers, the private investigator may lack the knowledge and experience to deal with particular problems effectively. That's why it's important to check out an investigator's background in terms of how effective she was in solving cases. (Over the years, I have met a few who had all the answers, but no solution.) You can always come straight out and ask whether or not she is competent to handle your particular case, because after all, you're interested in results.

It's important to find a private investigator in whom you have confidence and whose advice you can rely on. One may think that a theft case is simple to deal with. In fact, some are not, especially theft in the workplace. When a shoplifter is caught stealing, you can have the person charged or just thrown out of the store. But when a theft involves an employee, it's an entirely different ball game. You just can't throw workers out, as much as you might like to; everything must be done in accordance with the Criminal Code of Canada and the labour codes. As mentioned, for some, the firing process isn't an easy matter to deal with.

There are certain techniques a business owner can apply when dealing with troublesome employees who are not thieves but who, for one reason or another, create a great deal of stress among other workers, which is why you would like to rid yourself of them. First, we know that such employees are not content, because if they were, they would not be going about causing problems, right? A troublemaker—aside from not putting 100 percent of his or her focus into their work—leads other employees to also cause problems. A disgruntled worker isn't an asset, by any definition, and can be compared to a thief who spends a great deal of time thinking up ways to rip you off. If you have a piece of machinery that isn't functioning correctly; you either fix or replace it. The same goes for disgruntled employees.

One must keep in mind that it's all about honesty and productivity. An honest person is a loyal and productive person. Such employees are your best guarantee of satisfaction in the workplace.

And, as always, remember that there are proper procedures on both sides, designed to safeguard your rights as the employer and the rights of the employee. I would strongly recommend—trust me; it's to your advantage—to familiarize yourself with those procedures and laws. You may operate a small business with just a few employees or a larger business with a few hundreds— at the end of the day, the legal procedures are the same. They were put in place to protect all. Perhaps I sound repetitive here, but I cannot stress that point enough: it's essential to protect yourself legally. Think before you proceed. It could save you a great deal of emotional stress and money.

Handle matters problem by problem. Begin by taking care of one, then move on to another. If you have difficulty, as many have when it comes to dealing with a huge problem, dissect it. Chances are; you might then find it simpler to analyse. As an investigator, whenever I'm at work, I try keeping things simple. I find it less confusing.

CHAPTER 9
The Chester Encounter

A number of years ago, I was working a case involving two brothers who ran a family business. One headed the company as general manager, the other acted as his assistant. The general manager (we'll call him Chester) was always busy because he had three businesses to account for. His work kept him away from the main office a few days a week. While he was away, his brother (let's say his name was Allan) always made sure that things ran smoothly.

Chester was more of a family man and a few years older than Allan. Allan was known as a party man; he liked booze, women, and the race track. For a few years, things went well between the brothers. There were never any big problems between them. But one day Chester was having lunch with a business friend, who mentioned Allan had been seen dropping a bundle on the ponies. This was distressing news, because some months earlier, another friend had told him the same thing.

It bothered Chester. Knowing the salary Allan was being paid, he just couldn't see him being able to afford huge bets at the track. He checked the office books; everything seemed in order, but still Chester was concerned. Finally one evening, he mentioned his concern to a friend, who suggested Chester find someone to keep an eye on Allan, to see exactly how much money he was dishing out. The following day, Chester called me. I accepted the job, which was to follow Allan to bars, restaurants, and the race track to see how much money he was spending. I began on a Friday evening. When the night was over I hadn't seen him spend any large amount of money. He didn't go to the race track, but the following night he did, and I saw him lose a great deal of money. Each bet he placed on a horse was always for a huge amount, and he was never a winner. That night, I figured he lost more than two thousand dollars. The next day, I called Chester and gave him the information.

The following weekend at the track, Allan followed the same pattern. He'd bet large sums with lousy results. Again, at the bars and restaurants, Allan didn't seem to be overspending, but the race track—well, that was a different financial story. He seemed to have no control over his desire to bet on horses. After two weekends of observing Allan's spending, I met with Chester late one night at his office to present my written report. Chester was very confused by the fact that Allan was being paid six hundred dollars a week but was losing thousands on the horses. His question was obvious: where was his brother getting the extra cash?

I mentioned that perhaps Allan was involved with shylocks, people who lend money and charge a huge interest. Chester said he didn't think so, because Allan wasn't one to associate with such people. And if he was stuck for some extra money, he'd come to Chester, who would give it to him.

I still believed there was a possibility that Allan was dealing with the shylocks. Maybe he did not want to be seen with them, but when in dire need of money, people will make deals with the devil if they could. After Chester thanked me for my service, I left his office. I was walking out in the hallway when I noticed a man getting off the elevator. To my surprise, it was one of the men whom I had seen at the race track with Allan. He paid no attention to me as I stepped into the elevator. I looked back and saw him enter Chester's office. Now that was confusing; the more I thought about it, the more curious I became. And whenever a private investigator gets curious, a lot of questions begin to form that demand answers. Questions like, just who is that man? What connections does he have with Chester and Allan? Could it be that he had the answer Chester was searching for?

As I drove away, I thought about phoning Chester, but I decided to wait until the next day. I had to find out the identity of that "mystery man." After giving Chester a call the following day, I had my answer; he was the company accountant who had returned to the office to do some work. I told Chester I had seen that person at the race track with Allan, and he seemed surprised. He noted that was rather strange, because as far as he knew, Allan and the accountant didn't get along too well. I told him that from what I had observed at the race track, they seemed to get along very well.

At that point, I had another couple of pressing questions for Chester: how long had the accountant been with the company, and who had hired him? Chester revealed that Allan and the accountant had attended university together; Allan recommended hiring him eight or nine years ago. Hearing that, I told Chester he should really have someone go over the books. I was certain the answer to where Allan was getting the extra money for the race track was somewhere within the numbers in the company ledgers. I mentioned to Chester that I knew an investigator who worked in accounting and gave him his phone number. (Checking books wasn't part of my schooling, so I left that job to others.) The investigating accountant did most of his work in the wee hours of the morning when most people are home sleeping.

Chester seemed surprised when I mentioned the private investigator who was an accountant. A good number of people are unaware that we do have investigators who can function quite well in all types of work and conditions. Seventy-five percent of a private investigator's job is to gather information and evidence. The remaining 25 percent consists of putting it all together and making sense of it. At times, it's like a giant puzzle; you have many questions floating around in your head, and you work till all the answers fit nicely in place, little by little.

Chester wisely followed my advice and hired the investigative accountant to go over the company books. He was soon to learn that his brother and the company accountant were involved in a scam, ripping off the company with phoney invoices. For example, Allan took one of the company's old broken-down trucks and had a body repairman patch it up, repaint it, and change the interior a little. Allan then had someone act as an auto salesman and drive the truck over to the company lot and leave it there. Allan would write up a phoney invoice for a slightly used truck, and the accountant would write out a cheque. With that one scam, they ripped the company off for more than fifteen thousand dollars.

As for Allan and the accountant not getting along well around the office, that was just a scheme to help cover their tracks. A few months after it was over, out of curiosity, I gave Chester a call. He told me that his brother and the accountant were both let go. He mentioned that he and the family took it hard when Allan's fraudulent acts came to light, especially his father, who had a great deal of difficulty accepting what his son had done. His father didn't want Allan to remain in the family business, which he built up over the years with honesty, so Allan had to go.

Before ending our conversation, I asked Chester, if he had to do things over again, would he do anything differently. His answer was yes, adding that maybe if he had paid more attention to what was happening around the office, that whole unfortunate incident may not have occurred.

As I keep saying, it's all about taking care of business. If you're a fighter and you leave your guard down, you'll soon pay for it because you'll get hit. The same goes for business operators—if you let your guard down too often and don't take care of business, you could eventually take a blow where it hurts the most—right in the pocketbook.

As with Chester and Allan, ripping off one's own family member is nothing new. It's been going on for hundreds of years, maybe more so today, due to the fact that our needs and greed are greater. The cost of living has skyrocketed, and most people need that little extra cash in their pockets; where it comes from or how they go about getting it doesn't really bother them as long as they have it. Take, for instance, a person who's earning fifty thousand per year but is spending seventy-five; where are they getting the extra twenty-five?

If you have an employee who's driving around in a Cadillac, as with the receptionist who worked for the dentist, and you as the business owner can't afford one; wouldn't that send you some kind of message? If you have an employee who owns and lives in a three hundred thousand dollar home and you can't afford such a home, doesn't that tell you something? If you have an employee who's living the high society style of life—you know what I mean, an expensive car, plus wining and dining in big fancy restaurants while you may be going out to the much less expensive places such as the corner restaurant—doesn't that send you a message?

The extra cash these people need to continue living their life style—could that be coming from your pocket? Are you the one paying for their extra goodies without realizing it? And how about the gambling habit that your employee may have; is your money being used to feed the gambling machines? Could it be that a lot of your merchandise is leaving through your rear doors and you don't know it? If you're running a business where a great deal of money is changing hands, could it be that some of your money is also finding its way into your employees' pockets instead of your cash register?

Always keep in mind that if an employee figures out a way to rip you off, he will also find a way to cover it up. I have found that most employees who steal from their employers, let it be cash or merchandise; begin small. First they just take some small items. If they take money, they dip into the cash and take a small amount, with the intent of replacing the money the next day. For a period of time, they get away with it. Then the time comes when the employee is not satisfied just taking a few dollars here and there; now she begins taking bigger amounts of money, telling herself she'll put it back later.

When she can't put the money back because she doesn't have it, then she must find a way to cover the theft. Once she figures that out, she continues to pocket money, till the time comes when someone in management becomes suspicious and suddenly realizes that something is very wrong. By the time the employer finds that out, it's too late, because the employee has no way of repaying the stolen money.

How are you as an employer going to resolve that problem? Are you going to fire the corrupt employee so she can move on and get another job somewhere else, where she'll probably do the same, or are you going to get the police involved and let them handle the matter?

Chapter 10
Preparing Your Case is the Key

Before getting the police involved and having the employee charged with theft, this is what I recommend. When you are sure that a crime has been committed by an employee, before you approach the employee in question, you must first consider what your chances are of recovering part or all of the stolen money. It really makes no difference if the theft involved cash or merchandise; it adds up to the same thing—money. What are the possibilities for recovering your loss? If it's a huge amount, check to see what the employee may own of value—a new car or a nice home or an extra piece of property. Maybe your stolen cash is hidden away somewhere, or he may have a wealthy family member. If it's a younger person who still lives with parents, check out what they may own of value and then contact them; it should make no difference who pays you the money. The important thing is recovering the money, in part or all of it. It's better to recover some than none.

Whenever you question an employee, using the simple words "getting the police involved" does wonders. Whenever it comes to getting corrupt employees to cooperate with you, the justice system should also be considered. If the police get involved, there's always the possibility that some of your losses could be recovered through the courts. A judgment may be handed down by the court requiring the employee to make restitution, though that does not guarantee that you'll see any of your money.

Here's how I go about dealing with corrupt employees, depending on the amount of money or merchandise involved. First, I try to recover the stolen merchandise or money. When that is accomplished, I then turn the problem over to the police department and let them deal with the thief or thieves.

I will now discuss certain details and preconceived options that one should consider before getting the police involved or taking certain matters too far. If you get the police involved and a person or persons are charged with a crime, if you later decide that you may have made a mistake and no crime has been committed, that could cost you a huge amount of money, even if the criminal charges are dismissed. Bear in mind that civil lawsuits are costly, because they can go on for years in the courts, possibly at your expense. Be sure that you have the evidence needed to get a conviction.

As a business operator, you must protect yourself, because today, employees are well protected by unions, labour boards, acts, and regulations. Trying to rid yourself of an employee can become a struggle, so it's wise to be both precise and aware of their rights. Follow correct procedure when dealing with employees who are caught committing a crime in the workplace. I have seen many business operators get themselves in a good bit of trouble because they thought if they wanted to rid themselves of employees, they just had to pay them off and show them the door. No, no, no! Not today—maybe years ago you could have gotten away with it, but times have greatly changed. If there's no labour union involved, you may encounter problems with a labour board, and those people can be just as verbally nasty to deal with as any labour unions. As mentioned, be wise, protect yourself, and follow the correct procedures whenever dealing with employees.

If small business owners are to survive, they must arm themselves with tools and skills and the realization that planning is where it all begins. I believe that over 60 percent of people who venture into small business will fail within five years, due to lack of business knowledge. The failures can be credited to poor management. Small business operators put heart and soul into it, but without management skills in all aspects of running a successful business, they are doomed to failure. Their devotion, their love for their business, will be little comfort once the doors are closed. The tools to be used and the skills one needs to be successful in business are available to all; you just need to reach out and ask and gather information on how to achieve success. Hire a firm or individual with effective viable options to your problems. Don't put it off, waiting till your financial crisis has already occurred. Then it's too late.

Business education is a must. Equip yourself with the tools and expertise needed to establish a positive path for financial business success. And you can begin your path to understanding business management better by participating in management seminars and courses, to avoid drifting slowly into bankruptcy.

Another important factor in my experienced is pre-employment background checks. I found that employers sometimes quickly hire a person, making a decision based only on the potential employee's work application, without doing a pre-screening to check if the individual has a criminal record. Criminal record searches can reveal applicants with serious criminal histories; if hired, such employees may impact many aspects of your business, including the safety of other workers. These matters must be taken into account, because business wise a poor hiring decision could result in very drastic consequences.

Take, for instance, the individual who obtained his job without the employer having done a background criminal record check; he was given the position of managing a restaurant. Sometime later, after that individual no longer worked at that restaurant, he and another man walked in one night intending to rob the restaurant; they forced seven employees into a walk-in-freezer. They were bound and gagged, and then all seven were shot. Two survived, five died. Both gunmen had previous criminal records, yet both were able to secure employment, one at a restaurant, the other at a clothing store. The employers did not do background checks. If background checks had been carried out prior to their employment, especially on the individual who at one time managed the restaurant where the incident took place, they probably would not have been hired, and the senseless killing of the employees may never have occurred.

The same can be said regarding what took place at a shopping mall, where at one time I was employed as the mall security manager. One night after closing, a disgruntled restaurant employee forced four employees into a walk-in freezer, then shot and stabbed them to death. The next morning when the restaurant was about to be open for business, an employee made the gruesome discovery when she opened the freezer door and saw the dead bodies. The employee who committed the brutal murders had a long criminal record of violence, but no background check was done on him. He just walked in off the street and was hired—another dangerous example of hiring people without first doing a background check.

Today, criminal organizations are always trying to get some of their gang members hired into positions where they have access to sensitive customer information, especially in financial institutions.

Take what's happening today with political officials within our own government, with their scams that cost the taxpayers hundreds of millions of dollars in payoffs to business associates and friends. Now the government is spending millions to have certain corrupt political officials investigated. The investigation will linger on for years, and by the time it's completed, most of the general public will have forgotten what the fuss was all about. What will happen to those corrupt politicians who pocketed millions of stolen money through their illegal acts? Will these political crooks ever be prosecuted for their crime? Well, it's not that simple. Let's say that a politician wrote himself a cheque for a million; some months later, he was asked to account for that money, and he couldn't. We'd know that he stole the money, and there would be no problem having him prosecuted for that act of theft. If the same politician instead used a roundabout way to get that million, then the matter would be more complicated and not simple enough to have him charged.

The roundabout way goes something like this: let's say I'm a businessman who owns and operates an advertising firm. I'm a good friend of a certain politician. One night over a few drinks, we get to talking a little business, and the politician tells me that his government will soon be in need of some media advertisements. They'd need someone knowledgeable in the advertisement business to handle an account of roughly three million dollars, but there's a little catch. My friend the politician tells me that for his services, I must agree that whenever my advertising firm receives the cheque for that government money, I would have to pass one million of it on to him.

We know that the politician used fraudulent means to get the million, but the manner in which he went about achieving his goal would be hard to prove in court. First, I would have to be charged with some kind of wrongdoing, which will not happen because I didn't do anything illegal. Perhaps I could be charged with something; it was kind of a scam, and to be honest, very little of the millions were spent on advertisements, because very little work was ever done. As for my friend the politician, besides losing his job, what can they do to him? Even if the time comes that we are both charged with a fraudulent act and have to serve a few months in jail, it's no big deal. After all, serving a few months in jail for a couple million dollars really isn't a bad deal, especially if I still have part of the money stashed away somewhere, where they can't get at it. Besides, it's all a big embarrassment for the government, and they would like to see it go away. Knowing that, I'm confident that eventually their investigation into wrongdoings will quietly be swept under the rug.

As for politicians these days, whenever I hear a politician using the worn-out "my interest is for the people" slogan or "we'll fight for your rights"—that is a bunch of crap. Don't get me wrong. A good number of elected politicians have the public's interest at heart, but others are well known for their greed and manipulations, which are an embarrassment to their colleagues.

I am 100 percent for trusting people, but the problem is I don't know who to trust. Take for instance, I want to put my trust in a police officer. First, I'd have to find one of the honest ones, because as you and I are aware, some policemen are corrupt (and for the record, I'm not referring to any one particular police officer or police department or precinct. It's just an unfortunate reality that we do have crooked cops, just as we have some dishonest security personnel and private investigators). If we have a problem putting our trust in certain people, who's to blame? If you say they are, you're right on the money, so to speak. Security officers today are stealing money and doing it while in uniform; ditto for certain policemen. In fact, most such petty crimes are committed while in uniform; in other words, some are out there stealing while otherwise doing their job, serving and protecting the public.

I want you to visualize the following. Let's say I am a cop, out patrolling the city, town, or village in which I work. In the wee hours of the morning, I get a call from the dispatcher asking me to respond to a burglar alarm. After getting the name and address from the dispatcher, I rush to the location, which turns out to be a corner grocery store. After checking the front doors, which are locked, I proceed around to the rear doors, and I find one open. I carefully walk in and manage to locate a light switch. No one is to be found, so I radio the dispatcher and give her the information. She tells me the owner can't be reached by phone and I should stick around while she tries to reach someone else. While waiting, I walk around the store, checking for broken windows and such. I realize the rear door was forced open but not damaged. The door lock is still in place; when I push the door closed, it locks. Because the door can be locked, rather than wait around, I go to the counter and use the phone to call the dispatcher. That's when I notice packs of cigarettes on the floor.

I tell the dispatcher the story and say that I will return when the store opens for business to take a report as to what was stolen. After the call, I take another look at the smokes but then I walk to the rear of the store to turn the lights off and make my exit. But hey, what the heck—I turn back and take a few packs of cigarettes, stuffing them into my jacket before heading out.

Stealing the cigarettes doesn't bother me, but one thing does: when I arrived at the store and checked the burglar alarm key pad, it was not on. That means whoever forced the door open and went in must have had the code to turn the alarm off—maybe an employee. Who else would have a code? Good question, and I will check it out later. As for the stolen smokes, as far as I'm concerned, the person or persons who broke in did the stealing. Who will know otherwise?

What if it had been a jewellery store instead of a grocery store? Would I have stolen a nice watch or maybe a ring? I'm sure I would have. It would all depend on the opportunity. A good number of break-ins that occur at jewellery stores are of the smash-and-grab variety; the floor is littered with jewellery. Yes, I could easily pick up a few pieces from the floor and pocket them. Who would know the difference? Again, it would all depend on my opportunities. If I'm capable of stealing a few packs of cigarettes worth whatever the price is right now, you can bet I'm also capable of stealing a few pieces of jewellery, which may be worth thousands.

Keep in mind that police officers and security guards, as well as people like me, have the ways, means, and knowledge to rip you off. The good news is that in today's high-tech world, there's a significant decline in that type of theft, because thieves never know when the "magic eye" is staring down upon them, recording their actions. Problems arise when people forget or have knowledge that there are cameras placed above the ceiling. Some may be hidden and others in plain view, but some people explicitly involved in illegal actions and compromising positions are caught on tape (and I'm not just referring to people such as office personnel who are caught on tape stealing). Every now and then, we hear people complaining because video cameras in the workplace infringe on their rights to privacy. To that I say, "What privacy?" When you get right down to brass tacks, they don't really have any in this day and age. Maybe while using the washroom, they have a little, but even then, I wouldn't bet on it. Take for instance a story that made the news in New Brunswick a few years back, about an employee who worked in the office of a government department. He had hidden a small spy camera in the trash can of the ladies washroom. When the camera was discovered by one of the women, it caused huge turmoil among the office employees, especially when they realized one of their own co-workers had placed the camera. A couple of weeks later, the man who was responsible committed suicide rather than face the disgrace he brought upon himself, his family, and fellow co-workers.

That incident took place in the office of no less than the Minister of Justice and involved persons who are directly responsible for enforcing laws in place to protect people from sick-minded individuals. Like I said: what privacy? If women can't find a little privacy in their own workplace washroom, especially when employed by the Justice Minister's office, what woman office worker wouldn't have concerns? Spy cameras can be placed almost anywhere.

CHAPTER 11
Hidden Cameras and Panic Buttons

Some of these tiny cameras are found in school washrooms. I was at one of the local schools checking out a problem, and I went to use one of the washrooms. I happened to notice a small hole in the wall. Taking a closer look, I saw a lens of a small camera hidden within the wall of the washroom. The camera lens was very small, about the size of a pencil lead. That type of camera lens is known as a *pinhole lens* because it is very tiny and can be concealed almost anywhere. Some perverts are known to use such types of cameras attached to the end of a walking cane, with a video recorder hidden inside their clothing. They are used in shopping malls, elevators, and especially on escalators, where people are grouped together. The pervert stands behind a young girl or woman and places the tip of the cane near their feet. Images of their lower body under their dress is recorded by the camera and later viewed by the sick-minded pervert. And there is no way of knowing where the video images will end up. A good number of them could end up on the Internet to be shared with other perverts. It would be wise for women using elevators or escalators to pay attention to what is placed next to their feet. They may find the eye of a camera starring up under their dress.

As for the camera I found hidden in the wall of the school washroom— after leaving that school, I decided to drive over to another school to check the washrooms for hidden cameras. I also found a camera hidden within the walls of the second school. Disturbed by my findings, I decided to speak to the local police chief and tell him about the cameras in the washrooms. The chief said that he would look into it. I also contacted the local news media and gave them that information, along with the pictures I took showing the lenses of the hidden cameras. I expressed my concern about why certain schools were using hidden cameras within the walls of the students' washrooms. Within a couple of days the story of the cameras appeared in the newspaper, along with the pictures. Later, I received calls from concerned parents as to what was taking place within their children's schools. As for the police chief, I never heard anything from him, but I was satisfied that the newspaper brought the story of the cameras to the attention of the parents and the public. I suggested that the concerned parents who phoned contact the principals of their schools and question them as to why the hidden cameras were in their students' washrooms.

Over the years, I have often used such lenses while gathering evidences, but placing them in washrooms or bedrooms is something I don't agree with. Especially placing them in school bathrooms; the children are unaware that someone is sitting back in the school office watching their activities. This is comparable to the incident in the women washroom of the justice minister's office.

I found it interesting and at the same time very disturbing that both incidents concerning hidden cameras in washrooms were carried out by government agencies: the justice department and public schools.

As a private investigator I'm well aware of some of the wrongdoings by corrupt employees within the government that have been going on over the years. The incidents I mentioned only touch the surface of the wrongdoings and deceit that go on within our government agencies, at the tax payers' expense.

I believe that that having video surveillance cameras in the workplace is an asset for business owners. Besides being a deterrent to both dishonest shoppers and light-fingered employees, videotapes record a fair and accurate representation of an incident. I recommend the use of surveillance cameras, especially in businesses that are open at all hours of the night. Not only are the cameras a deterrent to shoplifters, they are also an asset in protecting the employees from harm by a would-be robber who's in need of fast cash.

Let's say that I'm going to rob a convenience store; am I going to walk into a place where I know in advance that they have surveillance cameras? No. Instead I will choose a place to rob that I know does not have surveillance cameras. Most persons who commit robberies don't just rush into a store without first eyeing the place. A thief may go in and buy a small item, look around, and then leave, returning later to commit the robbery. If I were the person who was going to commit the crime, would I, after noticing the eyes of cameras staring down upon me, return later to commit the crime? No, I won't want to risk being caught on camera, so I'd choose a place without a camera.

Cameras have a huge deterrent effect on would-be robbers, shoplifters, and corrupt employees. The crooked-mind very seldom rests; it is always at work thinking up new ways and schemes to rip people off. I have heard business operators say, "I'm one-step ahead of them." Some may think so, but I can assure you that if you are only keeping up with an employee with crooked intentions, you are doing well. To do so, one must have the ability to think as a thief. In other words, reverse your positions—let's say you're the employee. How are you going to go about ripping off the employer? If you have the ability to think like a thief, then you may be wiser about what they're up to. But to be one step ahead of a thief or a corrupt employee—I don't believe that's likely. As mentioned, the crooked mind very seldom rests. It's always at work, thinking and figuring out ways to outsmart you. It's like a game; you try to keep your money or merchandise, but the people around you continuously wait for the right moment to steal it away from you, and you never know when they're going to try. They are like a snake, waiting for the right moment to strike out at you. The disadvantage you have is you never know when they're going to strike. When they do, will you be prepared to deal with the situation?

I have always been concerned about the safety of employees at small businesses like convenience stores that are open during the night and into the wee hours of the morning, often with just one employee. I feel that there should be regulations in place to prevent store operators from having only one employee on duty; a person shouldn't be expected to work alone. It's bad enough that most such workers are underpaid, but to have them work alone, their life potentially in danger, is another question. The same can be said regarding coffee shop operators, though for some reason they are not at high risk for being robbed. It could be due to the steady flow of customers and policemen coming in and out at all hours of the night.

It's up to the owners to see that their employees are working in a safe environment. As it is now, a great number of these stores don't have panic systems and surveillance cameras in place, which could reduce the risk of harm or death sometimes inherent in a robbery.

I have spoken with a good number of employees who work all hours of the night. Whenever I asked what was in place to protect their safety, their reply was "Nothing," or "I don't know." Some said there was a button at the counter near the cash, but they were never told what the button was for. The button is referred to as a *panic button*. When an employee presses it, it activates a device that sends a special signal that a robbery is in progress over the phone line to a monitoring station. The monitoring station then relays that information to the police. The problem is that sometimes these panic buttons are placed at service counters but are not connected to anything. It is just placed there to give an employee a false impression that the button is there for her safety. In reality, if she presses that button in hope of summoning help, no one will respond because it is not connected to a monitoring station or the police department. The store owners and operators do not realize that they could be held responsible if an incident occurred where an employee gets harmed during a robbery.

It is the responsibility of the owners and managers to see that their employees have some form of protection. Placing panic buttons that do not function at service counters doesn't contribute to an employee's safety; that is being very deceitful, and management can be held accountable for their actions. My advice to employees who work at service counters is that if they notice a panic button, which is usually placed near the cash register, and management did not tell them their proper function, the employee should ask why the buttons is there. If a panic button is operational, how it functions should be explained to the employee, along with what to do and not do in case of a robbery. If placed there under false pretenses, the manager should tell the employee it has no function.

I know of many managers who forget to explain the function of these panic buttons to new employees, and that can lead to drastic consequences. For instance, an employee working at a convenience store was told that in case of a robbery, she was to push the panic button. One night, someone entered the store with a gun, and a robbery took place. The woman at the counter handed the money over to the person with the gun. As he turned to walk away, she pressed the panic button to summon help, but instead of getting help the robber turned around and shot her, killing her. If she had not pressed the panic button, the robber would have left the store, and no harm would have come to that employee.

The owner had rigged up his own little panic system that was not connected to a monitoring station; instead it was hooked up to a siren that was activated within the store whenever someone pushed the button. Hearing the loud siren go off, the robber knew that the employee had pressed the panic button, so he turned around and shot her. I'm sure that if the employee had known beforehand how the panic system functioned, she would not have pressed the button till the robber had gone out the door into the street. That mistake cost her life because an owner, to save a few dollars, had hooked up his own little gadget without giving any consideration to what could happen to an employee who pressed that panic button. In that incident, the cost was huge—a loss of life. A wife, a daughter, a mother gone forever—for what? To save an employer money.

This should be a lesson to other store operators who may have similar audible devices that function with a panic button. If it is audible, get rid of it and get connected to a monitoring station. The correct system could save a life.

If the store owner who rigged up his own little device had been the person at the counter when the robbery took place, would he have put his life in danger by pressing that panic button, knowing that it had an audible siren, when a person with a gun was still in the place? I believe the answer to my question would be no; he would not have touched that panic button while a robber with a gun was still in the store. But his employee did. Could it be that the woman who lost her life wasn't made aware of how that panic system functioned? Was she told to never press the button until a robber was out the door and onto the street? Was it explained to her if she did happen to press the panic button while the gunman was still in the store, it could endanger her life?

There's a huge difference between explaining to an employee how a panic system correctly functions and just saying to an employee, "If ever there's a robbery, just press the panic button." Are employees putting their lives at risk by pressing a panic button? Employee safety should be an employer's first concern; part of that is informing employees that if a robbery occurs, they should do what is needed to protect themselves from being harmed. Never confront a would-be robber who is armed. *Armed* refers any type of weapon, including a gun, knife, or any object that can be used against an employee. Why should employees put their lives at risk by confronting a robber? If the operator is insured, the owner or owners will be compensated for their loss by the insurance company. If the operator does not carry such insurance, that's their problem. If I were an employee working for minimum wage, in the event of a robbery, I would service the would-be robber as I would a customer—give him what he wants. Don't be aggressive—that could mean your life.

Keep in mind that most people who commit robbery are cowards, and cowards are known to strike out quickly. So don't give a robber a reason to do so. Most importantly, once you have handed over the money, quietly move back from the counter and keep your hands in full view of the robber to show that you have no intention of doing anything, and that will put the robber at ease. That could save you from bodily harm or even death. If you position yourself close to the counter and your hands are not in view, the robber may get the impression that you are contemplating something and take drastic action. Keep in mind that people who enter a store to commit an act of robbery want to get in and out as quickly as possible; no action should be taken by an employee to antagonize the robber. As long as the robber is still in the store, the employee's life could be in jeopardy. Any employees who think that they may become heroes by trying to prevent a robbery in progress could be contributing to their own death; once they are buried, such heroes are quickly forgotten.

To contribute to the safety of their employees, owners should have a dependable surveillance system in place, which should consist of good quality cameras with a good video recorder programmed to record all activities during store hours. The problem with video recorders is the fact that they must be serviced to ensure it is in good working order. In many cases, after a robbery has taken place and the videotapes are reviewed, the images on the tapes are not of good quality. The videotapes were reused too many times and very seldom replaced with new ones. I recommend the use of a digital video recorder in place of a tape recorder with a DVR. There is no tape; all video images are recorded on a hard drive. The recorded images are very clear when reviewed. If an incident such as a robbery ever occurs, the police may need to use the video recording as evidence. For police officers to submit video recordings in the courts, the recording must be of good quality and accurate. Distorted images of a video cannot be used in the courts of law as evidence.

If panic buttons are placed at service counters, these emergency systems should be connected directly to a monitoring station or a police department. As previously mentioned, there should be laws and regulations in place that will force all such owners and operators to install these two systems.

The person who shot and killed the store employee who set off the alarm by pressing the panic button was found and convicted of the murder and later electrocuted in a Florida state prison.

For some years now, insurance companies insist that certain businesses, such as convenience stores, have a security system in place before they'll issue an insurance policy. To get the insurance, many owners reluctantly get an alarm system installed and pay out a monthly fee to the monitoring service. With that done, the business owner gets the insurance policy at a discount. Often, some months later, the business owner cancels the monitoring service for which he received a discount on his insurance. When the alarm system needs servicing, nothing is done. Then the alarm is not useable. When the time rolls around to renew the insurance policy, the insurance provider renews the policy and the discount, assuming that the policyholder still has a functioning alarm system connected to the monitoring service.

Regarding government fire inspectors and municipal fire chiefs—some of the situations I have encountered over the years are unbelievable. As an example, when someone wants to go into the business of providing a special care home or a senor residence, the fire inspectors make sure that the building is equipped with safety equipment such as a fire system, along with magnetic hallway door holders, etc. This equipment must all be in place and functional before the residence can open for business. The problem arises a year or so later, when no follow-up is done by either the government or municipal safety inspectors. I believe it is part of their duties to check these places annually, making sure that such safety systems are still functioning properly. They check if the operators have a qualified person to verify that the fire alarm system was working correctly. Once that has been done, the person who performed the maintenance inspection then leaves a signed certificate of verification, with the date showing when the verification was done. It's the responsibility of the owners or operators to see to it that safety systems verification is done annually.

Because a fire system is a life saving device, especially in a residence such as special care and senior citizen homes, then someone with authority, such as a safety inspector, must see to it that a fire alarm system is in place and in good working order. Such systems need to be inspected and verified annually, which involves no manual labour on the inspector's part other than to walk into these places and check for a verification date when the maintenance of these systems were last carried out. And if they find that no annual verification has been done, then it's their responsibility to see to it that the owner or operator gets it done. They should return later to the location and make sure that the maintenance on the system was completed. In a significant number of incidents, the safety inspector makes the request, but the safety inspector fails to return to see if their demands were carried out in accordance with the safety regulations.

There's a great difference between a fire system that is in place to assist in saving a life and one to save a building without occupants. If a building is insured, then it's up to the insurance company to see to it that the maintenance service is done annually and the fire systems are in good working order for the businesses. If businesses can't prove that they had the annual inspection, their insurance policy shouldn't be renewed. I feel that the insurance provider, before issuing a renewal on an insurance policy, should have someone visit the location of the policy holder and verify that the annual maintenance service has been done on the fire system. As it is now, many insurance policies are renewed without anyone from the insurance provider checking to be sure that the policy holder still has a, functional fire system in place in accordance with the safety standards and regulations.

Each year thousands of people die due to smoke alarm and fire system failures, just because someone was too busy or didn't bother to check and make sure that those life-saving devices were in good working order. Can you imagine losing your children to fire and knowing that maybe you could have prevented that if you had only taken a few minutes just once or twice a year to change the batteries? What a cruel way for a child to die. As I write, somewhere a child is dying due to someone's laziness and stupidity.

While I am on the subject of smoke alarms, if you intend to put up a Christmas tree when Christmas rolls around, I strongly recommend that you visit a hardware store and buy an inexpensive gift for your family that only cost a few dollars—a smoke detector. Connect the battery to it and place it under the tree among the other gifts. One never knows, but that could be the gift that saves you and your family if the Christmas tree catches fire.

Some years ago around Christmas, a young woman was visiting her parents, and she placed a few gifts under the Christmas tree. On Christmas morning, the mother opened the gifts; one of the gifts was a smoke alarm. The mother placed the alarm back into the box. When Christmas was over, she placed the box that contained the smoke alarm in her bedroom closet. A month or so later, in the wee hours of the morning, the parents were awakened by a buzzing sound coming from the closet. The mother got up and walked over to the closet to see what was making that sound. As she approached the closet door, she noticed smoke coming out from under the door. She quickly opened the door and removed the boxes and other items from the closet floor to find where the smoke was coming from. It was coming through a hole in the floor, so her husband rushed down into the basement and found the garbage can was on fire. No damage was caused because it was a metal can. The smouldering fire was quickly put out.

Returning upstairs, the husband found his wife sitting in the living room tearfully looking down at the smoke alarm—the Christmas gift from their daughter that probably helped save their lives—in her hand.. If her daughter hadn't connected the battery to the smoke alarm, the outcome of that story could have been drastic. Even though the smoke alarm was still in its box, once it sensed a little smoke, it activated the buzzer, awaking the parents.

Since hearing that story, I have acquired five or six extra smoke alarms in addition the ceiling-mounted ones in my home. I put one behind my computer just above the power bar and the electrical wiring, and one at the rear of my TV and VCR, as well as one on our bedroom dresser. They are there for extra protection. The ceiling-mounted smoke alarms should always be maintained and the batteries changed once or twice a year. These alarms are life-saving devices, and the life they save maybe yours or that of a loved one.

The thought of dying in a fire really scares me, so for safety reasons I always keep a golf putter in the corner next to my bed. If there's ever a fire and we can't get out the bedroom door, that putter will be used to smash the glass from the bedroom window, enabling us to get out. A steel putter could be used to bust a hole through the bedroom wall. I got the idea about the golf putter one day while I was visiting an elderly lady who lived alone. I had stopped by her home at the request of her son, a friend of mine. He was out of town for a few days and was concerned about her; she had problems getting around due to her age. While there having a coffee with her, I glanced up and noticed a smoke detector and asked her if the detector was working. She said that she didn't know and had never checked it because she couldn't use a ladder. When I asked her when the last time was her son or someone else had changed the battery, again she replied she didn't know, adding that no one bothered with it. Hearing that, I walked over and picked up a broom. With the handle I reached up and pressed the smoke alarm test button; nothing happened. It was dead.

Not one of the four ceiling-mounted smoke alarms was in working order. I was pissed off. Her son told me that he was concerned about his elderly mother's safety, yet he didn't have the brains to see to it that she had working smoke alarms in her house. This made me wonder how really concerned the son was about his mother's safety. She had no batteries, so I went to the store and bought some. Before leaving her home, I made sure that all the smoke alarms were working. While in her bedroom replacing the alarm battery, I asked her what she would do if a fire broke out and she was caught in the bedroom. She said that she would not know what to do. I explained if she was unable to safely get out through the bedroom door, she was to quickly dial 911, pick up something and break the window glass, and yell out for help to get someone's attention. With a puzzled look she said, "Well, I can't pick up a chair. It's too heavy."

I said, "Use anything you can get your hands on and just stand back and drive it through the window." As she slowly looked at different objects in the room that she could use, I got an idea. I went out to my car and picked up a golf putter. I returned with it and placed it in her hand. I asked, "Do you know what that is?

"Yes," she said, "it's for golfing."

"You're right," I said. "As you can see, it's made of steel. Keep it near your bed, and if ever you need to break the window to get help, use it."

As I was about to get into my car and drive away, I heard a smoke alarm sound, so I returned to see what was happening. When I opened the door, there she was, using the broom handle on the smoke alarm test button with a childish smile. She said, "Just doing what you told me to do." I laughed and walked away, thinking she was going to be okay. As for the son who was so concerned about his mother, I had a few well-chosen words for him, and they weren't too nice.

As for safety devices like residential smoke alarms, I feel that there's never enough said about the importance of having working alarms in the homes. As one fire chief emphasized, an average of three children a day, approximately 1,100 children under the age of fifteen, die each year in house fires, and about 3,600 children each year are injured. He stated the fire was the number two cause of accidental deaths among children under the age of five, placing them at double the risk of dying in a home fire as the rest of the population. The most startling aspect of these tragic statistics is the fact that 90 percent of fire deaths involving children occur in homes without working smoke detectors. These statistics refer to the United States; can you imagine if Canada and other parts of the world were included in those statistics of children dying due to fires in homes that have no working smoke alarms? The children who die in fires don't die because of their own stupidity; their deaths can be attributed to the stupidity of their parents, the very people children rely on for their protection and safety. I cannot visualize a more cruel death for a child than being trapped in a burning house, surrounded by smoke and fire.

Smoke detectors that have dead batteries or none at all may cause not only the occupants of the homes to die. Firemen all over the country are losing their lives by going into burning homes to try to rescue children and get them to safety. Nationwide, firemen are urging parents and kids to adopt a simple, potentially lifesaving habit— to change the batteries in their smoke detectors whenever they change the clocks back to standard time. This simple act could be the most effective in making their homes a little safer each year.

I do not fear death, but death by fire, I do fear. It's a slow and horrible way to die. And as a father, if one of my children were to die due to my neglect, I would have that on my conscience for the rest of my life. I'd never forgive myself.

Chapter 12
Shoplifting

Speaking of the responsibilities of parent and elders to safeguard children, I include teaching children by setting good examples for them to learn and live by. I witnessed one of the most troubling encounters involving children one day when I was employed at a store. A woman came in, followed by three young children. She carried nothing but her purse; one of the children had a large shopping bag, and as the woman went from counter to counter looking at different merchandise, I noticed the woman glancing around as if to check if anyone was watching her, and I became suspicious. As she walked around the store, I kept at a safe distance so she wouldn't notice me. At one counter in women's lingerie, I noticed her placing a bra at the edge of the counter. Just as she was about to walk away, the young child who had the shopping bag reached up, grabbed the bra, and dropped it into the bag. Then they moved over to another counter, and the same procedure was used to steal another item of clothing.

As she left the store, a woman security officer and I stopped her when she stepped out onto the street with her children. Once we had her up in the security office, we called the police, as we usually did when we'd catch a thief. If small-priced items had been taken, we'd typically give the thief a lecture about what could happen if they continued stealing, and then we would put them out of the store. In the case of the women and her children, the police were called because of the young children she was using as part of her thievery.

When teenagers are caught stealing or have other problems concerning the law, how often do we hear parents say, "I don't know why they went wrong; I did my best with them." Is that what the woman with the children will say one day, after one or all of them end up behind bars? "I did my best to teach them what's right." (Oh! Really?)

As parents, we don't realize always it, but the fact is that most of us teach our children something about stealing at very young ages, and the teaching I'm referring to often goes something like this. You're at the mall shopping with your child, and you walk into one of the large grocery stores, grab a shopping cart, and proceed to do your shopping. You pick up an item, say something as simple as a grape, and you put it in your mouth. You may even offer your child one. A few aisles down, you may reach into the cookie box and get yourself one of those sweet little cookies to munch on, and again, you may be thoughtful and hand your child one. After all, what parent would walk around a grocery store munching on goodies without sharing some with their child, especially when it's costing the parent nothing?

That young child is always learning, and a good part of their learning comes from examples from their parents. When parents do such things in the presence of their children, they quickly pick that up. Seeing their parents do it, the children get the impression that it's okay. But it's not okay. Actually, when parents walk around grocery stores munching on items that aren't paid for, that's theft. If you take something you do not own and put it to your own use, or the use of others, you are actually stealing. If grocery stores wanted customers to help themselves to free samples, that would be no problem. But grocery stores don't do that. At times, people may hand out samples of new items, to get the customers' opinion on the new product. But as for customers walking around munching, the store owners don't want that.

After seeing that no one is watching or paying you any attention, how about if you causally slip an item in your pocket and leave the store without paying for it? The employees or other customers may have not seen you pocket the item, but your child did. Later in life, that child may begin stealing because of the examples set forth by his parents. Children think it was okay for their parents to do it, so they begin stealing small items here and there. As time goes on, the children who witnessed stealing by their parents become teens not satisfied with just stealing small items; they move one step higher and begin stealing clothing and other high-priced items. Eventually, they'll steal about anything they can carry away. When they end up in jail, ask yourself, *What did I do wrong?* Then recall the days when you walked around the store munching on things you didn't pay for. Don't forget the occasional can or bottle of beverage you may have opened and drank while pushing your cart around. Again being a thoughtful parent, you'd give your child a sip or two. So far there's no problem with that, because when you get to the checkout counter you'll hand the empty container to the clerk, who will charge you for it. That is a good example you set for your child, the correct thing to do—you drank the beverage and you paid for it. But many shoppers are known to take the empty container and place it on the shelf among other items. As the clerk is passing your items through the scanner, are you going to say, "Oh, by the way, while I was shopping, I drank a can of beverage, which I want to pay for"? No, you won't, because if you intended to pay for it, you wouldn't have hidden the empty container on the shelf. If you were in the presence of your child, with those little bright eyes watching every move you make, it's clear your child was learning from your example.

One day, I observed a young boy walk around a retail store stuffing items in his pockets as if he were an experienced thief. Once we got him up in the office, I asked him where he learned how to steal. He smartly answered, "From my mother." After talking with the young boy and learning more about him, I phoned his father at his place of work and told him that his son had been caught stealing and to come to the store and get him. I didn't want to phone the home, because I didn't want to talk with the mother. I wanted the father to hear what the boy had told us. When he arrived, I asked the boy to tell his father what he had told us about the mother who had taught him how to steal. Sometimes she'd send the boy into a store to steal items while she waited out in the car for him to return with the stolen merchandise. On that day, the mother wasn't outside waiting. If she had been, I would have gone and gotten her, and the police would have been called. After hearing what his son had to say, the father was in tears. He found what he heard from his son very difficult to accept. It was plain to see by the father's reaction that he had been unaware of what was going on between the young boy and his mother. That was just one of many disgusting incidents that I have experienced over the years involving children, teenagers, and parents.

It is astonishing and hard to believe that parents would have their children commit a crime for them, but it happens all the time. And not only the poor, but the very wealthy are doing it.

In my years working in private security, the most dangerous types to deal with were professionals who stole for a living. I have dealt with some who thought nothing of killing. One such person was Tommy, whom I had met one night at a western bar. Sometimes I'd stop in and have a few drinks and listen to the western singers. At the time, Mom's Tavern was the place to go. Unknown to me, Mom's was also a place where hoods and people like Tommy hung out. This was brought to my attention one night while I was seated at the bar talking with Terry, the owner and one of the barmen.

That night, after Terry had finished serving a group of men who were seated in a dark corner of the tavern, he quietly said as he placed a beer on the counter in front of me, "Fred, don't look around, but if I was you I'd leave, because there's a man back there with Tommy who knows you."

I asked Terry, "Why should I leave? I'm not bothering them." Just as I said that, I noticed one of the men from the table where Tommy and his group were sitting approach the bar. He walked up, stood next to me, and ordered a drink. He looked at me and said, "Hey, don't I know you from somewhere?"

"You may," I said. "I've been coming here for a while."

"No, no," he said, "not from here. It will come back to me later." With that, he walked back to Tommy's table.

I recognized him.

A few years back, he had tried to leave Simpson's store with a five-thousand-dollar mink coat. We managed to grab him just as he was about to exit the store with the coat. He put up a struggle and took a swing at me; he missed, but I didn't. Once we got him to the security office, the police were called, and he was taken to jail. He later served time for the attempted theft; he had a long police record involving acts of theft.

As I was deciding what to do, Terry said as he wiped the counter, "One of your friends one night mentioned that you were good with your hands, but Fred, no matter how good you are, you will not win with these guys. They don't fight one-on-one, and you're going to get hurt. Where's your car parked?" I told him at the front. Terry then told me, "Let on you're going to the washroom and then use the back door, and don't wait around."

I told Terry that I would leave, but through the front door.

After finishing my drink, I got up and walked toward the door. As I did, I noticed Tommy and his gang eyeing me. Paying no attention to them, I made my way down the stairs and got into my car, which I had parked close to the entrance. Just as I pulled away, I looked back in my mirror and saw a few of Tommy's gang rush out. If my car had been parked farther away, I wouldn't have made it. I later learned from Marc, a policeman, that Tommy and his gang were professional thieves and heavily into drugs.

It is said that at one time, Tommy shot and killed a man and had gotten away with it without having any criminal charges laid against him by the police. One night, he and some of his gang were at a ski resort up north. It was a place where they'd often go partying during the winter months. That night, Tommy had an argument with a man who, along with his girlfriend, went there to spend a few days skiing. The argument began when the woman, who had a little too much to drink, got overly friendly with Tommy. Anyway, after the incident, the man and the woman left, saying they were going to another place to have a drink. Tommy, who was in a rage over what had occurred and also had a few drinks too many, said loudly, "That bastard should be shot." That is precisely what happened.

The next morning, the man was found dead in his car a few miles outside of the village, with a bullet hole in his head. The woman wasn't with him. She told the police that he had left around three that morning to get some cigarettes. She went to bed.

Tommy did the killing, but there were no witness to the murder. The police chief met with Tommy and told him if he and his friends left the village and did not return, there would be nothing more said about the murder. That is what took place. Later in the criminal investigation into the murder, Tommy and his friends moved out of the village.

Tommy went around boasting to other gang members that he blew that guy's brains out. He said that after the ski resort had closed, he and his buddies left to go find another bar to continue partying. As they drove by a car that was pulled over on the side of the road, one of them noticed the man who was standing at the rear of the car having a leak was the same person Tommy had the argument with at the ski resort. Tommy had the driver stop the car, and they backed and stopped alongside the parked car, which was about to drive off. Tommy got out and walked up to the car. As the unsuspecting man lit up a cigarette, Tommy pulled out a gun and shot him in the head.

After the incident with the four thieves at the western tavern, I later met up with Tommy and his gang again, under very different circumstances.

When I first got started in private security, I quickly learned that it wasn't simple and easy work. My first experience came one day as I walked by the Simpson's store and came upon two women who were struggling with each other over a shopping bag. I paused, as others did, and watched the women. I found it amusing to see the two women fight over a shopping bag. As I stood and watched, I was suddenly pushed aside. The man who had rushed up from behind me grabbed one of the women by her arm and pulled her away from the other. As he did, the bag tore open, and the contents dropped to the street: women's panties, bras, and other underclothing. Those who stood watching laughed. I didn't feel like laughing. I was a little pissed off at the man because he pushed me aside roughly. So as he and the woman rushed by me, I stuck out my foot and tripped him. They both fell to the ground, the woman on top of him. As they pulled each other up, I said to the man, "Next time, watch who you're pushing." Just then, a police car drove up, and two officers rushed out. A woman who was picking up the clothing from the ground yelled out to the officers, "Stop them! They just stole that stuff from the store." The officers rushed down the street and grabbed the two.

As I was about to walk away, the woman who had yelled to the police pointed toward me, then one of the officers came up to me and asked if I had witnessed what had taken place. I told him what I had seen and explained why I had stuck out my foot and tripped the man. I was told by the officer to wait. After they put the man and woman in the police car, the officer who had spoken to me came back and asked for my name address and phone number. Thinking that something was going to happen to me, I said to the officer, "I guess I'm in trouble."

"No," he smiled, "we just need that information in case we need you as a witness." I went on my way and thought no more of it.

CHAPTER 13
Security

The following day I received a phone call from a Mr. Poitras, who said he was with Simpson's. After thanking me for what I had done, he asked if I was working anywhere. I told him that I had just quit a job I no longer liked. Mr. Poitras said that if I were interested, he might have a job for me. When I told him I was interested, he told me to come to the store and see him.

The next day, I went to the store and was taken to Mr. Poitras's office. When I entered, he introduced himself as one of the store's directors. He asked about my previous work. I told him that for the past two years, I had worked in the collection department of a company, mostly driving from place to place, trying to get money from people who didn't have any. Mr. Poitras laughed and asked, "What made you decide to leave?"

"Well," I said, "one day, I was given an account to collect, and I drove up to a broken old home. After knocking a few times, a woman opened the door, asking what I wanted. I told her that I was there to collect money that was owed. 'You want money,' she said, opening the door wide, as if she wanted me to see inside. 'We got no money, come in,' she said. 'I want to show you something.' She opened a beat-up refrigerator, which was empty, and then pointed to the four children at the table, eating nothing but dry bread. Seeing that, I asked her where her husband was. She said, 'At the tavern.' Because the children had no food, I took a twenty dollar bill from my pocked and handed it to her. I told her to go buy some food for the kids and left. That's when I quit. I had enough!"

Mr. Poitras said, "You're soft-hearted."

"Not really. I just don't like to see children go hungry."

"The woman who you saw outside the other day trying to make an arrest—Mrs. Gibson—she and her husband are police officers; they work here at the store in their spare time."

After filling out an application, I was told that within a few days someone from the store would be in touch with me. At the time, I didn't know what store security work consisted of. But after four days without getting a call, I figured I blew it, because the work application asked if I had a police record. I wrote *yes*, because I did. An incident occurred back in the latter part of the fifties. While working in Toronto, I was charged and convicted of obstructing a police officer.

While I was walking home one night, for no apparent reason a police officer got out of his patrol car and asked me my name. When I questioned him about why he was asking, he grabbed hold of me and pushed me in the back seat of the police car. (I will elaborate more on the incident later.)

So I figured I wouldn't be getting the security job. I was a bit disappointed, but on the fifth day I received the call from Simpson's and was told that I did get the job. I was to report for work the following morning. My first week was spent assisting other security personnel and familiarizing myself with the store, which had six floors. In the sixties it was considered one of the larger stores, along with Eaton's, in the downtown area, and it was always packed with shoppers and thieves.

At first, I found it very confusing as to how a store detective could spot a shoplifter among so many people, but as the days passed and I made my first few arrest, I quickly got on to it. It was mostly about body language and shifty eyes. In my first six months, I made over one hundred and forty arrests.

After being with Simpson's for a year and a half, I decided to take another job at the Windsor Hotel as a security officer. Working at Simpson's was a good experience. In the beginning I found it hard to believe the type of people we were picking up for stealing. They came from all professions and walks of life. Besides the down-and-outers, the people with no job or money, there were also people like the man I took to the office for shoplifting. Usually, we'd have suspects empty their pockets and put the contents on the desk. The sharply dressed man with a five- or six-hundred-dollar suit on had stolen a wallet and a pair of leather gloves worth around forty dollars. When I asked him for some ID, he opened up his wallet and handed me his driving licence. As he did, a business card fell out. The business card read Doctor of Psychiatry. I noticed it carried the same name as his driver's license. "Is that you?" I asked, handing him the card. "You're a doctor?"

He smiled and said, "Yes, I am." I stared at him, disgusted, for a moment, and then said, "You mean to tell me that you are a psychiatrist who treats people with mental problems, and here you are, a bloody thief, stealing!" He just stood there with a stupid grin on his face. "You are disgusting! I should have you put in jail," I said, handing him his driving licence. "Get the hell out of the store, before I change my mind and call the police." As he was about to walk out of the office, he took his business card and placed in on the desk and said, "Here—keep my card in case you're ever in need of my services." At the time, I didn't find it funny, but when I mentioned it to another officer later, we laughed. I would have called the police and had him charged, but the store had a policy: if the theft was under fifty dollars and the person hadn't caused any trouble, the police were not to be called. We were just to give them a lecture on stealing and send them on their way.

A few days after leaving Simpson's, I started at the Windsor Hotel. It wasn't really the type of security work that interested me, but it would be a different experience for dealing with people and problems. And that is what I wanted: knowledge in different aspect of security work. A few months before deciding to leave Simpson's I was having coffee with Mr. Poitras. Before working for Simpson's, he was a sergeant with the Quebec Provincial Police. He mentioned to me that for someone to be licensed by the Justice Department to operate their own private agency, they would either need five years' experience in different aspect of security work or to be an ex-police officer. As I wasn't an ex-policeman, if I someday wanted to operate my own business I'd need to learn from the ground up, and that meant on-the-job training. You learn as you're doing the work.

The Windsor Hotel had an interesting history. After it was built in the later part of the eighteenth century; the nine-story structure was acknowledged as the most luxurious hotel in the Dominion, with two huge, fabulous ballrooms, a twenty-foot ceiling, crystal chandeliers, the French renaissance-style salon de Versailles, and the Victorian salon. The Windsor was the fitting symbols of Montreal's historic ancestry. It has played host to royalty, including: King George VI, Queen Elizabeth, and politicians, such as Sir John A. McDonald, Sir Winston Churchill, Charles DeGaulle and John F. Kennedy, as well as celebrities, including Sarah Bernhardt, Rudyard Kipling, Jean-Paul Sartre, and Mark Twain, who in his speech at a banquet in his honour said, "You couldn't throw a brick without breaking a church window." He had noticed many churches from his hotel window. The ballrooms were always in demand for banquets, weddings, conventions, corporate meetings, and press conferences. The salons had hosted some of the most lavish social occasions the city had ever witnessed, among them, the wedding of former Prime Minister Brian Mulroney's daughter and that of Prime Minister-in-waiting Paul Martin's son.

Speaking of noted celebrities, I must mention the wedding of the daughter of one of the known mafia bosses. Around the latter part of the 60s, I was on duty the night that Mr. Cotroni hosted the wedding reception for his daughter in one of the ballrooms. Back then, Vincent and Frank weren't as well known to the general public as they would later become. In the 60s and earlier, Vincent had ties with Meyer Lansky, a powerful known Mafia leader in the United States. In a newspaper article during the latter part of the 90s, the police described Frank Cotroni as a Mafia boss and one of the most powerful drug smugglers in the world.

The night of the daughter's reception, as I was observing the hotel lobby through the one-way mirror from the security office, I noticed on different occasions a few men hanging around the front entrance of the hotel. They'd go out for a few minutes and then return and stand near the doorway, as if watching who was coming and going. At the time, I was aware of who the Cotroni brothers were, because one night when we were talking about criminals, Marc had mentioned that the Cotroni brothers were the most dangerous people to deal with.

Later that night as I walked through the hotel lobby, I noticed one of the Cotroni brothers talking to another man near the ballroom doorway. I approached him, told him that I was with the hotel security, and mentioned the men who were hanging around the front entrance. As he looked me over, Mr. Cotroni said, "They are okay; they are with us, but thanks anyway."

When the reception was over and the guests were leaving, as Mr. Cotroni walked by, he stopped for a brief moment and asked "What's your name?"

"Fred Hudon," I said.

"Thanks again," he answered, smiling as he walked away.

As with Tommy and his gang, some years later I would again meet with the Cotroni brothers—mainly Frank, who in later years would replace his older brother Vincent as the Montreal Mafia boss.

I found hotel security work was less stressful. I wasn't always running around in search of potential thieves. At Simpson's it was crazy; every day there, people were ripping the store off. For each one caught stealing merchandise, four or five would get away with it, and that wasn't including the dishonest employees who were steadily ripping off the store. At times, it was unbelievable the amount that some employees would steal.

After we caught one such employee stealing from the store, we went to search his home for stolen items. This young man had enough stolen merchandise stashed in his home to start a small store. He had over five thousand dollars' worth of jewellery hidden away in his bedroom. When it was over, we recovered over fifteen thousand dollars' worth of stolen merchandise. After he was caught, this young man squealed on other employees who were also ripping off the store. We had him believe that another employee had informed us about his stealing; when he heard that, he got angry and told on the other employees also involved in stealing.

When the investigation was over, five employees were dismissed and two were charged with theft; the other three, less serious offenders, were just fired.

Some cases stand out in my mind. One involved a woman who worked as a reporter for one of the French newspapers. Each time she came into the store, we'd see her eyeing any employees who were near her, and we believed from her actions that she was stealing. We spent weeks trying to catch her in the act. One night, when she was seen walking around the store, we explained to one of the young female employees what we wanted her to do. She was to put on her coat and walk around near the woman. We gave her a shopping bag with a few items to carry, to make it seem as if she was shopping. We asked that she try and keep an eye on whatever item the woman picked up. If she saw her place any item in her shoulder bag, the employee was to remove the hat we gave her to wear. Mrs. Gibson and I watched from the upstairs one-way mirror. The young employee approached where the woman was standing. From our vantage point, we could see that the young girl was doing okay. She walked around, picking up items and placing them back, as all shoppers do. After ten minutes or so, we saw the woman step on the escalator to go up to the second floor. About the fifth person behind her was the employee. She was smart to not get too close to the woman.

Mrs. Gibson and I made our way to the second floor to watch their movements. At times, we'd lose sight of them both because of the huge pillars, but most of the time, we had them in sight. After she spent some time looking over some blouses, we saw the woman pick two of them and walk toward the fitting room. It was out of view from where we were, but we could still see the employee. After about ten minutes, we noticed the woman returning with the blouses. She laid them on the counter and walked away. As she did, we noticed the employee go over to where the woman had placed the blouses. She picked them up, and as she laid them back down, she removed her hat.

Mrs. Gibson went out on to the floor, while I stayed and watched the woman's movements. After she spoke with the employee, Mrs. Gibson came back and said that the girl told her the woman had four blouses in her hands when she went into the fitting room, but she returned with just two. Mrs. Gibson asked the girl to check the fitting room to see if the woman had left them in there; if she saw them in there, she was to remove her hat again. When the girl came from the fitting room she didn't remove her hat. We both went out to the floor and spoke with the girl, making sure that she actually saw the woman leave the counter with four blouses. The young girl assured us that the woman walked into the fitting room with four and returned with just two. We then walked around looking for the woman; we had lost sight of her while talking to the girl.

It was a Friday evening, and the store was busy. There were many shoppers. Mrs. Gibson decided that when the woman left the store, she'd stop her because she believed what the young girl said about the four blouses. She was sure the woman would have the blouses in her carrying bag. First we'd have to find her. We walked around, searching for the woman, and the employee came and said that she had located her over in the lingerie department.

Then it was a matter of keeping our eyes on her till she stepped onto the sidewalk. We thanked the young employee, and she went back to her work. We continued to keep tract of the woman at a safe distance; when she got on the escalator going down to the main floor, we were closely behind her. As she stepped off and headed for the doorway, Mrs. Gibson was by her side. I kept a few feet back. When the woman went through the doors, Mrs. Gibson stopped her. Showing the woman her police badge, Mrs. Gibson said, "Please come with us."

The woman said in a strong French accent, "Madam, what for? What did I do?"

"Come along." said Mrs. Gibson. "I'll show you. Follow me." The woman followed, and I walked behind her to make sure that she didn't remove any stolen items from her shoulder bag and drop them among other things on the floor. Some are known to do that. If they weren't closely watched, when you'd search them, you'd find nothing on them. Some were known to sue for false arrest and get away with it, not only at Simpson's but other stores. Eaton's had the same problem.

Professional thieves would go from store to store, trying to be falsely arrested, so they could get money. Most stores would settle out of court rather than spend a good deal of money in legal fees. It was possible for the stores to win their case in court, but the store would have to show that the accused claiming to be falsely arrested had a past history of suing for false arrest, and that was hard to prove.

One gimmick was that they'd walk into a store where they knew most of the security officers by sight. Those professionals would walk around the store; if they noticed that they were being followed, they'd purposely pocket an item or place the item inside their coat, making sure that the security person saw them taking the item. Then the thief would continue walking around the store, knowing that she was being followed. Sometimes a second person was involved in the scheme; the individual who had pocketed the item would sometimes smoothly pass the item to the second person as they walked past each other. This was hard for a security officer to detect because sometimes they'd lose sight of the scheme artist. The second person, who the item was passed off to, would then walk out of the store with it. The individual who did the actual stealing would be arrested after leaving the store. This person, before going willingly back into the store with the security officer, would purposely cause a scene to attract the attention of shoppers going in and out of the store. The security officer would take the individual up into the security office and frisk him, finding he had no stolen merchandise on him. Yet the security officer saw him steal an item. He then would threaten to sue for false arrest. He wanted the police to be called in. The person would be told to leave the store. A few days later, the manager of the store would receive a phone call from the individual or a lawyer. It is often the store policy that if a security officer witnesses someone pocketing an item lost sight of them for any period of time, the person in question was not to be arrested.

As for Mrs. Gibson, neither of us saw the woman take the blouses, and as far as I was concerned Mrs. Gibson should not have arrested the woman. But Mrs. Gibson was a police officer. After we got the woman to the security office, she kept repeating: "But madam, I did nothing wrong. I'm a reporter, madam, I don't steal. I work for a newspaper, madam."

"Open your bag," Mrs. Gibson told her. I stood back and watched. There was more "Madam! Madam! I don't steal!" She placed her bag on the desk and opened it. To Mrs. Gibson's amazement, there were no blouses in the bag, only her personal items.

"See, madam!" said the woman, "I have nothing, I'm not a thief, madam!"

"Where did you leave the other two blouses?" Mrs. Gibson asked. "You went into the fitting room with four, but you returned with only two."

"Yes, madam, but I put them all back on the counter." As the woman spoke I noticed Mrs. Gibson looking her over very carefully. Mrs. Gibson said to me, "Fred, please leave us alone for a few minutes." I left the office and waited. After about fifteen minutes, Mrs. Gibson opened the door, and I went back in. There on the desk were the two blouses. "She had them on under her sweater," said Mrs. Gibson, adding, "This madam is very smart. She said that she was writing a book on shoplifting and had just taken the blouses to see what would happen. If she had not been caught, she would have returned the blouses to the store later." Mrs. Gibson said, "Well, madam, if you want to learn something about shoplifting, we'll help you." With that said, she picked up the phone and dialled the police. When the police arrived, Mrs. Gibson said, "She stole these two blouses as an experiment for a book she said she was writing. If she's looking for information for her book," added Mrs.

Gibson, "let's help her by charging her with theft. When she stands in front of a judge for her crime, that will be another experience she can write about." As the police led the woman away Mrs. Gibson said, "Madam! Madam, have a good night in jail. Whenever you finish writing your book, madam, please send us a copy."

Monday morning, I was called to Mr. Poitras's office. He asked me what had taken place regarding the woman. I explained precisely what happened. Mr. Poitras said that he had asked for me because Mrs. Gibson wasn't working till the weekend. He mentioned that he had received a phone call from the editor of the French newspaper asking to have the charge of theft against the woman dropped. Before leaving Mr. Poitras's office I asked, "Will the charge be dropped?"

"Absolutely not!" he answered. The following Monday, in court, the woman pleaded not guilty to the charge of theft; the case was set for trial. Two weeks later at her trial she repeated the same story to the judge: that she was experimenting for the book she was writing. When asked by the judge how far along she was in her book, she answered, "Well, I'm just in the process of doing the research."

"And part of that research," said the judge, "included you stealing the two blouses?"

"Well, I didn't really steal them, your honour," she answered.

The judge then asked, "When you were stopped by the security officers out on the sidewalk, did you have the two blouses with you?" She paused for a few seconds and said, "Yes."

"Did you pay for these blouses?" the judge asked.

After a pause, as if to think about the judge's question, she answered, "No."

"Well, madam," said the judge, "I find you guilty as charged. You just told me that you left the store without paying for the blouses. You committed a crime. If it was done as part of your experiment for your book—well, you learned you can't just go around stealing and say, 'Oh I'm just doing this as an experiment'."

After the judge found her guilty, he told her to return to court in two weeks for sentencing. When questioned about her background at her trial, she said that she was married and her husband was an army corporal living in France. In six months, he was coming to Montreal to join her. That may have been their plan, but it wasn't the way it worked out. On the day of her sentencing, the woman did not appear before the court. It was later learned from the French newspaper where she worked that she had returned to France. The police also verified that. If she ever returned to Canada, she'd be arrested.

When Mrs. Gibson heard that she had left the country, she said: "Good riddance! The bitch! Her and her *Madam! Madam!*"

Another case that stands out in my mind was not very serious, but at the time, I found it kind of funny. I had a lovely-looking young woman in my office. She was picked up for stealing a small item costing twelve dollars. As always for petty thefts, we gave a lecture before letting them go. As she sat at the desk across from me, I placed my hand on the phone and said to her, "What do you think will happen to you if I call the police?"

She looked at me with a grin on her face and said: "Do you ever watch that TV show *Let's Make a Deal?*" I laughed and told her to leave the store.

As I've mentioned, thieves come from all walks of life and professions. One day I watched a man and young boy in the sports section of the store. I noticed the man try on a motorcycle cap. He placed the hat on the young boy's head. The boy removed it and handed it back to the man. Again the man put the hat back on the young one's head, and again the boy took it off, shaking his head as if to say no. The man took hold of the boy's shoulder and shook him a few times and then once again placed the biker hat on the boy's head. He then guided the boy in front of him toward the checkout counter. I walked out of the store and watched them through the window at the cash. After paying for a small item, the man walked out of the store with the boy, who still had the hat on. I approached them, showed my security ID to the man, and told him that the hat the boy wore wasn't paid for. The man shook the boy roughly a few times, saying, "What did you do that for? Sorry," he said to me, taking the hat from the boy's head and handing it to me. He then added, "He's going to get it when I get him home."

I said to him, "You'll have to come back into the store with me."

"Why?" he asked.

"Well, sir," I answered, "that's the store's procedure and the policy."

"Look," he said, removing his wallet from his coat pocket, "I'm a policeman, a sergeant with the provincial police."

I looked at his badge and said, "It makes no difference, sir; you still have to return to the store." He reluctantly came back in. As we walked up to the security office, he hollered at his son, "Just wait—you're going to get it." The boy was in tears. I felt like punching that man. There he was, blaming his son, whom he had forced to walk out of the store wearing the hat. Once I had him in the office, I told him, "Look forget about your bullshit, because I saw you place the hat on his head. Then you forced him to walk out of the store in front of you wearing it. Forget about your cheap con story—you're a thief, one of the worst kinds, using your son like that. You should be ashamed of yourself—you a police officer!" After I took his name from his ID, I told him, "You're lucky I'm not calling the police and having you charged. For that, you can thank your son, because if he wasn't with you, that's precisely what I would do. You're a policeman—I don't need to explain what would happen to you if I did make that call." While I spoke, he just stood there with a stupid look on his face; he knew he was caught, though I didn't charge him.

Because his young son was with him, I also took into account that if I had called the police and had him charged, he would have pleaded not guilty, and then there would have been a lengthy court trial. There would be the issue that he wasn't the one who walked out of the store in possession of the stolen item instead of the son, even though the son was forced to do it. But that would be a question for the court to decide. Because he was a police officer, that could have influenced the judge's decision. I was quite sure if I charged him, he'd get away with it. That incident was another disgusting example of parents who use their own children to commit crimes.

In another case filed, it was the same story, theft, but that time it was a bigger fish—an inspector with the local city police precinct. After he stepped outside a Canadian Tire store, I pointed to his pocket and said to him, "You forgot to pay for an item you have in your pocket." He looked me over, as if sizing me up, and said, "Oh, really?"

Pointing to his coat, I said, "The item is in that pocket."

Placing his hand in the pocket, he pulled out the item and handed it to me saying with fake surprise. "Oh, Jesus! I'm sorry; I must have put it there while looking at another item."

I said, "You mentioned that you were a precinct inspector?"

He said, "Yes, I am," and he took out his police ID badge and showed it to me.

"Well, sir," I said to him, "because you are a police inspector, you are aware that walking out of a store with a concealed item that you did not pay for is committing theft."

He replied, "Like I said, it was a mistake. I just forgot about it. I'll go in and pay for it, and that will be that."

I had news for him. As he entered the store, about to walk over to the checkout counter, I said, "First, you need to come with me to the office."

"Look," he replied, "it was a mistake, like I told you. I'll pay for it."

He was getting a little agitated, so I said, "Sir, if you're going to cause a scene, the police will be called, and you are aware what will happen." With that, he willingly came with me to the security office. Once there, I asked him to empty his pockets. He hesitated, and I told him, "Sir, there are two ways of doing this; the easy way is for you to do what I ask and empty your pockets. If you refuse; then I have no other alterative but to call the police."

Again, he hesitated, and I reached over and picked up the phone. Convinced that I wasn't going to fool around with him, he reached into his pockets and placed other items he had stolen on the desk. I said, "And I suppose you also placed these other items in your pockets by mistake?"

In total he had about fifty-some dollars' worth of stolen merchandise. I took down information from his identification card; to this day, I don't know why I didn't call the police and have him charged. He even tried to bribe his way out of it, telling me that if I ever needed his help, he would be there for me. At one time, I asked him if he carried a gun. He said yes and then added, "Would you like to have one?"

"No," I said, "I already have guns."

Anyway, I decided to let him go, and as he left I said, "Inspector Albert, if you're ever caught stealing here again, believe me, you will be charged." With that said, the inspector thanked me and left.

A week or so later, I got together with my friend Marc for a few drinks. Because Marc was a policeman, I told him about Inspector Albert. Marc asked if I had called the police and had him charged. I told him no, that I had just given him a warning. Marc gave me shit for not calling the police. A few days later, I received a phone call from an Inspector Haché, who said that he had been speaking with Marc and wanted to know more about what happened with Inspector Albert. I explained what had occurred, and again I was told that I should have had him charged with theft. I wasn't too popular for letting the inspector off. For some reason, it seemed that Inspector Albert wasn't too well-liked among his fellow policemen.

My first six years working in the security industry went rather quickly. I had worked at Simpson's and then the Windsor Hotel for about the same length of time, and then I was offered employment and more money by the Laurentian Hotel, which was part of the Windsor Station, owned and operated by the Canadian Pacific Railway. I took the job, knowing that I wasn't going to make a career in hotel security.

The Windsor Station was a huge complex. After completing the first transcontinental railway in 1887, the Canadian Pacific began building Windsor Station. It was known as the Viger Station and Hotel. When completed in 1889, it played time an important role in Montreal's historic city centre, with its office buildings occupied by subsidiaries and its underground station later linked by corridors to places such as the Laurentian Hotel and restaurants and bars. One lounge was called The Gilded Cage; often when well-known celebrities were in town, they would gather for a few drinks, including the popular NHL hockey referee Red Story. He was well liked but very loud; he always had a few stories to tell.

As did other railways, the Canadian Pacific had its own policemen patrolling the underground station, but in the hotel complex, it was the responsibility of the hotel management to employ their own security personnel. The problems we encountered and had to deal with were the same as with the Windsor Hotel. At times, obnoxious hotel guests, after having a few drinks too many, would roam the lobby or hallways in a drunken stupor. On most occasions, we'd direct them to their room, or if they persisted in being unruly, we asked them to leave the hotel and go somewhere else.

When we felt that a guest was getting offensive toward us or other hotel guests, the police would be called, and the guest would be ushered away. It wasn't a major problem to deal one-on-one with a disgruntled hotel guest, but when they came as a group, that was a different story. Some would party all night, going from one room to another, and when other hotel guests would call the desk to complain about the noise that was keeping them awake, we'd go up and try to quiet them down. After being told that we had received complaints, most would quiet down. But there were others who'd just continue partying; after the second warning the police were usually called if they didn't settle down and behave, because we didn't want to expose other hotel guests or ourselves to harm.

The worst time for hotel security officers was when huge conventions with hundreds of people were held at the hotel. The problems we typically encountered were not with the guests attending the conventions but the thieves and prostitutes who showed up whenever conventions were held. The thieves were our main concern; they were mostly interested in stealing expensive jewellery from the guests when they were away from their rooms. In those days, hotels didn't have sophisticated door locks as they have now. Back then an experienced thief could open a hotel room door in seconds and quickly grab whatever he was after; within a minute or two, he would be out on the street again. After getting rid of the stuff, he would return and rob another room. With a packed hotel it was very difficult to pick out a thief among all the guests steadily going in and out of the hotel. The same was true for the prostitutes; some came in off the street, while other prostitutes registered as guests and used their rooms for their illegal activities. Many of the men who attended the convention brought their wives, girlfriends, or mistresses along. If a prostitute was in the hotel lobby among them, as a security officer, I was often unable to pick out the prostitute, because most of the prostitutes who followed the conventions, especially the ones registered as guests, were very sharply dressed. The majority of them were much more attractive than the wives, girlfriends, or mistresses.

On some occasions, male guests, knowing that we were hotel security officers, would approach us and enquire as to where they could get a hooker.

I would tell them to go just over to one of the local bars, such as the Esquire show bar, where they should have no problem finding one. I learned that many of the businessmen who came to the hotel preferred calling one of the escort services rather than going out to clubs. As one businessman put it, he would rather phone and have a prostitute come over to his room than go out in search of one. One such person, known to us as Sam the Meat Man from Moncton, came once a month and stayed at the Laurentian Hotel for a few days. Each time, we would notice a beautiful blonde walk in and head up to his room; an hour or two later, she would return to the lobby and leave. Each time the Meat Man was at the hotel, he always had the same woman visit him. From her looks and the fancy white convertible she drove, we could tell that the Meat Man was dishing out big money for her services. He didn't hide the fact that she was a hooker.

Sam was friendly and often stopped and chatted with us. One afternoon after the blonde had visited him, he came down to the lobby. One of the security officers said to him, "That's a good-looking girlfriend you have."

"Shit," said Sam, "don't say that! I'm a happily married man; she just comes over to give me a massage. It seems to relieve the stress." From the content smile on his face, we believed that the blonde was giving him a little more than just a massage.

Many businessmen who stayed in hotels often used the services of prostitutes; as one married businessman put it, "There's no love involved. I pay for their sexual services, and they are gone. It doesn't affect my marriage, whereas having a continuous affair with another woman could. So whenever I need it, I pay for it, then I forget about it. Girlfriends and mistresses can become very expensive, because you continuously need to supply them with money for their needs and upkeeps. With a hooker, it's a one shot deal; you pay, and she is gone."

We had no problem when prostitutes came into the hotel to visit a guest in his room. If they came in and solicited men in the lobby or bars, that was a different matter—we would not tolerate it, and we asked them to leave. Some would sometimes sit in the lobby, pretending to be waiting for someone. When they spotted a man who looked like a potential customer, they waited until he was getting on the elevator and then they would also get on and proposition the man. Sometimes we would set up a trap to catch them.

As hotel security officers, we didn't wear uniforms. We dressed casually, so we could mix among the hotel guests without them being aware of who we were. When we saw a woman hanging around the lobby eyeing men, we would get a key to a vacant room and a couple of marked twenty dollar bills. One of us would leave out the side door to the street and re-enter the hotel. Seeing the key, the prostitute would think that he was a guest. After exchanging a friendly smile with the prostitute, he'd walk over to the elevator. As he was about to get on, she would rush over and also get on. After exchanging some small talk, she would ask with a friendly smile if he was interested in having company. He'd say, "How much will it cost?" After she said twenty dollars, or sometimes forty, he'd show her ID and escort her out of the hotel.

In some cases, the security officer on duty didn't do it quite that way. Late one Friday night, after one of the officers was propositioned by a prostitute on the elevator, he took her to one of the rooms he had a key for. After paying her, they had sex, and when he was finished, he showed her his security ID and took his money back. He escorted her down to the lobby. As she was about to leave, she hollered out for all to hear, "You filthy pig! You used me and took your money back, and now you're throwing me out." Before she could say any more, the embarrassed officer quickly took her arm and rushed her out the door. She wasn't yet quite finished with him. Later she called the hotel and cursed the night manager for what the security officer had done. A few days later, the security officer was fired, because it wasn't the first time that management had received complaints about him, including using guests' rooms to have sex with prostitutes.

As hotel security officers, we sometimes had to deal with unusual incidences, like the time I came upon a couple having sex in a hall closet. As I was making the rounds that night, I noticed a young man and a woman who were staying at the hotel with a Russian dancing group get off the elevator. About ten minutes later, after checking the hallway, I was about to get on the elevator when I heard some moaning and groaning coming from the small hallway closet where the cleaning staff kept their mops and buckets. I walked over and pulled open the door. I found the couple I had seen earlier getting off the elevator locked in each other's arms having sex. One would think after seeing me, they would quickly get out of there, but no, they just continued. When I told them to get out, the young man, in broken English, pleaded with me to leave and close the door. I almost broke out in laughter while he pleaded for me to go away. They were like two dogs in heat clutching each other. Finally, after seeing how desperate they were, I told them that I would be back in a couple of minutes and they had better be out of there.

The dancers were four to six to a room and had no privacy. Some would walk around the hotel, on the lookout for somewhere they could hide and have sex; some would try and stop the elevator between floors for a few seconds; others would disturb other guests with their noise. After getting a call from the front desk most guests would settle down. If they continued, we would pay them a visit.

On occasion, there were some humorous incidents, such as the time I was called to the front desk and asked to go up to a room and bring the registered guest down to the office. He had been staying at the hotel for a few weeks and owed quite a sum of money. Each day he would tell them that he would pay but wouldn't. I went up to the room. After I knocked on the door, it opened, and, to my surprise, there stood a giant of a man, staring down at me. He was well over seven feet tall and weighed well over four hundred pounds. For a few moments, I just stood there looking up at him. Finally he asked, in a heavy French accent, "What do you want?"

With a smile, I told him that I was with hotel security, and he would have to come down to the office with me. In broken English he asked me why. Nervous, I told him I didn't know why, except the manager wanted to talk with him. He told me that he would be down in a few minutes. I told him that I would wait because he needed to come with me. With that said, he stepped back into the room and picked up a jacket, put it on, and we took the elevator down to the office. He seemed very friendly. On the way down, he kept looking at me with a smile; he seemed to sense that I was a bit nervous.

As soon as he opened the room door, I recognized him. I often watched wrestling on TV, and a few times I had seen him wrestle. He was André the Giant from France. At the desk, I listened as the manager spoke to him regarding the money he owed, which was over a thousand dollars. The Giant told the manager that he was going out to get some money that was owed to him and that he would be back later to square things up. He was asked for his room key and told if he didn't return that day with the money, that items he had in his room would be put in storage till he paid. He handed the key to the manager, saying he would be back. I watched as he went out, got into a cab, and was driven away. The Giant didn't return that day, so his belongings were removed from the room and put in storage. It was a few weeks before he returned.

I was on duty when he came back. He had another wrestler with him who was known as Mad Dog. He was also a big man, but he looked like a midget besides the Giant. I was at the counter when they walked in, and I moved away as he approached the counter. The Giant looked at me with a grin; I waved a little to say hi. He asked the clerk about the amount of money he owed and he handed him the documented receipt. André reached into his pocket, took out a handful of money, counted out the amount he owed, and handed it to the clerk.

I was asked to go to the storage room and retrieve his belongings, which consisted of some clothing and other small items. When I returned, I handed him his suitcase, again with a smile. In his broken English he said, "Thank you." He spoke with the clerk, and I went over and stood near the doorway.

When the Giant walked by me to leave, he reached over with his huge hand and placed it on my head, messing up my hair, which he seemed to get a kick out of. Then he walked out laughing. I didn't know what he was up to; for a moment I thought he was going to grab hold of me.

Some months later, while having a smoke meat at Ben's, I got to meet André again. I asked him as to why he returned to the hotel and paid over a thousand dollars to retrieve items that had very little value. He said that he liked the hotel and was treated well. He hadn't returned on account of his belongings but because he owed the money and wanted to pay.

Some guests would check into the hotel with the intention of obtaining food and lodging and leaving without paying. Back in those days, hotels didn't require a credit card when a guest checked in. Today, whenever guests come to a hotel, they are asked for some kind of credit card; if they don't have one, the desk clerk requests that the room be paid for in advance, with some exceptions, especially if the person is known to the hotel and had previously stayed there.

Some con men were very smooth and practiced at ripping off hotels. In the old days, a con man would come in with a suitcase or two and pass himself off as a businessman. After registering at the desk, the bellboy would take his luggage up to his room. The guest would give the bellboy an impressive tip—that was the beginning of his con, giving a huge tip. Later he would do the same after a drink or two at the bar or a meal at the restaurant; he would pull a roll of bills from his pocket and pay, again handing the waitress or barman a huge tip. Later down in the lobby, with a business briefcase in hand, he would stop at the front desk and have a friendly chat with the clerk, saying that he expected a few phone calls from business associates. If they happened to call while he was out, the clerk was to tell them that he would return their call when he got back to the hotel.

His reason for giving huge tips was that he wanted the hotel employees to remember him as a person with money. As we know, a person who hands out huge tips to a bellboy, barman, or waitresses will always be remembered. The big con came later in the evening, when he returned to the hotel accompanied by a lovely young woman. Before going up to his room, he and the woman visit the bar and have a few cocktails. When he leaves, he charges the bill to his room, giving the barman a good tip for his service. From his room, he orders food and expensive champagne and again charges it; as with the barman, he pulls out a wad of money and tips the room server. In the course of a night, the con man charged over three hundred dollars to his room. When checkout time came the following day, he was gone. When his room was checked later, the two suitcases he had come with were still in the room; they contained only a bunch of old phone books.

This was a common scam that con men used. Prior to going to a hotel, they'd visit a pawnshop or second-hand store and purchase a cheap piece of luggage and then fill it with stuff like phone books to add weight; if the suitcase were empty, the bellboy would notice that the suitcase was empty upon lifting the case to take it to the room. If the case contained useless items such as phone books, the bellboy would think it was clothing and other items.

One person who was known to pull off that type of scam was Zuba, who was in sales; he travelled all over the country scamming hotels big time. In a few days, he'd run up a six or seven hundred dollar hotel bill and then skip out without paying. He picked the top hotels to stay in and pull off his scam. Some of the hotels he had ripped off were owned by the railway, which is how we first heard of him. The railway hotels were notified by the head office to be on the lookout for him. If he happened to show up, we were just to put him out and tell him he wasn't wanted in the hotel. We learned later that Zuba was harmless and not a violent person. He hadn't caused any problem with the hotels other then stiffing them.

At no time did any of the railway hotels called the police and place fraudulent charges against him, because when he had registered at the hotels he'd always use his real name and the company he represented. A few days after he left one of the hotels without paying, staff phoned his place of work and spoke with the manager, who was told that Zuba had left the hotel without paying for his lodging. The manager made some kind of an excuse, saying that he had to leave town in a hurry and had forgotten to return to the hotel. A week or so after speaking with his boss, the hotel received a cheque from the company for the amount owed. Zuba continued doing the same thing, and hotels would have to phone his company to get paid. Otherwise, the hotel bill would never have been paid. Eventually Mr. Zuba was barred from all railway hotels. He pulled the same stunt at different hotels; some got paid when they could trace him, and others got stuck with the bills.

One day I called the Chateau Frontenac in Quebec City; while talking with the security officer regarding another con man who had ripped off the Laurentian for food and lodging, I happened to mention Zuba's name. When the officer heard the name, he said, "He's a real con man. He stiffed about every hotel around the city. The last time he was here for a few days, after he left, we had young women come to the hotel looking for him. He told women that he was working with a modelling agency, and if they were interested in modelling to come see him at the hotel." The security officer went on to say that one day one of the hotel workers was home on her day off. Her doorbell rang, and she opened the door, and a salesman handed her a Bible and began giving her a sales pitch. She recognized him from the hotel. It was Mr. Zuba, the Bible salesman who moved from town to town conning people. I laughed when he mentioned the Bible salesman who was passing himself off to young women as a scout for a modelling agency.

Today, Mr. Zuba would need a credit card to check in. As for him conning the young women with his modelling pitch, today I don't believe they would go for it. The young women are much wiser, although some are still gullible, especially when faced with a smooth talker who can tell a woman what she wants to hear.

The Windsor was a lovely hotel, owned by a Mr. Webb, who also owned other hotels in Toronto, where he lived. One night while working the night shift, I was told by Mr. Heff, who was in charge of security, that the following morning when I'd finished my shift I would get to meet Mr. Webb, because he was coming in from Toronto.

I was looking forward to meeting him because the employees spoke highly of him. Later that night, in the wee hours as I was checking each floor, I came upon an elderly man staggering around the hallway in a drunken stupor, with only his undershorts on. As I approached, I asked, "Sir, where is your room?"

"Why?" he mumbled. "Who are you?"

"I'm the hotel security officer, and you need to quickly get back to your room, sir."

"Oh, really!" he said, steadying himself up against the wall.

"Yes," I told him. "You can't walk around the hotel hallways with just your shorts on." As I spoke, I noticed one of the room doors was ajar. I said, "Sir, is that your room down there?"

"Yes, I guess it is." He began walking toward the open door as if walking around a hotel half-naked was an everyday thing with him. Before entering the room, he turned to me and said, "What if I don't want to go in?"

"Well, sir," I said, "the police may have to be called, and you may be removed from the hotel." As he closed the door behind him, I heard him say: "Ridiculous. He's going to have me removed from the hotel."

That morning around 7:30, after I finished my shift, I was standing next to the elevator talking with Mr. Heff when the elevator door opened and the man stepped out. Mr. Webb said, "Mr. Heff, I would like you to meet Fred Hudon. He's our new security officer." To my amazement, Mr. Webb was my partially naked friend. As we shook hands, Mr. Webb said, "Didn't we meet when I came in last night?"

"No sir," I answered, "not when you first came in." As he walked to the stairway that went down to the Captain's Cabin, Mr. Webb glanced back toward us and then continued. After he was out of sight, I couldn't help but laugh. When Mr. Heff asked what was funny, I told him about what had happened. Mr. Heff also laughed, especially when I mentioned the part about Mr. Webb closing his room door, saying, "Ridiculous! He's going to have me removed from the hotel."

"He will not remember a thing," said Mr. Heff. "After he has a few, he's in a world of his own."

The Captain's Cabin was a lavish place for influential people to gather. It had a lovely small dinning room, along with a bar and lounge. Whenever Mr. Webb came to town for a few days, that was where he'd spend most of his time. Quite often, he'd be there in the mornings when the place opened and would be one of the last to leave when it was time to close for the night. He was always neat and very sharply dressed. Well, come to think of it, I wouldn't say that Mr. Webb was *always* neatly dressed; after all, I did find him strolling along the hallway wearing just his undershorts.

While employed at the Windsor, I was involved in four notable incidents besides the daily routines of a security officer. One such incident took place one night and involved certain members of the Royal Canadian Mounted Police (RCMP) who were staying at the hotel as escorts for the security general of the United Nations, who was at the hotel for a few days. While the security general was speaking in the ballroom at a banquet luncheon, a Jewish man stood up and said, "Please help our people." After repeating that twice, the man was grabbed by four RCMP and forced out of the room into the hallway and then escorted out the front door of the hotel to the street. As the man was being forced outside, the police had the man held by both arms, and a news reporter tried to take pictures. The RCMP quickly grabbed his camera. The reporter was thrown down the cement steps onto the street.

Later, the incident involving the man who was forced from the banquet luncheon and the news reporter was reported in the newspaper. The RCMP headquarters quickly launched an investigation regarding the incident. A few days later, the hotel manager told me that the RCMP officer who was conducting the investigation wanted to talk to me in the rear office. When I entered the office, I quickly recognized the seated police officer. After asking me to sit down, he began asking me questions about what I had seen the night of the incident. I paused for a moment, then said, "Well, sir, I saw the same that you did. You were right there with the other police officers."

"I'm sorry," he said, "but you must be mistaken. I wasn't here that night.

"Well," I said, "you must have a twin brother who is also a policeman;

because the night in question, before the incident took place, I was asked by one of your officers if I would have a few drinks brought up to the room. I was the person who took the alcohol to the room." From the look on his face, he didn't want to hear that, especially when I mentioned alcohol. With that said, he told me that I could leave. I specifically remembered him being up in the room sharing drinks with the other officers, because he was the one who thanked me for getting the drinks. I didn't like what took place that night. The police officers used excessive force on the man and also the reporter who was brutally pushed down the stairs onto the sidewalk.

Before leaving work that day, I was told by the hotel manager, who preferred to be called the Senator, that it would be in my best interest if I'd cooperate with the investigating officer. I told the Senator, "That officer already knows what I have seen because he was there. He was part of it." They expected me to say that I had not witnessed any unnecessary force or other wrongdoing by the Mounties. That I would not do, because I didn't care for people who brutalized others, especially police officers who had sworn to protect people. In the end, nothing came out regarding the investigation.

Another incident concerned a hotel guest who had checked into the hotel from New York City. Two days after he had registered, the hotel received a couple of long distance phone calls from a woman asking to speak with her husband. Each time the hotel operator tried his room, there was no answer. Later that night, the woman called again, asking to be connected to her husband's room. When he didn't answer, she asked to speak with the manager. The Senator was working the front desk that night. The lady told the senator she was concerned about her husband because he wasn't answering his phone. She asked him to see if her husband had checked out. He told her that he was still registered and that he would have someone check his room later and let her know.

The Senator had a few personal problems. One of them was his memory. If he didn't mark everything down that he was to do later, at times he'd just forget about it. That happened the night he told the woman caller that he'd have someone check her husband's room. When his shift ended, he left the hotel without mentioning anything to anyone about the woman caller and having her husband's room checked. Around 3:00 am, as I was checking the floors, I walked by that room, which had a do not disturb sign out. I heard some faint noises coming from within the room, as if someone was gargling and then breathing heavily. At the time I thought no more of it and continued on. Later, when I was down at the front desk, I was told that a woman had just called looking for her husband; when they tried his room number, he didn't answer. She asked if we'd check his room.

I got the room number and went up to the forth floor; to my surprise, it was the same room I had previously heard the gargling sounds come from. As I stopped and listened, I could hear the same gargling sounds. I knocked a few times, but no one answered and the sounds continued. Sensing there was something wrong, I rushed down to the front desk and got a passkey for the room. Returning to the room, I once again knocked; when no one answered, I used the passkey to open the door. I could only open the door a few inches, because the night chain was connected to the door, preventing it from opening.

Through the opening, I could see the man lying on his back on the floor, his mouth and chest covered with vomit. I rushed down and got a chain cutter, at the same time telling the night clerk to quickly get a doctor to the room. I cut the door chain and got in. I could see that the man was choking on his own vomit; I tried to get him to talk, but there was no response. I rolled him over on to his stomach and waited for help to arrive. The room phone rang. It was the desk clerk telling me an ambulance was on its way. She also mentioned the man's wife had called again. I told her if she received another call from her, she was not to mention anything about her husband just yet. We'd wait till morning. On the night table next to the man's bed, I found two empty pill bottles. It looked as if he wanted to commit suicide. As the ambulance attendants took him away, he was still breathing, but very faintly.

That morning when the day manager came in to work, he was told what had happened. Later, he called the hospital and was told that the man would pull through, but he'd have to stay for a week or so. The man's wife was called, and she was told that her husband was in the hospital. When I returned, I was told that if I had not entered the room and turned him over on his stomach, he would not have survived till morning.

The most disgusting thing I encountered at the Windsor involved the Greek chef. One Friday night, I was near the kitchen when I overheard the hotel chef tell someone, "No! We'll serve it to the group of niggers who are coming tomorrow from the States. I'll put some sauce on it; they will not know the difference."

"But the meat is three days old!" said the other person.

Not liking what I had heard, after the chef and others had left for the night, I got the key for the kitchen and went down and checked to see what meat they were talking about. Opening one of the refrigerators, I saw part of a roast beef, which was cut up in slices. There was enough to serve about ten or twelve persons. I took a small piece and tasted it. It wasn't fresh, and I knew it, because I had eaten a lot of roast beef over the years.

When I returned the key to the front desk, I checked the reservation list to see what groups would be coming. There was a group of ten from the United States that would be arriving at the hotel around lunchtime. Pointing to the reservation list, I asked the clerk, "Are these people white or black?"

She looked at the names and then said, "I believe they are black. I see a reverend's name here."

That Saturday morning, I finished my shift and went home. As I tried to get some sleep, I kept thinking about what I had overheard the chef saying, about serving the niggers the meat with his sauce, because they would not know the difference. It bothered me. So around noon, I drove to the hotel. I would have to make some kind of excuse, because I wasn't due for work until seven that night.

Arriving at the hotel, I saw the group of black people sitting around the lobby, talking and laughing among themselves. As I went past the dining room, I noticed that a table was being set up for lunch. I went down to the kitchen doorway and glanced in. I saw the beef dinner plates lined up on the kitchen table, ready to be placed in the heating oven. One cook was brushing each plate with a light sauce, and another was placing the plates in the oven. I returned to the hotel lobby and sat for a few minutes, pondering what I should do. I glanced at the black group enjoying themselves. I noticed one of the men was wearing a clergy collar. He was seating alone reading a book. I stood up, walked over, and sat on the chair next to him. As I did, he looked up from his book and, with a big smile, said, "Good day, young man!"

I smiled back and said, "Getting ready for lunch?"

"Yes," he answered. "We're starved. We drove here from New York, and on the way, we didn't eat very much, because we were in a hurry to get here, so we didn't want to make too many stops."

"What are they serving for lunch today?" I asked.

"Oh," he said. "Today we're having roast beef." While he spoke, I was trying to figure out a way to let him know about the beef they were about to be served.

"By the way," I said, "I have a friend who eats quite regularly in the restaurant section of the hotel. One day he mentioned that he was served roast beef that tasted noticeably different. Figuring it was the meat sauce, he scraped it off, and after taking a bite he found that it was the beef and not the sauce that tasted strange."

"Well, thank you, young man," said the jolly minister.

Later that night, when I returned for work, I asked the Senator, "How are things going?"

"Very quiet," he answered. "But early today, they had a slight problem with a group who felt they were served staled meat and refused to eat it.

"Really!" I said.

"Yes," he replied, "but the chef took care of it by replacing the beef with chicken."

As I walked away, I laughed to myself and thought, *The sucker got caught with his special sauce and stale beef.* I took a quick dislike to the hotel chef for what he had tried to do. One day as I saw him leaving through the rear door of the hotel with a bag, I stopped him and reminded him that all hotel employees, after finishing work, must leave the hotel using the front door, not the rear. The chef said that he was using the rear door because he had his car parked out back. Noticing that the bag he carried looked kind of heavy, I said to him, "What have you got in the bag?"

"Oh!" he answered, "it's only scraps for my dog."

"Open it and let me see the scraps," I told him. As I reached for the bag, he hesitated and said, "Look, I'm the chef here, and I can leave or come through any door I please."

"Maybe so," I said to him, "but right now, I want to see what you have in that bag. If you don't open the bag, I'll take you to the office."

He reluctantly opened the bag, saying, "Here. You see; it's only scraps."

I reached in and pulled out a steak about an inch thick. He had six large steaks in the bag. I said to him, "Oh, boy! I wish I was your dog." Taking hold of the bag, I said to him, "You need to come with me to the office." As we walked through the lobby to the front desk, I could see the embarrassment on his face. I loved it, especially when I opened the bag and showed the senator the steaks. I said, "I got him leaving through the back door with these steaks. He said it was just scraps for his dog."

"Well," said the Senator, "they are a little more than scraps." Handing the bag back to the chef, he added, "Take them back to the kitchen and leave through the front door." As the chef walked away with the bag, other employees of the hotel stared at him with a questioning look, wondering why I had taken him to the office.

Before I had finished my shift, I made sure that other employees knew what he had tried to get away with: stealing steaks and trying to pass it on as scraps for his dog. The management did nothing about it. The chef wasn't even called to the office. A few days later, I said to the Senator, "I bet if that was any other employee they'd be fired."

"Basically," said the Senator. "Good head chefs are hard to find; other employees are not."

Anyway, I had the satisfaction of showing the management and other employees that the chef was a thief.

After that incident, the chef didn't stroll around the hotel like a peacock, as if he were a distinguished member of nobility, wearing his huge white chef's hat. When I knew he'd be leaving the hotel, I would purposely position myself near the doorway and eye him as he passed by. I could see that that bothered him, and I liked that. After all, it was part of my job to check employees for stolen items. Because he was a known thief; it was only fair that he would be my prime target. To be quite honest, when it came to the chef, I did push it a little; after what he tried to get away with—mistreating the black hotel guests as he did and stealing steaks. There he was, serving hotel guests stale food, while he stole prime steaks to take home to feed his family. Quite often when I'd catch employees trying to leave the hotel with small stolen items, I would just give them a talking to and not report them to management, but the chef was a special case and, as mentioned, I enjoyed it.

Another incident involving Mr. Webb stands out in my mind. It happened one night while Mr. Webb was down in the Captain's Cabin having a few drinks. Around 10:00 pm, as I walked through the hotel lobby, I happened to glance up at the security office, which was located on the second floor. As I did, I noticed a slight movement in the window, as if someone was watching. Because the window was a one-way mirror, it was hard for me to really see, but I did know that someone was in there watching. If a person positioned himself too close to the window, even though it was a one-way mirror, you could tell someone was there if they moved a little. Thinking it was the security chief, Mr. Heff, checking up on me, I paid no more attention to it. A few minutes later, to my surprise, I saw Mr. Heff walking in the hotel. I asked him if he had been up in the security office. He said no, that he just arrived. I told him about what I had noticed. Mr. Heff asked if I had seen Mr. Webb. I told him no, but earlier I was told by an employee that he was seen down in the Captain's Cabin.

Mr. Heff picked up the desk phone and called to check if Mr. Webb was still down there. He was told yes, he was. Mr. Heff and I took the elevator up to the second floor; when we got to the security office door, we heard someone within the office moving around. Mr. Heff quietly used his key and quickly pushed the door open. To our amazement, there stood a young teenage boy at the window with a rifle in his hands. Reaching his arm out, Mr. Heff said, "Tod, give me that gun."

With tears streaming down his face, Todd handed the rifle to Mr. Heff, saying hysterically, "I'll kill the bastard! The son of a bitch deserves to die."

"Fred!" Mr. Heff said. "You keep him here. I'll be right back." When Mr. Heff left, I said to him, "Why do you want to kill him?"

"I want to kill the bastard, because of what he has done to my mother. He turned into a drunkard, a pot smoker, and then he threw her out." As I was trying to calm the boy, Mr. Heff returned with Mr. Webb, who seemed to have had one too many.

When Mr. Webb saw the boy and the gun, he flew into a rage and tried to grab hold of the boy; but Mr. Heff intervened by pushing Mr. Webb back, saying, "What do you want done with him—do you want the police called?"

"Hell, no," said Mr. Webb. "I don't want the police involved. If the news media gets a hold of this, I'll be hounded for months. Just call his mother. Get her over here and get him the hell out before I kill him. Make sure they use the rear door. I don't want anyone to see that f***** in the front lobby."

While I watched Mr. Webb yelling and cursing at the boy, I felt a little sorry for him. At the time, I didn't understand what ties the boy had to Mr. Webb. As Mr. Webb angrily opened the door to leave, he saw me with the rifle. He said, staring down at the boy, "I bet the idiot didn't have the brains to put a bullet in it."

"You're wrong, sir," I said, showing him the six bullets I had removed from the gun. Seeing the bullets, Mr. Webb angrily reached down to grab hold of the boy, who was seated on the floor. Again Mr. Heff pushed him away, saying, "Mr. Webb, if you want to keep this quiet, I think it's best for you to leave. I'll take care of it." Slamming the door behind him, Mr. Webb said, "The little bastard—I'm not finished with him."

Later, the mother was called, and she came and picked up the boy. After things settled down, Mr. Heff mentioned that the seventeen-year-old boy was Mr. Webb's stepson. His mother and Mr. Webb had been married; but for the past year or so, they had been separated and were in the process of a divorce. Mr. Heff said it would cost Mr. Webb a few million to rid himself of the arrogant woman.

I was told that if I hadn't noticed the stepson in the security office window, Mr. Webb could have been killed. From that window, the boy with the high-powered rifle would have had a clear shot at Mr. Webb as he reached the top of the stairs. "Because Mr. Webb would have been only about fifty feet away," Mr. Heff said, "I don't believe he would have known what hit him." Everything regarding the incident was kept quiet; no police were involved. There was no news media story concerning the stepson trying to kill his stepfather. It was later rumoured that not too long after the incident took place, Mr. Webb did divorce, and the ex-wife was successful in getting a few million as part of the settlement. The incident with the stepson and the gun seemed to help bring matters to a quicker resolution as far as the divorce and the ex-wife's demands.

If I were Mr. Heff, I would have summoned the police and had the young man charged with attempted murder. As the security chief, I felt that it was Mr. Heff's responsibility to do so. Rather than doing the right thing and calling the police, he did what he was told by Mr. Webb, and that was to do nothing, exactly what Mr. Heff and the security chief did—nothing, covering it up as if it never happened. The hotel employees who were aware of what took place were told not to talk about the incident; if they did, it could cost them their jobs, so the employees kept things to themselves, and soon the matter was forgotten.

Speaking of guns, one incident I found a bit scary stands out. It took place when I was employed at a Canadian Tire store. One busy Friday evening, up in the security office I received a call from the front service counter that there was a suspicious young man hanging around near the checkout counters. I went down and watched the young man from a distance to see what he was up to. While he walked around checking out certain items, he often eyed the cashiers as they were serving customers.

After a while, I noticed him reach into a watch display case. He quickly grabbed a watch and put it into his pocket. I walked out and waited for the young man to leave the store, and as he did, I stopped him and asked for the watch he had pocketed. He didn't say a word; he just removed the watch from his pocket and handed it to me and then turned to walk away. As he did, I took hold of his arm and told him that he'd have to come back into the store with me. "Why?" he asked, a glazed look in his eyes, as if he was on some kind of drugs.

"Because you walked out of the store with a stolen item, so you need to come with me," I told him. I took hold of his arm, and we began to walk back to the store. As we neared the entrance I noticed him put his hand into a shoulder bag he carried. I quickly let go of his arm and grabbed his shoulder bag, and I placed my hand in the bag on top of his hand. I felt the barrel of a gun that he had a hold of. He let go the gun. I took possession of the bag and the gun and took him to the security office. I asked him what he had intended to do with the gun. "Were you going to use that gun to shoot me?" I asked him. He sat across from me with a stupid look.

"No," he said, "I just wanted to get rid of it. I was going to drop it into the garbage can near the door." When I removed the gun from his bag, there were no bullets in the chamber, though nine bullets were in the gun clip, which was in the gun. He said that the gun belonged to his brother, and he had been just going to return it to him. When I asked why he stole the watch, he said he didn't know why. Believing that he was on drugs, I felt it was useless to question him any further, so I called to the front desk to summon the police. When they arrived, I handed the gun over to them and explained what had taken place. I was asked if he had made any threats with the gun; I told the police that he hadn't made any threats of violence other than reach into his bag for the gun.

When questioned by the police, the young man told the police the same story: that the gun belonged to his brother and he had only reached into his bag to get it and put it into the garbage can. As for the watch, I told the police that we weren't interested in laying any charge. As they left the office with the young man, one police officer commented as he placed the gun in the bag; "This could be your lucky night. If he hadn't been on drugs and his actions were a little faster, the outcome could have been very different." It seemed that the police had previous dealings with him, because when they entered the office and saw him, one said, "You again." After they left, I thought of what the police had said about it being my lucky night. It was a little scary to think I could have been shot over a thirty-dollar watch.

When such incidents happen, when you might be putting your life in danger, you don't think what the outcome could be. You just do your job and deal with problems as they occur. Later when it's over, reality sinks in, and that's when it bothers you.

Another such incident took place, again involving a gun. That time the rifle was stolen from a store gun rack; a man was seen cutting the chain with a chain cutter. By the time security was called, the man had left the store with the gun. As we rushed out into the parking lot, the employees who had seen the man steal the gun saw him get into a truck and drive toward the exit to the street. Just as the truck was to make its exit, the truck stopped for a red light. I quickly ran up to the truck, opened the passenger door, and reached in and grabbed the barrel of the rifle, which was lying on the seat. I pulled it out of the truck as the driver hit the gas peddle and sped off into the street. I went flying backwards, the gun clutched in my hand. I picked myself up from the pavement and walked back to the store. Onlookers didn't know what to make of it. Seeing the gun in my hand, some quickly moved away. The thief got away, but he didn't get the gun.

Later, when I realized what I had done, it suddenly dawned on me how stupid what I did was. I had reached into the truck and grabbed the barrel of the gun, which was aimed directly at my cheek. If the thief had had a bullet in the rifle chamber, he would have only had to reach down and pull the trigger, and I would have been a dead security officer. As I said before, you get a little shaken up when you realize what might have taken place, because the action of man and gun can be quick and deadly. As for the man who stole the rifle, it was later learned that he had also stolen a box of bullets for that gun and could have easily placed one in the gun, which could have meant bye-bye security man.

When trying to apprehend a thief, you never know who you are dealing with. The danger and problems arise when you confront the thief and he doesn't want to be caught. It could be that he previously had trouble with the police or there's a warrant out for his arrest. In that case you have a problem on your hands; he's not going back with you willingly.

Four of us once arrested two men for stealing more than two hundred dollars' worth of merchandise. When we confronted the two in the parking lot, they realized they were outnumbered, and they returned willingly to the store. We had extra help just in case they put up a struggle, because one of them stood over six feet tall and weighed about two hundred and fifty pounds. An employee got suspicious when he noticed one of the men enter and leave the store a few times without buying anything. Later we learned they would pocket items, leave the store, place the stolen items in their car, and then return to the store to steal more merchandise. After we got the two men into the security office, they offered to pay for the merchandise. I told them the store had a policy; for anyone caught stealing for the amount they did, we had to call the police. As I said that, I reached over and picked up the phone, and all hell broke lose. One of the thieves, the bigger one, jumped up from his chair, grabbed a store employee who was standing in the doorway, and threw him across the room. He then quickly pushed the other two aside and rushed out of the office, down the stairs, and out of the store. As for the other man, we managed to hold him and keep him in the office. He didn't put up much of a struggle, but his friend was a bull. As soon as the word *police* was mentioned, he went wild. A few days later, we learned why. One of the police officers who came and picked up the other thief returned to the store and told us it was too bad that we hadn't held the other thief till they arrived.

The police had been searching for that man for a couple of years. He was wanted for attempting to murder a police officer. As I mentioned, when it comes to thieves, you never know the type of person you're dealing with. We were lucky four of us approached them out in the parking lot. If there had been only one or two of us, we would have been in big trouble. When it comes to dealing with thieves who have guns or knives, you never know what the outcome could be. In many situations, security officers are at a high risk for getting hurt or even killed when confronting criminals. A criminal with a gun may think twice before taking a shot at a police officer, but when it comes to a security officer, it's a different story.

CHAPTER 14
Collection

Over the years, I have gotten myself involved in a few unpleasant situations; that was the case when I got involved with Chuck while I was employed at the Windsor Station Complex. Chuck had come to the Complex with a few friends and had a few drinks at the bar. He was in his late twenties, likeable and very friendly, and quite often he would stop and chat with the security personnel. He was a big man, always neatly dressed and impressive-looking.

A month or so later, I met him again; he walked in as I was leaving one night after my work shift. Noticing that I was about to quit for the day, he invited me to join him at the bar for a drink. I didn't usually drink at my place of work after work hours. If I felt like having a drink and relaxing a bit, I'd usually stop in at the Monetary Bar, which was just up the street from the hotel. That night, I accepted Chuck's offer and had a few drinks with him. He mentioned that he had seen me before when I worked at the Windsor Hotel. One of the security officers at the Windsor had mentioned to him that I had previously been in the collection business. It seemed that Chuck was more interested in talking about the collection business than my work as a security officer. He asked questions about how one would go about finding people who had skipped town owing money. After a few drinks, I left. A few days later Chuck showed up at the hotel and said that he had a proposition for me. Would I meet him after work to discuss it? I agreed.

I met him at the bar. After ordering a drink; Chuck suggested that we move to a table, where it was more private. At the time, I didn't know anything about Chuck other than he was in the finance business, which another security officer told me. At the table Chuck asked if I was interested in going back into the collection business. I laughed and said, "Hell no! I had my fill of chasing people around, trying to collect money from people that have none."

"No," said Chuck, "you wouldn't have to chase anyone. I'm interested in opening an office, and we'd be fifty-fifty partners in business. Because you have the experience, you'll manage things. As for me, I will be a silent partner and put up the money to get things going."

I considered his proposition and found it interesting. I wondered why he had chosen me. I thought he knew nothing about me except that I was a security officer. I quickly learned that he knew quite a bit about me. He said he had a friend who was from the same town as me in New Brunswick and spoke highly of me. I would later learn that that friend was the ex-wife of a man I knew back home. The husband had divorced her after he came home one night and found his wife making out in their bedroom with her boss after work. After the divorce, she moved to Montreal and later met Chuck and moved in with him.

The offer Chuck made sounded too good to refuse, but I said, "Give me a few days to think about it." I decided to take Chuck up on his offer. When I spoke to the security manager and gave my notice that I was leaving; he told me that if ever I wanted to return, he would have a job for me.

Within a week, Chuck and I had an office; he paid for everything, including the bond and liability insurance needed to operate a collection agency. I chose the name for the business: The International Collection Agency. During our first week of operation, Chuck walked in one morning with a stack of past due accounts to work on. When I asked him how he got those accounts, he said that they were from different people in the poultry business who supplied restaurants with chickens. Chuck referred to these accounts as "chicken accounts," which at the time I found kind of odd.

In the first week of operation, we had two employees working on the phone, and the following week, we had six: four young women and two men. Chuck had hired all six. Before that, I had mentioned to him that we needed to place an advertisement in the paper for workers; he said that there was no need for that, because he knew of people who were looking for employment.

We had been in operation for a few months. Late one night, I returned to the office and found Chuck and a few men sitting around talking and having a drink. Just as I was about to walk in, I heard one of the men say, "Chuck, that was a good idea you had opening that place; we should do good."

I walked in, and Chuck said, "Freddie, I want you to meet some business acquaintances of mine. I invited them over to see our operation." I was introduced to the men and had a few friendly words, and then I left, telling Chuck I'd see him in the morning.

As time went by, I discovered that Chuck was frequently using the office at night with his friends. During the day, he would seldom come around, other than to drop accounts off to be collected. For most accounts that Chuck gave us for collection, I noticed that the invoices weren't regular. The majority of them were hand-written, showing the person's name and address and the amount owed. When I questioned Chuck regarding these so-called invoices, he just laughed and said that the original invoices were lost and not to be concerned, as those people listed knew that they owed the money. I began to notice that whenever I questioned Chuck regarding an account in collection, he seemed to get a bit annoyed, and he always gave the same answer: "They know they owe the money, so collect it." Then he would quickly change the subject.

As I said, I knew very little about Chuck other than he was in the financial business. One Sunday afternoon, I stopped by the office to get something. I picked up the phone to make a call; just when I was about to dial, I heard a click on the line. Thinking that Chuck was in the back office and had picked up the phone, I opened the door of the office. He wasn't there; there wasn't anyone in the office but me. Again I picked up the phone, and I heard the same click. As I put the phone down, I thought to myself, *The phone line is tapped. Who would bug the phone line?* Then it struck me: the police. But why? I was about to pick up the phone to call Chuck, but I decided instead to use a public phone. After dialling his number a few times without getting an answer, I decided to call my police friend Marc. I mentioned to him about the phone being bugged and asked him if there was any way he could check to see if it was the police. Marc asked for the phone number and under whose name it was listed. When I gave him the number and the name the International Credit Bureau, he asked, "What have you got to do with that business?" I told him that I was part-owner with Chuck Rosenberg. When I mentioned Chuck's name, Marc asked, "How long have you been mixed up with him?"

"Eight to nine months," I answered. He said he would see what he could do; he would call me at home later. I hadn't spoken with Marc since getting into the collection business. As far as he knew, I was still doing security work. I didn't like the sound of his voice when he asked, "How long have you been mixed up with him?" I got the impression that he already knew Chuck.

Returning home, I sat around waiting for Marc to call and wondered why someone would bug the phone line. I remembered an incident when I was employed with the Windsor Hotel. One night I was called to the front desk and was told by the manager that the police were on their way over. When they arrived I was to take them down and unlock the door to the electrical room. Shortly, two city detectives showed up. I took them to the basement and let them into the electrical room. I was told that they'd be in there for awhile; when they'd finished, they would let the manager know. As I left the electrical room, I glanced back and saw one detective begin checking the telephone connections to the hotel rooms. Later, when I returned the key to the front counter, I said to the night manager, "They said that they would be there for awhile." I added, to see if I would get any reaction from the manager, "I guess someone's room is about to have the phone line bugged."

"Yeah," he answered. "I'll call you when they are finished to lock the door."

As I was making the rounds, checking each floor, I wondered which room was being bugged. Later, when the night manager was away from the desk, I quickly glanced through the index file of the guests who were staying overnight. When I saw the name V. Cotroni on the guest list, I knew which phone line the police were interested in.

On another occasion, two police detectives came to the hotel and spoke with the manager. I was asked to take them up to an unoccupied room. After unlocking the room door, I was told to wait out in the hallway; they would be in there just for a few minutes. They came out, and as I was locking the door, one detective removed a room key from his pocket and opened the door to the room next to the one they had been in. I was about to walk away, but one detective asked, "Are you working tonight?"

"Yes, till midnight," I answered.

They entered the room and closed the door. Later, I would learn that the room they had spent a few minutes in would be occupied later that night by two men from New York who were known to have ties with organized crime. Prior to their arrival, the detectives hid a listening device that would enable them to listen in to and record the men's conversations from the next room.

A few hours after I phoned Marc, he called back and said that he had some information, but he didn't want to discuss it on the phone. I met him at a nearby restaurant. I found what he had to say very disturbing. He said that the phone line at the office was indeed tapped by the police because of Chuck's involvement in criminal activities. Marc went on to say that Chuck had a long police record and was one of the biggest shylocks in Montreal. He and his associates would loan money to people at a huge interest rate, and if a person didn't pay or was unable to repay, he would have them taken care of. They would end up with a busted leg or arm, especially men. For women, they would use other means to get them to pay, perhaps committing theft or prostitution to earn money to repay their loan. Marc said that when I had registered the collection agency with the City and had put Chuck's name as a business partner, the police soon learned of it and began bugging the business phone line. At night, the police would watch the office to see who Chuck was meeting with.

When I mentioned to Marc the type of accounts that Chuck was bringing to the office to be collected—information scribbled on a piece of paper without any invoices that he had often referred to as "chicken accounts"—Marc said the accounts to be collected weren't from customers. Chuck's and his associates had made loans and were using the collection agency as a front to collect and launder money. I was told some disturbing things about Chuck; when Marc asked if I had signed any insurance policy regarding the business with Chuck, I told him yes. When we first started, we signed the partnership papers and also an insurance policy, which Chuck said was only to protect each other. Hearing that, Marc said, "Yes—if you happen to be found dead somewhere, Chuck will collect on the insurance policy." Later that Sunday night after I met with Marc, I went to the office, picked up my personal things, and wrote myself a cheque for an amount that I felt was rightfully mine. I signed another blank cheque and left it on the desk.

Early the next morning, I went to the courthouse and met with the lawyer I had previously dealt with to draw up the partnership agreement between Chuck and me. I told the lawyer that I wanted to dissolve the partnership. I explained my reasons, and he said that he would have my name removed as Chuck's business partner. After I left the courthouse, I went to the bank and cashed the cheque I had made out to myself. Then I got a cab and headed to the airport. At the airport, I called Chuck and told him that I had been to the courthouse and had our partnership dissolved and about the police having the office phone tapped. I also mentioned what I was told by Officer Marc regarding the illegal accounts Chuck brought for collection. Chuck cut in and said, "Freddie, come to the office and we'll talk about it."

"No," I told him, "I'm finished." I told him about the blank cheque that I had signed and told him to use it to close the business bank account at the bank. Chuck said, "Come to the office and we'll talk about it" a few times. He was aware that I was at the airport, because as we spoke, he could hear the planes taking off and landing.

Less than an hour after talking with Chuck, I was on a plane to Toronto. The lawyer had said that it would take a few days for the partnership to be dissolved, and I didn't want to take any chances with Chuck, especially after what Marc had said about the business insurance policy. Two weeks after I left Montreal, I returned and went back to doing security work. A couple of years later, Chuck was shot and killed by policemen after breaking into a home in Hampstead. I heard that he and another man entered the house of a wealthy family, thinking there was no one home, and as they did, they came face to face with the owner, who had activated the panic alarm.

Within a few minutes, the police had the house surrounded. Chuck jumped through a window, and as he did a piece of glass cut into his throat and pierced the main artery. As he was trying to get away from the police, he was shot and later died in the hospital. Before he went to that residence, Chuck was aware that the house was protected by a burglar alarm system connected to the Hampstead police station. The plan was to cut the outside telephone line before entering the house, but they must have forgotten. I would later hear that Chuck broke into the home to steal some valuable paintings and jewellery.

I liked Chuck; he treated me fairly, except for him planning to have me done away with to collect on the business insurance. I'll never know if he would have followed through on that idea or not. Maybe I was lucky, because after what Marc told me, I didn't stick around to find out.

Years after Chuck was killed, I would once again be approached to go into the collection business as a partner. The offer came from the big boss, Mr. Frank of the Montreal Mafia. In the movie *The Godfather* about the Mafia, when the Godfather says, "I'll make him an offer that he can't refuse," *can't* is precisely what he meant. To refuse an offer from the boss-man isn't wise; it's an insult. Anyone who refuses the offer might end up dead or pay for it, one way or other.

After the short business venture with Chuck, I went back to working in security. After a year, I decided to apply for a licence to operate my own agency. The requirement to be granted a licence was a good employment record and either five years of on-the-job experience or to have been a policeman. I had over seven years' experience, and as far as I was aware my past employers seemed satisfied with my work. I applied. I was decided that if my application was refused, I would get out of private security. I was fed up working for others. I did the work, and they got the credit. If I was licensed to operate my own business, I would be able to choose the type of security work I wanted to be involved in. When working for someone else, that wasn't possible. A month after applying, I received my licence as a private detective.

CHAPTER 15
Private Detective

For a while before I got my licence, I worked for a private detective agency. In the beginning I found it intriguing, but as time went on I discovered the job was nothing like the private detective shows you see on TV, with flashy cars and beautiful women. I found that in the real world, being a private investigator, dealing with dirt and corruption, wasn't as glamorous as portrayed on TV. Following spouses wasn't really the type of investigating work that interested me—as they say, it was not "my thing." The money was good, but I didn't fancy being involved in emotional messes, especially divorce cases.

You may have heard stories about the wealthy housewife and the milkman or the businessman who felt that his wife was going out and having an affair while he was away on business. Well, as far as the milkman, he was supplying more than milk to the housewife; and as far as the businessman, he was right—his wife was having an affair, but she didn't have to go out looking for it. His golfing buddy, who lived next door, took care of that. He'd sneak over after dark and use the back door so he would not be noticed by other neighbours. When that was reported to the businessman, he seemed stunned and repeated to himself. "Chris is my friend. We're always out golfing together—it couldn't be Chris." Oh, yes, it was his friend Chris, his golfing buddy. One never knows what goes on in the neighbourhood, especially when the spouse is away. As they say, if only those bedroom walls could talk. If they could, you can be sure that a good number of the neighbours wouldn't be on very friendly terms.

And how about the lawyer who was making out with his client's lovely wife whenever he was away? Yes, that cliché is also true—the man was paying the lawyer big bucks to handle his business affairs, and his lawyer was taking care of more than his business affairs—he was also taking care of his client's wife's needs. Shameful but true. If a person can't trust his personal lawyer or his next-door golfing buddy; who can he trust?

When I first applied for the licence to operate my own security agency, Sgt. Martin, the police officer whose job was to interview applicants who applied for licensing, asked if I had any previous police training. I said no, but actually, I did have a little experience in some aspects of police work, back in Toronto during the latter part of the fifties, after I'd been employed with the McLean-Hunter Publishing Company a few years.

CHAPTER 16
The Mag Salesman

Before elaborating on the subject of my police work, I would like to mention a little about my stay with the publishing company McLean-Hunter, first as a salesman, and later as a sales supervisor. At the age of eighteen, I was travelling around the country, knocking on doors and selling magazines. When I was first hired I didn't really know what kind of work I was getting involved in. I read an ad in the newspaper that said Young men wanted. If you're free to travel and want to earn good money, we have the job for you. I applied for the job, along with a dozen or more other young men. Qualifying for that job was rather simple: as required, I was free to travel, able to read and write, and neat in appearance. When I was being interviewed by Mr. Nelson, the circulation manager, he said, "You'd be good at the job. It is in sales, and with your looks you should do well." That said, I was hired and told to show up Monday morning, ready to leave town for a week or so.

I didn't know what the job was about, other than it was in sales. The following Monday morning I arrived at the McLean-Hunter building; a group of us was taken out into the parking lot, and there we were split up in two groups. Bob, who was the sales supervisor, chose who he wanted to travel with him in his car from the group. I was selected, along with five others, Bob said to Vic, his brother, who was the driver of the second car, that we would meet up in North Bay. As we drove out of the city, Bob kept reassuring us in an upbeat manner that we were going to love our job and have fun doing it.

That was interesting, but I had not yet been told what the job was about, other than being in sales. Mike, who was seated next to me, asked Bob, "What kind of sales is that? What are we going to sell?"

"Well," said Bob, "as you know, McLean-Hunter is in the magazine publishing business, and our job is to sell their magazines." He then handed each of us a sheet of paper. "Here, read this, and study it, so when we get to North Bay you'll be ready for work." With that said; we quietly sat back and read what he had given us. It was a sales pitch with nothing but bullshit and lies. In part it said we had to tell people that we were students working our way through college. When people bought the magazines from us, we would get various points toward winning a scholarship to college.

We read it over for a few minutes, and Mike, who seemed more outspoken than the rest of us, said, "What's that about working our way through school?"

"What it is," said Bob, "is just a sales pitch that will help you sell magazines. Later on, once you've gained a little experience; you can make up your own pitches."

I didn't like what I was hearing. I just couldn't picture myself telling people that I was working my way through school. After a few hours of driving, we got to North Bay and meet up with Vic. We had a coffee, and each of us was handed a receipt book and shown how to fill it out. Then we were dropped off in various locations in the town to knock on doors. As Bob left each person off, he said that he'd be back in a few hours to see how we were doing. I was the last of the group to be dropped off. As I stepped out of the car, Bob pointed to the row of houses along the street and said, "Freddie, work your way down one side and then up the other, and knock on every door." I reluctantly agreed, and then he drove away.

For a minute or two, I stood there, looking at all the homes along the street; I felt very nervous and uncomfortable. It felt like from each home, eyes were staring out at me. I took the sales pitch out of my pocket and quickly read it over again. *No*, I thought to myself, *I can't do that. I'll wait till Bob returns to pick me up, and I'll tell him that I have decided to return to Toronto because I'm not interested in this type of work.* Knowing that it would be a few hours before Bob returned, I walked around putting in time till he showed up. I knew that I would have to take a bus or hitchhike back to Toronto. That didn't bother me, as long as I got back.

While I walked around passing time, I came across a new subdivision: about two dozen newly built homes. I walked along and saw a lot of activities going on. Some people were out seeding their new lawns; others were working in their gardens; carpenters were working on more houses. When I got to the end of the street, I sat on the curb and watched the carpenters doing their jobs. After a while, I noticed a few young girls, around fourteen or fifteen, walking toward me, laughing and talking amongst themselves. As they approached, I looked at them and smiled. "What are you doing?" one asked with a grin.

"Nothing really," I answered. "I'm just watching the men working."

"Do you live around here?" another asked.

"No," I said. "I'm from Toronto."

"Oh, really? Are you selling something?" she asked. I felt that they were just trying to be friendly, so I jokingly said with a laugh,

"Yes, I'm selling magazines. Do you want to buy one?"

"No, I don't," she quickly replied, "but I think my mother would be interested, because last night, she mentioned something about buying gardening magazines. Do you have gardening magazines?"

"Yes, I do," I told her, and I reached in my pocket and took out the list of magazines and handed it to her. "Here, pick out all the magazines you want. Go ahead," I told her. "I'll be here for a while." I wasn't trying to sell her any, because prior to being dropped off, Bob told us that for some reason or other we weren't allowed to sell to anyone under eighteen. I just gave her the list as if to say, *Yes, I'm selling something, now get lost.* The girls ran off with the list.

A few minutes later, they returned, telling me that their mother wanted to talk to me. Picking my ass up from the curb, I nervously followed the girls. When we got to their house, the mother was waiting at the door with the magazine listing in her hand. With a big smile, she said, "Lucky for me—this is just what I've been looking for, magazines for the home, and I see on your list you have the home and garden one that I'd like." The lady did most of the talking while I nervously stood there, listening to her questions about certain magazines that I didn't have the answers to, because I knew nothing about those magazines.

Seeing what was written on the back of the listing, which I hadn't noticed before, the lady asked, "What are these points about?"

Looking at the listing, I quickly answered, not really knowing what to say, "Oh! Those are the points I get depending on the number of magazines I sell."

She asked, "How much does a subscription cost?"

Not knowing what she meant by the word *subscription*, a word I hadn't heard before, I thought that she was referring to the cost of the magazines. I told her, "It's just ten cents a copy, ma'am."

"Okay," said the lady. "So if I buy twelve copies, that will give you twelve points, and if I choose fifty copies, that will give you fifty points."

Again, not knowing what the points were all about, I said, "Yes, ma'am."

"Well," she said, "fifty copies are a little too much, so I'll take thirty-six, and that will give you thirty-six points." I filled out the receipt with her name and address and the amount for the thirty-six issues that she was to pay me. When she then handed me the money, I found it hard to believe that I had actually sold an order for magazines without having to walk up and knock on doors and give a phoney sales pitch, thanks to the curious young girls who wanted to know why I was sitting out there watching the carpenters. I thanked her for the order and was about to walk away, when she said, "You go next door and see Mrs. Woods—tell her I sent you." After once again thanking her, I rushed up to the next house and knocked on the door. When the woman opened the door, without thinking anymore about my nervousness, I smiled and cheerfully said to her, "Hi, my name is Freddie, and I was just over talking with your neighbour Mrs. Edwards. She told me to come over and see you because I'm selling magazines, and she thought that you may be interested."

"Yes," the woman answered, "come in. As a matter of fact, I am interested, especially if you have some for the home." As with Mrs. Edwards, I sold another order for magazines. For next two hours, I continued to rush up to each home and simply say, "Hi there, my name is Freddie, and I was just over talking with your neighbour. I thought I'd drop by and see you for a moment." As I spoke, I'd hand them the cards. "I'm selling magazines. Would you be interested?"

With those simple words, out of the eighteen doors I knocked on, I sold fifteen orders. My pockets were bulging with money and cheques as I made my way back to the street where Bob had dropped me off. I took the sales pitch that he had given me, tore it up, and threw it away. When Bob drove up later, the first thing he asked as I got in the car was, "How did you make out?"

I said to him, "I got fifteen orders."

"What? You got fifteen orders?" he repeated, with a serious look.

"Yes, I did," I answered and reached into my pockets and pulled out the money and the cheques. Seeing that, Bob said, "Holy shit, you really did good! You must have run into a lot of marks." I would later learn that among mag salesmen, a mark was a person who was easy to sell to or someone who'd buy most anything. I also learned that Bob often used the word *shit*; it was always "shit" that and "shit" that.

As we sat in the car, Bob counted the money and checked over each receipt. "Shit, these orders are all big orders. You sold for over fifty dollars— that is something." Then he added, "And just in a few hours."

Bob drove around to pick up the others. As each one got in, he would ask how many sales they made. After everyone was in the car, Bob said to Mike, "You did good, Mike. You sold twenty-two dollars." Mike, a good-looking young man, very conceited and full of himself, sat up like a little peacock with a grin on his face, till Bob said, "Well, Freddie outsold all of you. He got fifty-four dollars' worth of orders." Mike's grin quickly disappeared from his face. Later, we would learn that he didn't like it when another salesman outsold him.

The rest of the week, ready with my simplified sales pitch and a smile, I'd say, "Hi, ma'am, my name is Freddie, and I'm selling magazines. Would you be interested?" If not, after the second no I would rush over to the next house. After a while of knocking on doors, I learned not to accept the first no, because I found that a lot of housewives would quickly say no when they heard the word *magazines*. "I don't want any magazine."

I would then say, "Well, ma'am, we've got some nice family magazines." Very often, after looking over the list, some would end up buying. When I got the second no, I would walk away, leaving them laughing, saying, "Okay, thank you. I'll be back to see you when I have a better sales talk."

Whenever a man answered the door, my pitch was very short. With men, I didn't wait for the second no; as soon as they said, "No, I'm not interested," I'd be gone. Sometimes the husbands would make smart remarks. After I was promoted to sales supervisor and had a new car to drive around in, one day after I'd knocked on a few doors, a husband answered the door. I told him that I was selling magazines; he said to me, "Wait a minute," and he walked back into the house. Within a few seconds he returned and handed me a newspaper. He said, "Here, check the want ads and go get yourself a job." For a fraction of a second, I didn't know what do or say. Then I looked at the old beat-up car that was parked next to the house.

"Is that your car?" I said.

"Yes it is. Why?"

"Well, sir," I said, pointing down to the end of the street where I had parked my car, "you see that new convertible with the top down parked down there?"

Glancing toward the car, he said, "And that's your car?"

"Yes, sir," I told him with a smile, "that's the car I drive." Handing him back the newspaper, I added, "And as for me going out and getting myself a job, I already have one, sir."

He stood there with a stupid grin on his face, not knowing what to say. Then he muttered, "You got that car by selling magazines?"

I stepped away from his doorway, turned, and pointed to his broken-down car, and said, "Enjoy driving your old wreck." He eyed me as I walked down the street and got into my car. He was still standing in his doorway as I started the car, and then I slowly drove past his house and gave him a friendly wave, as if to say *bye-bye*.

When I first got into selling magazines, the first couple of weeks were the hardest. We would stop around five; Bob said it was a waste of time working late on Fridays because most people would be out doing their shopping. After my first week, Bob handed me an envelope and said, "Here's your pay for the week." In the envelope was a breakdown of the magazine orders I had sold.

My first week in the mag business, I earned one hundred and twenty-seven dollars. Back in the mid-fifties, that was good money. And that was what kept me in the mag business—the money. I was with McLean-Hunter for a year and was promoted to sales supervisor; the nice, flashy car that the company provided me also helped to keep me knocking on doors.

One of the problems with that work was that I had to travel all over the country. One day I'd be in one town or city, and a few days later, I would move on to the next. I was always on the move with fellow salesmen, living in hotel or motels. At times we would be away for a few weeks, and then we would return to Toronto and work around the city for a week or two. Then we would take off again for another few weeks. I may have been a little shy when I first got into door-to-door sales, but working in that line of business and meeting so many different types of people in a short period of time, I lost my shyness.

Approximately 90 percent of the people we talked to were women, and a good number of them were young "frustrated" housewives; need I say more? Sometimes we'd have to quickly leave town for some reason or other. One night we learned that a man was driving around town with a gun searching for a door-to-door salesman who had an affair with his wife. At the time a couple of young men from Nova Scotia, who were able to handle themselves, were working with me. And before I left home at the age of seventeen, I fought a few times in the ring. But when it came to an angry husband with a gun, believe me, we wanted nothing to do with that guy. We quickly packed up and headed for another town.

Selling magazines door to door was a special education and a confidence builder. Most of the people I worked with over these five or six years would later go on to better things; others would stay. But those of us who were married while in the sales business eventually ended up separated or divorced. That was the sad part of being a mag man; travelling from one town to another for the job kept them away from home.

Regarding separations and divorces, one must keep in mind that "if you play, you must pay." That is precisely what happened to me. I played, and in time I paid. One Monday morning, feeling fed up with always being on the road, I walked in to McLean-Hunter and handed the car keys to Mr. Tony, who was then the general manager of sales. I told him that I was leaving. When I was asked why, I told him that I was tired of being away from home and always on the road; for the past three years I had very few holidays. Mr. Tony tried to change my mind by offering more money and saying that I could work within the city. Then I would have more time to spend with my family. I told him no, that I had made up my mind to leave. He said to take a couple of weeks off and return; we would talk again.

CHAPTER 17
Background

At the time I didn't know what other type of work I would find, but I knew that I wouldn't have a problem with finding a job. Jan seemed a bit joyful that I had left the magazine business. It was hard for her, me being away most of the time. Jan was from my hometown in New Brunswick. I had met her when I was sixteen; she was a year younger than I. I loved her dearly; she meant the world to me. Her parents, especially her father, didn't like the idea of us seeing each other. I didn't have much schooling and was known to be kind of wild, especially when it came to fighting. In earlier years, when I was in school, I was always being bullied by bigger boys.

When I turned sixteen, I quit school. My father got me a job at the lumber mill where he and my older brother Bill worked. Bill was ten years older than me and was into boxing. One night when I went over to the arena to watch him and other boxers training for an upcoming fight, I met Mr. Cormier, who asked me if I was interested in learning how to box. I told him yes, I would love to. He told me he could train me at his home and for me to come over the following night, which I did. Mr. Cormier, I learned later, was a boxer when he was in the army. He had the basement of his home equipped with boxing equipment.

When he first started training me, he told me that if I was good, he would enter me in a Golden Gloves boxing tournament that was to be held in Saint John in a few months. I spent the first night of training punching on the bag while Mr. Cormier watched and corrected my mistakes. The next night, Mr. Cormier put on boxing gloves too and told me to punch away at him, which I did, and he parried most of my punches with his gloves.

After a while we stopped, and he told me that I was fast with my hands, but I needed to learn how to correctly throw a punch so it would have more effect, rather than just punching with my arms. He said that I needed to put my weight behind a punch. He explained that if I weighed 135 pounds, he wanted to see me put that weight behind my punch. That could only be achieved by punching straight forward with my fist, not swinging wildly, as I was doing. He referred to it as *scientific boxing.*

For the next two months, I would go to his house each night and train for a couple of hours. One night he said to me, "Freddie, always remember that if a train is coming down the track and it runs into another train that is stationary, the train that struck the stopped train is going to cause a lot of damage. Now, let's say that the train that was struck was headed toward the oncoming train and was hit head-on; the impact and damage would be much greater. Well," said Mr. Cormier, "it's the same when two men get into the ring and fight. If your opponent weighs 150 pounds and you weigh 135 pounds, when he steps forward to take a punch at you and you quickly step into him and connect to his jaw with your weight behind the punch, that will have more effect because you're using his weight against him when he moves forward to throw his punch."

It was clear from the look on my face that I wasn't getting what he meant, so he said, "Okay, come over here to the bag." He stepped behind the bag and placed his hand to the sides of it. "Now I want you to throw a punch and put your shoulder and weight behind it." I threw a punch at the bag, and as I did, he held the bag firmly, so it would not move when I struck it. He had me repeat that a few times, and then he said, "When you punch, I'm going to move the bag forward, just as your fist makes contact with the bag." I threw a punch with my weight behind it, and just as my fist was about to make contact, he quickly moved the boxing bag forward. I then understood what he was trying to explain, because when I struck the bag I could feel the difference in my arm, like I had hit a solid object. After that each time I used the punching bag, he would always say, "Freddie, remember to use his weight to your advantage."

A few weeks before the boxing matches were to be held in Saint John, Mr. Cormier was away on holiday. While he was gone, a boxing match was held at the arena, and I was asked by the promoter if I'd like to fight that night. Without thinking, I told him that I sure would. He said that the guy I would fight was just a beginner, a bit taller and heavier than I was; but he assured me that I'd have no problem beating him. At the time, I wasn't worried about getting beaten; I just was happy that I was going to get into the ring and fight.

Before the fight night, I met Leigh while I was at the corner store. He said, "Freddie, I heard that you're going to fight Ed."

I answered, "I don't know his name."

"Well," said Leigh, "I boxed him, and he beat me. What do you think he's going to do to you?"

I looked at him and said, "I don't know. We'll just have to wait and see." Leigh was a couple of years older than me. I knew one thing about him; he was no boxer—a boaster maybe, but not a boxer.

On fight night, after arriving at the arena, I was okay but very nervous.

Don Spragg was the lightweight champ of New Brunswick and a very good boxer; he beat the best there was. He said to me, "Did you see the guy you're fighting?"

"No," I answered.

"Go out into the hall and take a look at him—he's standing there," said Don.

I walked out and saw him. I said to Don, "Shit, he *is* big."

"Don't let his size bother you," said Don. "Here's what I want you to do. I know you're fast with your hands. Just before the fight begins, he's going to reach out to touch gloves with you, and when he does, let on you're going to touch gloves with him. Instead, throw a good punch at him, and make sure it's a solid one."

"Isn't that illegal?"

"No, it isn't," he answered. "Boxers don't need to touch gloves before fighting." As he left the dressing room, Don said, "Don't forget—come right under and give him a solid one."

It seemed like hours before someone came in and said, "Get ready, Freddie, you're on next." A few minutes later, I was in the ring. As the announcer was introducing us, I kept looking over at Ed and remembering what Don had said. Ed was tall and about twenty-five or thirty pounds heavier than me. As soon as the bell rang, he did what Don said he'd do—as we stepped in the center of the rink, he reached out with his long arms to touch gloves. As he did, I stepped into him and got him with a right hand, sending him back four or five feet. He didn't go down, but I could tell by his eyes he was hurt, so I went after him. He got me a couple of times, but his blows had no effect; he wasn't hurting me. It seemed that my first punch took everything out of him. In the second round I got him with a few solid punches, opening a cut over his eye. In the third round, I never threw a punch at his stomach; they were all in the face area. When the bell rang, ending the fight, I was happy, because my arms were dead and I could hardly hold them up. I was awarded the fight. As I left the ring, I looked over at Leigh, who was seated a few rows away, and gave him a smile, as if to say, "He beat you. So what?" When I was in the dressing room changing, Ed came in and shook my hand, saying, "I didn't expect that—you're a hell of a fighter."

"Thanks," I answered. "You also did good."

Before leaving he asked, "Will you someday give me another match?"

With a smile, I said, "Sure, Ed, anytime."

Because of that fight with Ed I lost any chance of going to Saint John to fight, as Mr. Cormier had planned, because when he returned from his holiday and found out that I had fought Ed, it was the end of our relationship. He was very disappointed because I had been paid for fighting Ed. That would disqualify me from fighting in the Golden Gloves. If I had known that, I wouldn't have fought Ed, because I was looking forward to going to Saint John and fighting.

Before I left Bathurst, I fought in the ring two more times. Those two fights were much tougher than the one I had with Ed. In one in Campbellton, I was on the same card as Don. Don was boxing the main event, and I was boxing in one of the earlier fights against a guy who had once been a wrestler. Again he was much heavier than I was. In those days around New Brunswick, if a fighter weighed 200 pounds and you weighed 150 and it wasn't a title fight and you agreed to fight him, you fought him.

In the final round, as I was getting the best of fighter Gagnon, he pushed me back against the top rope, and I fell over on the marble floor, with him coming down on top of me. As he did, he got me in the ribs with his knee. I was in such pain I could barely get up from the floor. In the meantime, he jumped back into the ring, and the referee began counting, as I stood outside the ring holding my stomach.

Don, who was standing watching from the doorway of the dressing room, saw what was going on and quickly came out and told the referee that because I was pushed over the rope by fighter Gagnon, he needed to give me time to get back into the ring. When Don intervened, the referee stopped counting; Don came around to me and said, "Freddie, get back in there. You can beat him with one hand." I told Don that my ribs were damaged; he said, "The hell with your ribs! Get back in the there and beat the sucker." With some assistance from Don, I got back in the ring, and the fight continued. Because of my damaged ribs, I just kept jabbing Gagnon in the face to keep him away. Finally the bell rang, and it was over. I was awarded the fight, and the next day I went to the hospital to have my ribs strapped up. If it wasn't for Don, I would have been counted out by the referee, and he would have awarded the fight to Gagnon.

My third fight was the toughest one; it one took place in Chandler, Québec. I was asked to go there and fight with a couple of other boxers, including my brother Wild Bill. Howard, a local boxer with no great skill in the ring other than his size, was promoting the fight. He chose the boxers who would go to Chandler to fight. When he first approached me to go, I confirmed that the guy I would be fighting was a beginner with very little experience in the ring, and I accepted. We were to fight on a Sunday afternoon, so we arrived in Chandler on Saturday evening. While Howard and the other fighters went out on the town, I stayed in the room that I shared with my brother and went to bed early. When Wild Bill returned, he woke me and said, "Do you know who you're fighting tomorrow?" When I said no, Bill said, "You're fighting the lightweight champ of the Gaspé area."

"Howard told me that the person I was to fight was just a beginner."

"He's no beginner," said Bill. "At one time he even fought Don." I didn't like what I heard and told Bill that I wouldn't fight him. I felt that if he was good enough to fight a boxer like Don, I wouldn't have a chance against him. Bill said that as long as I was there, I should get in the ring with him and stay away from him.

I was seventeen years old, and he wanted me to box with a champ who was twenty-nine and had been fighting for the past nine years. Howard wasn't fighting; he was going to be the referee. I didn't see Howard that night, but if I had I would have taken a punch at him. I felt he had set me up to take a beating. Howard and I grew up together and didn't get along too well. He was big and could be very mean, especially when he was drinking. We had fought together a few times, and it wasn't in the ring. Even though he was a few years older and much bigger, he didn't come out the winner.

After hearing what Billy said about who I was to box, I tried to get some sleep, but I got very little because I kept thinking of getting hammered if I got in the ring with that guy. That Sunday afternoon at the arena, I met the fellow I was to fight and was told by him that he would take it easy on me. I decided to get in the ring and fight. Prior to the fight beginning, the announcer introduced us. He mentioned my name and where I was from, and he introduced the hometown boxer, Gustave Meunier, and mentioned that he was a champ. The crowd went wild. When the bell range to start fighting, I could tell Meunier was taking it easy on me as promised, and I wasn't throwing hard punches at him because I didn't want to get him mad. After the first round was over, we were pretty even, but when the bell sounded for the second round I quickly realized that Meunier was going to try to knock me out, because as soon as the bell rang, he rushed to the center of the ring and threw a punch at me with his right hand, which got me on the jaw and knocked me back a few feet. For a moment, I saw stars. When he saw that I was hurt, Meunier came at me with both hands swinging. When my head cleared a bit I thought to myself, *Well, if I'm going to go down, I'll go down fighting.*

Up till then I hadn't tried too hard. In the first round I wasn't throwing solid punches, but in the second round, when I saw he was trying to put me out, I made up my mind to fight. Meunier was fast with his hands, but after the first round I knew that I was a bit quicker. Meunier kept rushing at me with both hands, and as I parried some of his blows I thought back to what Mr. Cormier had taught me. Whenever Meunier took a step forward and threw a punch, I'd step in to him with my left hand, and each time I connected, I could tell he was feeling the blows. Then he stopped rushing me. At one point, he took a wild swing at me, and as he did, I connected with a solid blow to his jaw, knocking him down.

Howard began counting, and Meunier got up, I could tell he was hurt, but instead of going after him and trying to finish him off, because of lack of experience in the ring, I waited for him to come to me. Howard, seeing that Meunier was still hurt when he got up, came close to me and said, "Finish him off, Freddie, he's hurt." Even though Meunier was the hometown favourite, when I knocked him to the canvas, the crowd went wild, hollering, "Freddie, Freddie, give it to him."

When the second round was over and I went to my corner, I was told, "Freddie, just keep boxing him, don't get into a slugging match with him." When the final round began, Meunier connected a solid punch to my stomach, and I felt the pain. For a few seconds I had trouble breathing, but I didn't let on that I was hurt and continued throwing solid jabs to his face, keeping him away. When the bell rang, ending the fight, the crowd kept cheering, "Freddie, Freddie." Hearing that made me feel rather special, because in the beginning they had cheered for Meunier. I knew I had beaten him, but to my surprise, when Howard announced the winner, he said that it was a draw. Hearing that, the crowd stood up and booed his decision. Some hollered, "Freddie won—he beat Gustave."

Later, Howard would say that he called it a draw because since he and I were from the same town, he thought it would look bad. That was bull shit. As we were leaving the arena after the fights that day, people said to me, "Don't worry Freddie, we know you won the fight. You beat Gustave. You knocked him on his ass! Good for you, Freddie." It felt good hearing the fans say that, but I was very disappointed that Howard didn't award me the fight. On the drive back to New Brunswick, Howard and I almost got into it, but my brother Bill told me to forget about it, because he and the other fighters knew that I had beaten Meunier. What bothered me the most was the fact that Howard had lied about who I was going to fight. Instead of a beginner, like he had said, I had to fight a champ. Anyway, it was a good feeling knowing that at seventeen, I had beaten an experienced boxer who was twenty-nine.

Shortly after Jan and I made plans that she would come join me later in

Toronto, I left Bathurst. I felt if I stayed around Bathurst I would eventually end up losing her. As planned, when Jan turned eighteen and had graduated from high school, she came to Toronto to join me.

When Jan arrived in 1956, I had already been in the magazine business for a little more than a year. I hadn't mentioned to her when she first arrived that my work involved a lot of travelling and that I'd often be away for days and that she'd be alone. Within two weeks, Jan and I were married, and I worked around Toronto for a few weeks. Because I earned more money when I worked out of town, one night, I told her that I'd be going away for a few days. She didn't like to hear that. I understood how she felt, coming from a small town and suddenly being left alone in a large city like Toronto. After assuring her that I'd only be gone for a few days and that I would call her each night, I left the next morning.

When I returned, she told me that she didn't like being left alone. If I was going to continue going out of town, she'd prefer if I find another type of work. I said that I would, but I would need more time before giving my notice to the company that I was leaving. That was a lie, because I could quit at any time. I told her that I would work for another month, and then I'd leave and find another job. When the month came, I gave her another excuse as to why I want to continue for a bit longer. I told her before I quit, I wanted to save a bit of money; once I did, I promised her that I would leave.

In the meantime, Jan got pregnant, and I continued in the mag business, but instead of being away for just a few days; I'd be gone for a week or more, and I continued with my lies as to why I needed to stay in the business. Finally, when Jan was around six months' pregnant, she said that she'd like to return home and have the child there, with her parents. I thought it was a good idea, and a week later, Jan left. Within three months, she gave birth to our son, Brad. I later drove to New Brunswick and returned with her and Brad. Things went quite well for the next few years. When I was out of town, she kept busy with Brad. Then finally one day, she told me that if I didn't get out of the mag business, she would leave. I again promised her that I would, and that time, I meant it. Within a few days, I quit the job. While I looked for other work, Jan decided to return to New Brunswick and visit her family for awhile.

After Jan and Brad left for New Brunswick, I felt a bit empty and lost. So at night, I began to go out to the local bars. Two of the taverns I preferred were the Brass Rail on Yonge Street and the Horseshoe Tavern. There was always live entertainment, featuring the type of music and songs I liked, the westerns.

CHAPTER 18
Police Investigation

One Friday night after having a few drinks with Irvin, who was part owner of the Brass Rail, I was walking down Yonge Street on my way home when I came upon a bunch of people watching a policeman struggle with a couple of men. The officer was trying to keep them up against the wall. As I stopped to watch, I noticed another man who was standing behind the policeman remove something from his pocket. He was about to take a step toward the policeman when I hollered out to the officer, "Watch out behind you!" The officer quickly turned and grabbed hold of the man; just then a police car drove up, and three other officers jumped out and grabbed the other man.

I was about to continue down the street, but someone suddenly grabbed me from behind. Not knowing who it was, I reached up and grabbed hold of the arm that was around my neck and flipped the man over my hip onto the sidewalk. Then I realized that it was one of the police officers who had jumped out of the police car. The young police officer whom I had warned quickly rushed over. He said to the policeman, who was getting up from the sidewalk, "Charlie, that fellow isn't with the other guys. He yelled out to me to warn me about the guy behind me."

As the officer I'd flipped stood glaring at me, I said, "I'm sorry, sir, but I didn't realize that you were a policeman."

He just gave me a push with his hand and walked away. As he did, I heard one of his fellow officer say to him, "Charlie, he got away from you. You're losing your grip."

"Yeah, maybe that time," he answered, making eye contact with me as I turned away and left.

A week later, I got to meet Charlie again, and it wasn't a pleasant meeting, especially for me. Again it was Friday night. After the club closed, I was on my way home when I noticed a police car drive by and then make a sudden U-turn. It parked on the same side of the street I was on. As I approached, the policeman who was on the passenger's side got out and said to me, "You smartass, come here." I stopped, and I saw it was Charlie. I had a feeling the encounter wasn't going to be good.

"What's your name, asshole?" he asked. We stood face to face.

"My name is Freddie. Why do you want to know?" I asked him.

He grabbed my arm and opened the rear door of the police car and pushed me in, saying, "I'll show you what we do with a smartass like you." After he got in, he said to the driver, "We're taking him to the station." As the car began to move, I noticed that the driver was the young officer who had struggled with the men the week before.

I said to them, "What is this about? I wasn't doing anything wrong. As a matter of fact, I had helped the driver the other night when he was about to get hit."

I had just gotten the words out when Charlie turned and punched me in the face, saying, "You shut your f***** mouth. You're going to jail." Within a few minutes we were at the police station and I was charged with obstructing a police officer and resisting arrest. Later, I was driven by two other policemen to the Don Jail, and I was told that I would be there till Monday morning. Then I would be taken to court to face the charges against me.

The punch I received from Charlie didn't bother me; I had been punched before. It was the reason they had conjured up to have me locked in jail that really bothered me. I spent Saturday and Sunday locked away, dumbfounded. Those two days and nights, the only person I thought of was Officer Charlie. I hated that bastard. I came from a small town, and I had always respected and looked up to police officers, but now there was one that I would love to see dead: Charlie.

Come Monday morning, I stood before a judge and listen as the two charges were read off against me. Officer Charlie repeated his lies as to why he had me charged. When I was asked by the judge if I was pleading guilty or not guilty, I told the judge that I was not guilty because the policeman had lied.

"Well," said the judge, "you'll need to get yourself a lawyer."

I told him, "I don't need a lawyer. I was locked up for no reason, and I did nothing wrong." Looking down at his papers, the judge said, "I see that you've already spent a little time in jail. Are you married?"

"Yes," I said. "I am."

"Well," said the judge, "Seeing that you're not going to get yourself a lawyer, I'll tell you what I'm going to do. I'm going to find you guilty as charged, and your sentence will be time served." Not understanding what he meant, I asked, "What is *time served*?"

"Those are the two days that you have already spent in jail for your crime."

"I committed no crime, sir." That said, I was told that I could leave. As I walked out of the courtroom into the hallway, I saw the young officer waiting by the elevator. I walked up to him and said, "How could you do that? You knew he was lying, and I helped you."

Glancing around nervously, he said, "I'm sorry, but I had to. I'm new on the job, and he's my boss." He added as he moved away, "Leave, because he is going to come out any minute."

That morning, I left the courthouse with only one thing on my mind—I wanted to see that lying bastard dead. In the past, I had often heard certain people refer to policemen as *pigs*. Now I understood why. They were referring to police officers like Charlie. That was my first experience having to deal with a corrupt police officer. In later years, in my future work, I would get to meet and have to deal with many other policemen like Charlie. And in the end I would have a few words that would describe them all.

Back at my apartment, I tried to get a bit of sleep, because I had gotten very little the two nights I spent in jail. At the time, those were the two loneliest nights in my life. What made it sadder was the fact that I lived the next street over from the Don Jail. After a few hours of sleep, I went out, picked up a newspaper, and then walked over to a restaurant on Yonge Street. While I was waiting to be served, two uniformed police officers walked in and sat down directly across from me. Seeing them reminded me of Officer Charlie. Suddenly, I was no longer hungry, so I picked up my paper, about to leave, when the waitress walked up and handed me a menu. I stood and said, "I'll be back later." On my way out, I heard one of the policeman say to the waitress, "I guess he doesn't like our company." I felt like turning around and say, "No, I don't," but I decided it was best not to; I was afraid I'd wind up back in jail.

That week I mostly stayed around the apartment, thinking of what I was going to do. I knew that I would soon need to find work. It was more than a month since I left McLean-Hunter, and Jan was to return in a week's time. I was getting a bit low on money. I stayed away from the Brass Rail and Yonge Street for fear of meeting up with Charlie the prick again. I didn't fear him, but he was a policeman and I knew what he was capable of, so I figured it would be in my best interest to stay away for a while. I kept mostly to myself because I didn't feel like talking with anyone. After what happened with Officer Charlie and being out of work, I felt a bit lost.

As mentioned, during the previous three years when I was on the road,

I seldom took a holiday. Now out of a job, I found it hard, especially with Jan and Brad away. Some nights, I walked over to a nearby tavern and had a few drinks; I wasn't too fussy about the place. Most of the customers were elderly, and many were down on their luck, looking for a free drink, but they served good food, and I found most of the people easy to talk with. At the time, I didn't feel like talking with anyone, but as I sat among some of them and listened to their hard luck stories, I forgot about my personal problems for a while.

At the time, I wasn't much of a drinker, but as time marched on, I found many reasons to drink. At first it was to forget my problems, and later I'd use the excuse that it was Friday—even though I was not back to work yet, I felt that I deserved to relax and have a few drinks. I soon found many reasons to drink. I would drink whenever I had a problem or was in a bad mood or a good mood. Then I'd have a few because it was a lovely day, and if it was a dreary day, then I'd use that reason: the weather was bad, so I'd have a few to cheer me up. As time passed I could think of a hundred reasons to have a drink, but I never thought of one reason why I shouldn't.

A few weeks after the incident with Officer Charlie, I decided to go down to the police station and talk to the police chief about what he had done. I was asked by the desk sergeant why I wanted to see the chief. I told him that I was charged and jailed for a crime I did not commit. The sergeant walked away, telling me to wait a few seconds. Later he returned with another police officer dressed in a suit, who identified himself as Inspector Walker. I repeated my story to him and mentioned Officer Charlie's name. Inspector Walker took me to his office and told me that because I pleaded guilty to the offence, there was nothing he could do. He then asked about the punch I got from Charlie and whether I was hurt by the blow. I told him no, because I had a little experience in boxing; when I saw he was going to punch me, I quickly moved my head back.

He looked me over, and then the inspector asked if I was presently working and where I was from. I told him I was from New Brunswick and had recently left my job. He asked if I was married. I told him yes and that my wife and son were away. "It's too bad," said the inspector, "but now that you have a police record, you can't become a policeman."

"Me, a policeman?" I quickly said, "At my weight I could more easily become a jockey."

The inspector laughed, saying, "Yeah, you are a little on the light side, but you seem to have a lot of spunk." Later when I got home, I looked *spunk* up in the dictionary and found it interesting. For some reason, after talking with the inspector, I felt a little more at ease with myself. I believe that talking about what had occurred with Officer Charlie with someone with police authority like the inspector was helpful. I got it out of my system, but I would still have loved to see that pig dead. I knew there were a lot of good cops out there, but I also felt that there were others, like Charlie, who would use their position as police officers to have a person charged and convicted of a crime that they did not commit.

I decided to call Jan in New Brunswick, and I asked her if she would mind staying down there for a couple more weeks till I found work. She agreed that it was a good idea. Of course, she didn't know it, but I hadn't been looking for work.

After talking with her I went out and made the rounds of different bars on Yonge Street. One night I stopped in at the Le Coq d'Or to listen to a little rock and roll by the not-yet-so-famous rock and roller Rockin' Ronnie Hawkins, with his "Whole Lotta Shakin' Going On" and other great songs, such as "Mary Lou" and "Mama Come Home." For some reason or other, later he'd become known as "The Hawk" and went on to fame all over the world with his style of rockabilly. It was a pleasure to watch him perform; once he was on stage, within a few seconds the Le Coq d'Or would be rocking for the rest of the night. No matter which nightclub I began drinking at, I would usually end up at the Brass Rail and indulge till closing time.

As mentioned, I preferred western music. Terry Roberts and the Deans didn't go on to much fame, but they sure packed the Brass Rail with customers—especially lovely looking young women, who, like most of us, were just out to enjoy themselves and have a good time. At times the odd person would be looking for trouble. If you stayed around long enough, you'd be sure to find it.

Most Friday and Saturday nights, the place was jam-packed. In the centre of the club, people would dance, while others watched, admiring the young women with their shapely figures. It would take a few drinks to get some of the women going, but once they did, it was party time. I became friends with Irvin and got to know his partner, Maurice, who, like Irvin, was also Jewish. Irvin was single and a few years younger than his partner.

Sometimes after closing the club for the night, Irvin and I would go out to different restaurants. Quite often we would meet up with some of the young ladies who were at the club earlier. Irvin didn't believe in mixing pleasure with business, but after work hours, it was a different story. He was five years older than I and a good-looking person. He and I took a liking to each other, and we got along well together. At times at the club while mixing in with the young women, I would make a date for me and Irvin. After the place closed we would meet. I had got to meet Irvin's friends when they stopped by the club. Some men were in the clothing business and would at times bring their lovely models along. I sat with them and told a few jokes and added a few lies here and there. One night Irvin jokingly said to them, 'You should see the gals Freddie picks up; he sure knows how to pick them." Irvin may have been right, but one night I made a big blunder. I had arranged to meet two women later at a restaurant just across the street from the club. Irvin and I had been sitting with the women for a minute or two when one of the women looked up and said, "Holy Jesus, here comes my husband." Hearing the word *husband,* I turned and looked at the huge man who had just walked in. He was headed toward our table. I glanced over at Irvin, who was seated across from me, next to the man's wife. From the look on his face it was easy to see that he was very concerned.

As the man approached our table, he paid no attention to Irvin and I. He angrily glared down at his wife and said, "What in the hell are you doing here? You were supposed to be home hours ago." That said, the two women stood up and walked out with him. After they left, Irvin said to me, "Freddie, what are you trying to do, get me killed, fixing me up with a married woman?" I told him that I didn't know she was married. "Well," said Irvin, "before you try and latch on to a woman, you should ask, because there's no bloody way I want to get mixed up in a messy divorce case or get shot by some disgruntled husband or boyfriend."

One night at the club, a woman walked in and sat down next to me at the bar and ordered herself a drink. I had noticed her a few times at the Brown Derby. As I sipped my drink, I wondered why she had sat next to me; most of the other seats at the bar weren't occupied. Thinking she was just out looking for a quickie, I turned to her with a smile and said, "Hi! How are you?"

"I'm just fine, thank you," she answered, and then she asked, "Are you Freddie?"

"Yes," I said. "I'm Freddie, but there are other customers who come in here who are also named Fred or Freddie."

"No," she said. "I believe you are the right person." She added in a low whisper so the barman wouldn't overhear, "Do you know Inspector Walker?"

"Kind of," I told her. "I met him once."

"Well, he would like to see you. He tried phoning you a few times but got no answer. So he asked us to keep an eye open for you as we make our rounds."

Making eye contact with her, I grinned and said, "Making your rounds? Are you a hooker?"

Laughing, she hesitated for a moment and then answered, "No, I'm no hooker. I'm a policewoman." She took a sip of her drink, got up from her chair, and reminded me to get in touch with the inspector. Then she walked away with a friendly smile and said, "A hooker! See you later, Freddie."

Early the following morning, I called the inspector and was asked to go see him at the station. Thinking that he wanted to see me regarding Officer Charlie, I rushed down. And when I got there the inspector mentioned nothing about Charlie. Instead he said, "Mr. Hudon, a few days ago while attending a police convention, I met the chief of police from your home town, Chief O'Neil. Do you know him?"

"Yeah," I said, "I do."

"When I mentioned your name to Chief O'Neil, he said that he knew you and your family well."

I grinned and said, "Did you tell him that I was a known criminal?"

The inspector laughed and said, "No, not really. I just told the chief that I had met you."

As the inspector spoke, I thought to myself, *What the hell has this to do with my complaint about Officer Charlie?* The Inspector continued. I was surprised when he said that Chief O'Neil had mentioned something about me being sent away to an industrial school for delinquent teenagers for about a year at the age of fourteen.

I answered, "Yes I was, sir, but it wasn't for anything serious," wondering what that had to do with Officer Charlie.

He then said, "I spoke to the new officer, and he did say that if you hadn't hollered out to him, he could have been struck from behind. The officer did appreciate your help." Hearing that I thought to myself, *He sure didn't show any appreciation the night I was put in jail or in court when he backed up Officer Charlie's lies.*

"As for Officer Charlie, I have yet to meet with him, and until I do, I feel that it wouldn't be right for me to elaborate regarding that incident till I get to speak to him."

I said, "I understand." I was about to leave, when the inspector said, "Mr. Hudon, I believe I mentioned to you the last time we spoke that the police department is always on the look-out for new police officers."

"Yes," I answered, "you mentioned something about it."

"Chief O'Neil spoke highly of you, and he said that when you were young, you got yourself into a problem regarding a gun. What was that about?" he asked.

"That happened, sir, when I was fourteen. I had been out in the woods hunting near my home. When I came out of the wood, there were two police officers waiting. They charged me with hunting without a licence. Because I was a minor, I shouldn't have had the gun. In those days, sir, many young fellows like me hunted, and we knew nothing about needing a licence."

"You said the police charged you; what happened when you went to court?"

"The magistrate was told that my parents had a problem getting me to go to school and that I had run away from home a few times, because I didn't like going. The magistrate said that he knew just the place for a boy like me, and he sent me to the Boy's Industrial School in Saint John."

"How long were you there for?" the inspector asked.

"For about a year," I answered.

"Did you learn anything?" he asked.

"Yeah," I said, "a lot of schooling."

The inspector smiled and said, "Since then you have had no trouble with the law?"

"Not really," I answered, "other than the incident with Officer Charlie." I felt like saying "that prick Charlie," but I didn't.

He looked at me for a few moments, and the inspector said, "As I mentioned, I spoke with the other police officer, and he said that you flipped Officer Charlie over when he had his arm around your neck. Officer Charlie is a big man. How did you do that?"

"Well, sir," I answered, "when I was grabbed from behind, I didn't know that he was a policeman. I just wanted to get out of the hold he had on me, so I bent my body forward a bit and quickly moved my shoulder back. As I did, he loosened his hold on my neck, and I grabbed his arm and flipped him over."

The inspector seemed amused; he sat back with a grin on his face. "Like I said, we're always looking for good young men, and that is one of the reasons why I wanted to see you. As for you becoming a police officer, like I previously said, that is out of the question because of the police record you now have, but I do have work for you if you want it."

"What type of work is it?" I asked.

He said the job involved working four or five nights a week with police investigators who went out around the city getting into "blind pigs" and illegal gambling places. The term *blind pig*, he said, referred to places where they sold booze and had other illegal activities, such as bootlegging. I was aware of the type of places the inspector spoke of, but I didn't say anything about my knowledge. I just listened to what he had to say about the work. Most such places also involved prostitution. People from all walks of life would gather at those places after bar hours and party all night. Some places were just into bootlegging—you'd go there, buy whatever alcohol you wanted, and then leave. At other places, you could stay and do your drinking till the wee hours of the morning. At most of the after-hours sit-in drinking places, for a few dollars, a person could get themselves a quickie or two. Some of the homes were very nicely set up, with lovely furniture and deep rugs from wall to wall.

Some people felt more comfortable in those establishments than nightclubs. In those places, they could get precisely what they wanted: booze, sex, and, in some places, even drugs.

The inspector explained that my work with the police investigators would consist mainly of getting into those places and paying with marked money. Once I walked out of the place, the policemen would rush in and make their arrest, at the same time seizing the marked bills, which would later be used as evidence. Hearing the inspector explain how simple the work would be, after he assured me that I would be well-paid, I told him that I would give it a try. After all, I had nothing to lose. If I didn't like the work, I would just quit.

Before I left the inspector's office, he left me alone for a few minutes and then returned with three men and one woman. The inspector said, "Fred, I want you to meet the officers you will be working with." The woman was the same person whom I had spoken with the night before at the bar. Her name was Mary-Jean. She said with a smile to the other investigators, "Can you imagine? When I met him at the bar, he asked me if I was a hooker. The nerve of him!"

Robert, one of the other detectives, quickly spoke up and said, "Mary-Jean; it wouldn't be the first time that someone mistook you for a hooker." They all laughed. I was told that the following day, one of them would give me a call to arrange to meet and then I would learn more about the work.

Later, back at my apartment, I got to thinking about what I was getting myself into. Inspector Walker made things sound so simple—I'd just have to get into those places, have a few drinks, pay with marked money, and then leave. The more I thought about it, the more questions about the work came to mind. If the work was that simple, why didn't they use their own regular undercover policemen? Shortly after I began, I'd learn that that work wasn't as simple as the inspector made it out to be.

CHAPTER 19
My Formative Years

That night as I sat around, my memory quickly shot back to the day I stood in front of the court magistrate on the charge of hunting without a licence and for having a gun in my possession. On that day, as was often true, I was in the woods doing a little hunting for birds. After firing off a few shots from the .22 rifle, I headed back for home. As I walked out of the woods, two police officers were there waiting for me. Taking the rifle away from me, one officer asked why I was in the woods shooting; why wasn't I in school? I told him that I often went in the woods hunting, and as for not being in school, I said that I didn't like going to school.

Whenever I gigged school, I would pass school hours in the woods hunting. *Gigged* was a word used in the forties and fifties to refer to doing something else instead of attending school. After school was out for the day, I'd go home, and my mother would think I had been in school, but I hadn't.

The police officer said that he'd have to take me to the police station, because he had received a complaint that I was shooting at a horse's hooves, trying to make the horse dance, in a nearby field. I told the officers that I wasn't shooting at any horse, which I hadn't done. At the police station, they charged me with hunting out of season, plus shooting off a firearm near a residential area. I was then taken home. They explained to my mother that in a few days, I would have to show up in court to answer to the charges. At the time, I wasn't concerned about showing up in court. My concern was about the rifle that they kept and said that I wouldn't be getting it back. The gun belonged to Ross, who ran a small canteen not far from my home. After school hours and most weekends, I worked for Ross in that canteen, doing odd jobs. The canteen was the type of place where they served fast food, such as hotdogs and hamburgers, along with fries and different types of sandwiches. It was a busy place, especially at nights and on weekends, because a great number of people were interested in buying one item that wasn't shown on the menu, and that item was booze. This little canteen was more or less used as a front for bootlegging, especially after the war was over and men returned home.

Bootleggers were popping up everywhere in East Bathurst, which was known as Hell Town. Within a quarter of a mile, there were easily eight or ten bootleggers. The young men who had gone overseas to fight had returned, and most of them couldn't find work. Some were more fortunate than others; Ross and his brother both got jobs at the paper mill. The other less fortunate ones would find odd jobs, such as loading or unloading the large ships as they came.

Ross had a good location for his boozing business. His canteen was located next to his parent's business. They ran a grocery store. At the back of the store, they had a large ice house where they'd store their dairy products and other items to keep them fresh. At times, Ross's father, Mr. Wise, would go out to the ice house and find some of his son's booze hidden among the grocery products. When he did, you'd hear him cursing if you were nearby. He didn't like either his son's bootlegging or Ross using his ice house to hide his booze. The parents were good church-going people, especially Mrs. Wise. They'd always help others who were in need; men and women with families would go to their store, give them a hard luck story, and walk out with bags of groceries. They marked it down as money owing, but usually they'd never see it or the customer again. Ross ran his canteen in the same manner; he would give credit and many times never got paid. He would not bother to go after them for his money, though it was a different story if a person got booze on credit. If the man didn't show up to pay, the next time Ross met up with him, that person could end up with a busted jaw if he didn't have the money. Ross was easy-going, but if someone messed around with him, he could get mean and dirty. The two brothers were the same; anytime someone tried to pull a fast one on either one of them, in plain English, they would get the shit beat out of them. It was well known around town that if you messed with the two brothers, you're sure going to end up with a problem. Especially the younger one—he'd stand face to face with a man, and, quick as a flash, the man would end up on his ass from a fist or a boot to the face. He was fast, like lightning, with his hands or feet.

On weekends the two brothers would leave and go to the farm they had outside of town, which some referred to as the "party place." At the time no one was staying at the farm; the place was mostly used on weekends for wild parties. Come Friday night, the brothers and a few of their friends would leave early, and I would be left to take care of the canteen. Usually Ross would close the canteen around 1:00 am, but when I was there alone, I would leave it open till the wee hours of the morning. Men would come in; if they wanted a bottle of booze, I would pull up a floor board and pull out a bottle of Hermits or 999 wine and hand it over the counter. The person would stuff the bottle inside his coat and then quickly leave, because the police were always out cruising around. At times, they would stop in to have a quick sandwich or burger. Seeing me there alone, sometimes an officer would make a comment about why I was there alone instead of being home in bed. I'd say, "There's no school tomorrow, so I'm just here earning a little money." Some would ask my age; I'd say fourteen. I lied, because at the time I was only thirteen.

One Friday night, I was almost caught by the police for selling booze. I had just handed a bottle to a customer when I saw the police cruiser pull up and park near the entrance. I said to the man, "Get out, here come the police." The policeman met the man as he walked out. After greeting each other, the officer came in and asked for a Coca-Cola. Just as I stepped back from the counter to get his cola, I lost my balance and grabbed on to the counter. When I saw the officer drive up, I forgot to put the floor board back, and I almost stepped into the hole. Before the officer could say anything, I said, "That damn floor—they were supposed to fix it." If the officer had looked over the counter, he would have seen the hole and also the rum and wine bottles hidden away there. After I handed the cola to the police officer, he said to me, "By the way, do you know of any bootleggers around the area?"

I thought to myself, *He knows*. Then I got an idea. "Yes, sir," I said, "there's one just around the corner. He's a taxi driver, and he's always selling booze. Matter of fact," I added, "he keeps it in that little shed at the rear of his home. That's where it's hidden, especially on weekends."

"Are you sure?" said the cop.

"Oh, yes, I am, because I sometimes go there for my father for a bottle, and once I saw him go into that shed and come out with it." The police officer quickly left and headed for town. A short time later, I saw two police cruisers rush by, headed toward the taxi driver's home. The next day, I heard that the police had raided his place. I was pleased because I didn't like the cab driver, on account of him continuously supplying my father with booze. Any bootlegger who sold my father alcohol, I had no use for; so it didn't bother me. The next night, I told Ross what I had done and about the cab driver getting raided by the police. He just laughed and said, "Good! Now there's one less."

After I told Ross that I was caught with his gun and the police had kept it, he told me not to worry about the gun; he would get it back. When it came time for me to go to court, I went alone because my mother wasn't well. In court, as I stood in front of the magistrate, one police officer explained that I was shooting a gun off near homes and mentioned the complaint they had received from a homeowner. Staring down at me with his bloodshot eyes, the magistrate said to me, "So young man, I hear that you don't like to go to school, and you do like shooting guns."

"Sir," I said, "I like hunting with guns."

"Why are you here alone? Where are your parents? They should be here," he said.

"My mother is sick, and my father is working," I answered.

He asked the police officer, "Did the owner come get his gun?"

"Yes, he did," said the policeman, giving me a stern look.

The magistrate said, "You just can't walk into a man's home and take a gun without his permission. You're lucky he didn't press charges against you for theft."

I glanced toward the officer, dumbfounded, not wanting to believe that Ross had told the police that I took his gun without his permission, which was a bloody lie. He had told me that I could use the gun anytime I wanted to, because he knew I liked going hunting in the woods. I said to the magistrate, glancing over at the police officer who had picked me up, "You say he didn't want to press charges?"

"No," said the officer. "Mr. Wise was just interested in getting his gun back."

"I see," said the magistrate. "Well, seeing that you don't want to go to school and you take people's belongings without permission, especially a gun; I have just the place for young fellows like you. I hereby sentence you to the Saint John Industrial School for Boys, for a period of one year; and there, my young man," he added, "you'll have to attend school." As he spoke, I glared back at him and felt like shouting out, "You old f***** drunk, sending me away for something I didn't do." He finished by telling the sheriff to take me home and get my clothing and then to deliver me to the school in Saint John. The magistrate was well known around town for his boozing. That's why I thought of him as a drunk.

Arriving at my home, my mother met us at the door. The sheriff and she seemed to know each other. After he explained to my mother that I would have to go Saint John Industrial School for a year, she began to cry. He tried to comfort her by telling her that the school would be a good place for me. Besides going to school, I would have the opportunity to learn other skills. As they sat in the kitchen talking, I listened from the living room. At one point, hearing my mother crying, I thought of sneaking out the front door and running away, which I had often done before. But before I had a chance to do anything, Sheriff Aubé called me to the kitchen and said that he would be taking me to Saint John the next day, so I could spend an extra day with my family. It seemed that the sheriff could read my mind, because he told me if I ran away and wasn't there when he returned to pick me up, I would be just making things worse for my mother. Looking at her, as she sat there with tears in her eyes, I assured him that I would be there when he came to pick me up.

After the sheriff left, I sat with my mother, and we both cried. We were alone, as my sisters and brothers were still in school. We were a family of thirteen children, eight girls and five boys. My four older sisters were taken at a young age to be educated in the States by my grandmother. Another sister lived in Windsor; my oldest brother Billy was married; and Romeo, who was ten years older than I, left home for Ontario after having a fight with our father and wasn't heard from for years. That left six of us still living at home. Oscar was one year younger than I, and Donald was the youngest boy; Eleanore, Myra, and Noella were the youngest of the girls. I asked my mother not to tell them when they returned from school, or my father either, about my being sentenced to the Saint John School till after I had gone.

The next day, I was taken to Saint John. To my surprise, there were no huge fences around the property or a guard standing at the entrance as we drove in, as I had expected to find. The Industrial School was just a huge farm with about fifty or sixty other fellows, from twelve to seventeen years old. Arriving there, I was taken to Mr. Fergie's office, the superintendent, and the rules were explained and what the work involved. I would have to attend school classes every day for six hours. We were to be up at six am each morning. After breakfast, we were to do some farm work, including feeding the horses and cows and other livestock and a few hundred chickens. After milking the cows at nine o'clock, we would be in the classrooms, and after school, we would start the farm chores over again.

Being born on a farm, I was accustomed to farm work, so I didn't really mind it. But having to attend school every day this I wasn't too happy about. I was put in the sixth grade. My biggest problem was with spelling. As for reading and writing, I could manage. I was also good at math.

Whenever the teacher asked me to spell a certain word and I spelled it wrong, some classmates would laugh. That I didn't like, but I would have to sit there and take it. One smartass was a couple of years older than me, and he always found a reason to make fun of me. He was known to be a bully and to pick on others younger than him. A few weeks after I arrived there, the bully and I got into a fight, and both of us were taken to the superintendent's office. Both of us were made to drop our pants and bend over, and we were beaten on the ass with a belt. It was painful. After the beating, we were told if we were brought to the office again for fighting, the next beating would be more severe. Mr. Fergie didn't do the strapping; he had Mr. McFarlane, one of the school's supervisors, do it. He seemed to enjoy using the strap. Each time the strap made contact with my ass he would ask, "How do you like that? Do you want more?" and I didn't answer, so he'd come down harder with the belt.

I would later learn a few things about Mr. McFarlane. He was very sadistic. He would walk around the farm checking on us, and sometimes, for no reason, he would hit us a crack across the legs with a small tree branch that he always carried with him. If he didn't like you, he could make your stay at the farm very uncomfortable. Mr. Fergie's wife was our teacher; we later learned that Mr. McFarlane was having an affair with her. Certain nights, whenever Mr. Fergie was away, Mr. McFarlane would stay around much later that he usually did. Mr. McFarlane usually went home before six o'clock at night. When Mr. Fergie was away, he would stay around late into the night. Mr. and Mrs. Fergie lived at the farm. Mr. McFarlane did not; he went home at night. The night watchman, Mr. Scott, would start his shift around six o'clock, when Mr. McFarlane would usually leave.

One day as I was working in the kitchen stockroom, I heard the two of them talking near the doorway. Mrs. Fergie told Mr. McFarlane that Mr. Fergie would be away for the night, and she wanted to see him later up in the living quarters, located on the top floor of the building. After it got dark, I noticed that Mr. McFarlane had disappeared. So I went out into the ball field; from there I could look up at the top floor, so I knew the location of each room. As I watched from the back of the ball field, I saw the figure of a man near the living room window. I knew it was Mr. McFarlane. The lights were on in the living room and bedroom. Later, as I stood there watching both windows, I saw Mr. McFarlane's shape near the bedroom window. The shades were drawn, but I could make out it was him. The bedroom lights went out, and I couldn't see any movement in the living room. I returned to the building. From our sleeping quarters, I watched from the window to see when Mr. McFarlane went out to his car. An hour or so later, I noticed him leave, get into his car, and drive away.

That night as I lay in bed, I thought what would happen if Mr. Fergie knew about his wife and Mr. McFarlane. At fourteen, I knew enough to know that Mrs. Fergie didn't have Mr. McFarlane up in her bedroom to teach him his ABC's. Early the next morning, Mr. McFarlane was back ringing the big bell, the signal for us to get out of bed. Each morning, he would walk around. If any of us were not up when he reached our bed, he would hit us a crack with his little branch. At times, he would yell, "Get up, you lazy bunch of bastards. You have work to do." As I watched Mr. McFarlane making his rounds, checking to see if we had made up our beds correctly, I got an idea. When he approached my bed, I said to him, "Sir, last night when I was out in the ball field I looked up and noticed a man in Mr. Fergie's living room window." For a few seconds, he didn't say anything; he just stared at me. I then said, "Should I mention to Mr. Fergie that his wife had a man visiting her while he was away?"

"What were you doing out in the ball field after dark?" he asked. "You are not to be out and around after dark."

I answered, "I went out to get my ball glove that I had earlier left out there, sir." I hadn't mentioned to him that it was dark when I was outside. So I knew he knew what I was talking about. Before walking away, he gave the bed a few light taps with his switch and said, "The fellows around here usually mind their own business. If they don't, they could find their stay here very long."

Knowing what he meant, I said, "Yes, sir."

Later that afternoon, as I was leaving the class, Mrs. Fergie called me over to her desk. She said, "Freddie, I see that you are having problems with your spelling, so starting tomorrow, I will have you stay for a while after class, and I'll help you."

"Thank you, ma'am," I said and left the room. I figured that Mr. McFarlane must have told her what I had said about seeing a man up in her quarters while her husband was away. Every day for the next month, she kept me after class to work with me on my spelling, which helped a lot. I had no difficulty reading; it was the bloody spelling of certain words that was my main problem. I wanted to learn, so I continued trying hard. At night, when the other fellows were out fooling around, I would stay in and study. Quite often, I would fall asleep spelling words to myself. I found that after I had stood up to the farm bully, I made a lot of friends among the boys. There was no more laughing when I misspelled words in class. As a matter of fact, many boys who had fewer problems with schooling tried to help me, and eventually, between them and the teacher, I got the knack of it. After the school term was over, my marks were good enough to pass to the next grade.

Shortly after the school ended for the summer, I was called to Mr. Fergie's office and told that he had found me a job in town, working at a drug store, for the remainder of the summer. That was a program the school had each summer. Certain boys would be chosen to go out in the city to work, and the money they'd earn was put into a special account. They would get it when it was time for them to go home. For the remainder of my stay at the farm, I continued to work at the drug store. Each morning at seven, I would take the bus into the city, and at five I would return to the farm. This continued for three months. Finally, one evening I met Mr. Fergie in the hallway, and he asked me into his office. As he sat back in his chair, he said, "Freddie how would you like to go home?" Not finding any words to say, I just stood there looking at him. "You have been here for eleven months," he added, "and I feel that you are ready to return home." Before I managed to say anything, he said, "Tomorrow I'm driving through Bathurst, and I have decided to take you with me."

Later that night, as I gathered my stuff to leave, I had mixed feelings about leaving the farm. For eleven months, I was well fed and clothed, and at night, I had a decent bed to sleep in and didn't have to worry about my father pulling me out of bed and sending me out in the cold winter nights, with very little clothes on, to fetch him a bottle of booze from the bootlegger. Many times, when I couldn't find someone to sell me a bottle, I would return and hide out in the cold outhouse, freezing till my father got up and left for work. Then I would go in and try to get a couple of hours of sleep before being sent off to school. Often, I would fall asleep at my desk from lack of sleep.

No one besides my family knew the hell that all of us was put through on account of my father's drinking. Everything was well hidden; he only drank at home, so the neighbours weren't aware of what was going on in the house. He was like a Jekyll and Hyde. When he wasn't drinking he could be pleasant, but once he got into the booze, especially the wine, he would drastically change for the worse. When he drank, it was like living in hell for all of us. When he was sober, he was likeable, but when he got into the sauce, he was a completely different person: hateful and abusive, especially to my mother.

The next day, as we drove away from the farm, I felt like crying for some reason; there was a deep sadness inside of me. I should have been happy because I was going home, but I wasn't. As we drove along, Mr. Fergie sensed that and tried to cheer me up by saying that my family was going to be surprised to see me, because he hadn't notified my parents that I was coming home. When I thought of seeing my mother and brothers and sisters, I was glad that I was going home. The only contact I had with them for the past eleven months was a few letters. So thinking of seeing them again made me feel better.

Chapter 20
Returning Home after Industrial School

My arrival was a big surprise to my mother. Seeing me get out of the car, she rushed out and threw her arms around me saying, "Oh my God, Freddie, you're home." Within seconds of seeing me, she was in tears. Mr. Fergie came into the house, where my brothers and sisters were waiting for me to come in. I was so happy to see them that tears began to run down my face. Mr. Fergie sat for a while with my mother, telling her what I had accomplished in school and saying that for the past three months I had been working at the drug store. Before leaving, Mr. Fergie had me promise him that if I had any trouble, I would call him. I said that I would. Later, after he left and my mother got control of her emotions, we sat around the table talking.

I hadn't seen my father yet; he was still at work. My mother noticed that I had grown a couple of inches and put on a little weight. She kept repeating how good I looked. My dear mother—how I loved her. At times I wished that I could have the same feeling for my father, but that wasn't to be. When he arrived home from work, he just looked at me and said, "So you're back." As usual, he showed no emotion whatsoever; he didn't even bother to say that he was glad to see me. It was just as if I hadn't been away for the past eleven months. That hurt me, but I didn't let it show. Later that night, I soon found out that nothing had changed. He kept to himself, drinking up in his bedroom. The only time he came downstairs was to go out to the outhouse, then he returned to his bedroom to continue drinking.

Later, my mother and I sat in the kitchen talking about what I was going to do now that I was back. My father staggered downstairs and told me that he was going to get me a job at the lumber mill where he worked. I stared directly into his eyes and told him that I might not want to work at the lumber mill. By the look on his face, I could tell he didn't like what he just heard. For a few moments, he didn't know what to say. I hadn't spoken back or stood up to my father before. I surprised him. He just stood there with a dumb look on his face. My mother spoke up and said, "He just got home. Give him a few days, then he'll decide what he wants to do. I want Freddie to go back to school." I decided rather than go work with my father, I would return to school, which I did. At sixteen, I quit school, and a year later I left Bathurst for good, beside the occasional visit. On one occasion, I returned to see my mother on the day she was being buried at fifty-three years old. She died with a broken heart, but in doing so she finally found peace, and I knew she had gone on to a better place.

As for my father, he was alone. My two younger brothers and sisters had moved on with their lives. Oscar was in Windsor, married and working for Chrysler, and Donald stayed in Bathurst and married his little sweetheart. My sister Eleanore also stayed in Bathurst and married at a young age. My two youngest sisters, Myra and Noella, ended up in Montreal and eventually married.

Five years later, I would once again return to bury my father, age sixty-three. When he took sick, the doctors couldn't do anything for him because of his drinking. His stomach was damaged by the cheap booze he had consumed over the years. If after death there were such places as heaven and hell, I was sure of two things: one was that my mother was in heaven. As for my father, I couldn't visualize his soul going anywhere other than hell, where he rightfully deserved to be.

When I was young, if anyone had told me that later in life there was a possibility that I would grow up to be anything like my father, I would have told them that they were crazy, but time would tell.

CHAPTER 21
The City of Toronto

As for my work with the Toronto police, the first few nights went smoothly, but after that, the work got more complicated. The first night Officer Mary-Jean and I got into a couple of after-hour drinking establishments. At one place, we sat around for an hour or so. After having a couple of drinks and paying with marked money, we left and met with Jay, who was waiting up the street with two other policemen. After Mary-Jean told Jay it was a go, they headed up to the Blind Pig. Mary-Jean and I got into her car and watched from a distance as the police raid was carried out. In another part of the city, we later met up again with Officer Jay. Over a coffee, he mentioned that the next place might be a little more difficult, because they had already raided that place just a few months earlier.

I was to go up to the door while Mary-Jean waited in the unmarked police car. When someone answered the door I was to tell them that Rodney had asked me to pick up a bottle for him. After I got the bottle and paid with the marked money, I returned to the car, and Mary-Jean flashed the head lights off and on a few times, giving Robert the signal that we had gotten the booze. When the police moved in, we again waited till we saw Jay and the other policeman come out with the occupants of the house, along with a few cases of alcohol as evidence.

The following week, the work got a little more complicated. I had to go into night clubs and get friendly with certain men who were involved in running some of those after-hour drinking places. I had no problem with mixing in with people and getting information and later passing that information on to the police.

Besides the bootleggers and after-hour drinking establishments, there were the prostitutes and the illegal gambling places. The police were less concerned with the prostitutes, but sometimes the police didn't like certain ones for some reason, and they were set up and arrested. We would park near the hotel, and they'd point out to me the one they were interested in. I would later go into the hotel, have a few drinks, and get friendly with the prostitutes. Then I would wait till she propositioned me. We would go up to a room, and I would leave the door unlocked so the police could just walk in. That usually happened within ten minutes after we entered the room, giving me enough time to pay the prostitute with the marked money. When the police entered, I would leave the room and wait out in the police car till they called for a second police car to take the prostitute to the police station.

I continued doing that type of work for a few months. One night I was picked up by Robert and Mary-Jean. As usual, we began the night by having a coffee. That night, Robert said that Mary-Jean and I would go to the Famous Door Tavern, located on Yonge Street, and try to get friendly with a man named Whitey. He was known among the police to run an after-hour drinking place and also had a few prostitutes working for him. When Robert mentioned the Famous Door, I told him that I didn't like the idea of going in there to set anyone up, because I often went to the Famous Door and had friends there. "Well," said Robert, "if you go there often, maybe you know who Whitey is—that will make it easier."

"No," I told him, "I don't want to be involved in that one. Use someone else." He seemed disturbed when I told him to get someone else. He quickly said, "Well, Fred; that is part of the job." I repeated that I wouldn't do it. Seeing that I was serious, Robert said, "We'll put it off for another night." The Famous Door Tavern was located just a few doors down from the Brass Rail and there was no way that I was going to get involved in setting up anyone at either tavern.

Earlier, when Mary-Jean and I were alone, I was told that Robert wanted to get Whitey real bad, because at one time Whitey tried to run him over with his car. She mentioned if I helped to set Whitey up, it would be good for me. "No," I told her. "I will have nothing to do with it."

"Freddie!" she said. "In this type of work, you can't pick and choose what you want to do. You have to go along with what you're asked to do."

"No," I told her, "I will quit rather than try to set Whitey up. Let Robert do it himself. Let's assume," I added, "that I go along and set Whitey up. If that person already tried to run over a policeman, what do you think he would try to do to me? I am no policeman. Matter of fact," I reminded her, "I have nothing protecting me—no insurance, nothing. Each week I am handed an envelope with money, and that's it."

Later that night, Mary-Jean and I received a call from Robert. We drove over to the west end, where he was waiting with two other police officers.

Mary-Jean got out and spoke with them and then returned and said we are just going up the street to a house to try and buy a case of beer. The name we were to use was Tony.

Arriving at the house, Mary-Jean parked in front, and we went up and knocked; a woman answered the door. When I told her that Tony had said that we might be able to get some beer, she asked us in. An impressive-looking man in his mid-forties sat behind a desk playing cards with a younger man. "Tony sent them over," said the woman.

"What do you want," he asked.

"A dozen beers," I answered, removing my wallet from my pocket.

"Where's your car parked?" he asked. I said in front. "Drive it to the back," he said, "and Chummy here will bring it out to you." We left and drove the car to the back of the house. The young fellow was there waiting with the case of beer in his arms. He told Mary-Jean to open the trunk; we both got out of the car, and when Mary-Jean opened the trunk, he placed the case of beer right next to the police radio transmitter, which was in plain view. Realizing that, Mary-Jean quickly closed the trunk. We got in and pulled away from the driveway. Mary-Jean signalled with her car lights to Robert, meaning that we had made the purchase. As usual, we drove up the street and waited until Robert and the officers came out. Two of the policemen were helping the older man to the police car. For a moment I thought that the officers were struggling with the man, but when they got to the sidewalk, I saw that the man had only one leg; the other was cut off above the knee. As I watched, the officers placed him in the car. I felt sorry for him and said to Mary-Jean, "There are hundreds of other bootleggers; why him? He's only got one leg."

"Freddie," said Mary-Jean, "it's like I mentioned to you before—we don't pick or choose who to go after. As policemen, we just do what we are told."

"Well," I said, "Robert must do the picking. He's in charge."

"Yes," she answered. "He's one of many who makes the decisions."

As we drove back downtown, I didn't say much. I kept thinking of the one-legged man; I felt a bit sorry for him. We could have gone after able men, many too lazy to go out and work for a living; those types I felt no remorse about. But for the one-legged man, I did.

We had one more set-up to do that night before I went home. We parked on Yonge Street and waited for Robert. After he showed up he got in and gave us an address to go to. He said it was a drink-in place. We were to go there and try and get in; usually he'd give us a name to use, but that time he said, "Just knock and ask if you can come in. If you get in, good; if not, we'll try again another night." Approaching the house, Mary-Jean seemed to know right where to go, because I had the house number on a piece of paper and she didn't ask me the address. After parking, we both poured a few drops of cheap alcohol, which was kept in a small container, in our hands and then rubbed our faces with it, so when someone answered the door, they would smell the alcohol and think that we had been out drinking. We would often use the alcohol so people would think that we had already been drinking.

As we got out of the car, I said to Mary-Jean, "Fancy-looking house." I was about to press the door buzzer when Mary-Jean touched my arm and said, "Freddie, this is the home that Robert spoke to you about earlier." Before I had time to react, the door opened, and there stood Whitey, who I knew as Willard, from the Famous Door Tavern, a man who on many occasions I had sat and drank with, a man I considered a friend. From the look on his face, he was surprised to see me at his door. "What are you doing here, Freddie?" he asked?

Glancing at Mary-Jean, not sure what to say, I said, "Are you just going out?" As I said it, I nodded my head a bit as if to say yes, again glancing at Mary-Jean. He hesitated for a moment and then said, "Yes, I was just at the door getting my coat when I heard you coming up the steps."

Lost for words, I managed to say, "Okay, I'll see you later," and we turned and walked away.

I told Mary-Jean to drive me home; I was finished. When she got to Robert's car, which had been parked up the street with other policemen, she rolled down her window and told him that we didn't get in because he was just on his way out. I didn't bother to look over at Robert as Mary-Jean spoke to him. As far as I was concerned, he was just a prick for what he had done. As Mary-Jean drove toward my home, I said, "Why didn't you tell me before we walked up those steps? You knew where we were going."

"I am sorry," she said, "but I couldn't do anything. Robert is my boss, and I just take orders. As a matter of fact," she added, "I only decided to tell you when I saw you reaching for the door bell. If Robert knew, I would be in big trouble."

I thanked her for telling me. I now disliked Robert as much as I disliked the crooked cop Charlie.

Mary-Jean dropped me off around 5:00 am. That night, I received a call from her asking me if I had changed my mind about not wanting to continue working. I told her no, that I was finished. "Okay," she said, "I'll tell Robert." A week later, I hadn't returned to pick up my pay, and Mary-Jean stopped by. She said that because I hadn't picked up my envelope from the inspector, she decided to bring it over on her night off. In the envelope was my pay, in cash, for the nights I had worked. She stayed for a while, and we had a few drinks. I asked if she knew what happened in court to the one-legged bootlegger. She said that he pleaded guilty and paid a fine and that his sentence was suspended due to his health. I was glad to hear that he wasn't sent to jail. She said when she told the inspector that she was going to bring the envelope to me, he asked her to tell me to give him a call after I had rested up. "What did the inspector mean by *rested up?*" I asked her.

"I don't really know," she replied, "but I think Robert told him that you weren't working for a couple of weeks because you were tired of the night work."

I laughed and said, "Robert can't even be honest with his inspector."

When Mary-Jean left, she reminded me to give the inspector a call. That was the last time I saw Mary-Jean. As for Robert, I met him one more time. One night as I was having a drink at the Brown Derby, he and a fellow policeman walked in and sat next to me at the bar. He said hello and asked how I was making out and if I felt like going back to work. After finishing my drink, I said to him, "After what you did, forget about it." I got up and left.

A few days after meeting up with Robert, I called Inspector Walker and told him precisely what had happened between Robert and I. With that said, I thanked him and told him that I had decided to leave Toronto. I then called Jan, who was still in New Brunswick and had been for four extra months; I told her that I would be moving to Montreal and already had a job lined up, which was a lie, but I knew that I would have no problem finding one. After I promised to quit drinking and running around to bars at night, Jan agreed that after I got to Montreal and found an apartment, she and Brad would join me there.

CHAPTER 22
Arriving in Montreal

In 1960, I arrived in Montreal, and within a few days I was working. The problem was—I was back in the magazine business, again knocking on doors. There was one thing I liked about the magazine business; I knew that I could make good money even though I didn't like knocking on doors. As planned, shortly after arriving in Montreal, I got an apartment, and Jan and Brad came and joined me. And as I had promised, I stayed away from the bars and did very little drinking. When Jan first learned that I was back in the magazine business, she threw a fit. After assuring her that it would only be temporary, she said okay, but only for a while and as long as I didn't have to go out of town.

I may have been making good money, but I had to work twice as hard for it. Knocking on doors around Montreal wasn't like knocking on doors in Toronto. In Montreal, I had the language issue to deal with, and, after a while, I found that people weren't as friendly. It got to the point that whenever someone answered the door, before you'd have a chance to say anything, they would say "Okay, what are you selling?" Quite often there would be two or three salesmen on the same street, knocking on doors, trying to sell different products. Whenever that occurred, I would move on to another area of the city.

One day while I knocked on doors, I came across an Englishwoman who had just arrived from England. After selling a three-year subscription to the *MacLean Magazine*, her husband walked in just as I was about to leave. As I walked down the steps, I heard her tell him that she had bought some *MacLean's*. He said to her, "Dear, we are going to have a lot of tooth paste." At the time, I didn't know what he was referring to. Later I would learn that there was a toothpaste called MacLean's. So instead of them receiving a tube of toothpaste every second week, they would get a magazine.

Another incident occurred one day while I was working just outside the city. I drove by a huge house with a steel gate in front. Seeing that the gate was open and an elderly woman was working nearby in the garden, I decided to go in and give her my sales pitch. After I did, she said that she would like the *Chatelaine Magazine* now that it was published in French and that she would prefer receiving it by mail rather than buying it at the store. When I asked her how many copies she would like, she glanced at the list and said, "I'll take the two hundred."

"Madam," I said, "most people usually take the thirty-six copies."

"No," she answered. "If it will help you, I'll take the two hundred copies." Thinking that maybe she didn't realize the amount of money she would have to pay, I said, "That will be twenty dollars."

"Okay," she said, "come to the house and I'll get the money." In those days twenty dollars was big money to pay for magazines. Because she wanted it, I wrote the order up, and she paid me the twenty dollars.

A couple of weeks later, I was called to the office by the circulation manager. He said, "Freddie, that order you turned in for two hundred copies of the *Chatelaine* needs to be cut down a bit."

"Why?" I asked.

"Well," said the manager, "a subscription to a magazine for approximately seventeen years is a bit too long for a woman who's eighty-five."

"Sorry," I said. "I didn't know she was eighty-five." Glancing up at me from his desk, the manager said, "I bet." I was told that they had called the woman and decreased the order to thirty-six copies instead of two hundred and refunded her $16.40. Before I left his office the manager said, "Freddie, stay away from little old women with twenty-dollar orders for a magazine that is only published monthly."

The first time I wrote up an order for twenty dollars to an elderly person was when I was with McLean-Hunter. One day while out knocking on doors, an elderly woman answered. Because she was very old, I jokingly said to her, "Madam, I'm selling magazines, trying to raise enough money to get my father out of jail." Sometimes when someone answered the door and I felt that it was useless to give them a sales pitch, I would say just about anything and then move on to the next house. But that little old lady, she was very interested. When I mentioned that I was working to get my dad out of jail; she asked, "Why is he in jail?"

For a moment, I didn't know what to say; the first simple thing that came to mind was bootlegging. So I said, "Oh, he got caught selling booze, and now he's in jail and needs a lawyer."

"You poor boy," said the elderly lady. "It's so good of you to try to help your dad. For that reason," she said as she looked over the list I handed her, "I'll take the two hundred copies." I thought she would change her mind when I handed her the receipt; after looking at it she said, "You wait; I'll get my purse," and she returned, handing me the twenty dollars. She said, "I do hope your dad gets out of jail."

A few weeks later, when I had returned from out of town, I was asked into Mr. Tony's office. He said, "Freddie, what in the hell is going on with you?"

"Why, sir?" I asked.

"Well," Mr. Tony said, "you turned in an order for twenty dollars, which you sold to a woman who's in her nineties. When we phoned her in regard to decreasing the order, she said that she didn't really want the magazine, she just bought it to help the young man get his father out of jail. What type of sympathy pitch did you use on the woman?" Mr. Tony angrily asked.

"Well, sir, when she answered the door and I saw that she was elderly, I didn't give a pitch. I just jokingly said to her, 'Madam, I'm selling magazines to help get my father out of jail.' When I was about to walk away, she said 'Okay, I'll buy some'."

Warning me about giving elderly people a sympathy sales pitch, Mr. Tony said that the order had been cancelled and her twenty dollars returned to her. Personally, I thought it was funny, but Mr. Tony certainly didn't think so.

I continued knocking on doors around the Montreal area, till I felt getting sales was too hard. It seemed that the city was infested with door-to-door salesmen. One evening, I talked with Jan about going out of town with a crew of other salesmen; she didn't like the idea but agreed, as long as I would only be away for a few days. I continued making excuses to stay in the mag business and go out of town to work.

It began with being away only a few days at a time, but as time went on, once again I was spending more time out of town than I did at home. On the road I was also back to drinking a bit heavier. During the day, we would sit around the bars drinking. With me, it was always the same. I would start out intending to just have a couple of drinks, but usually I would stay till the bar closed. This continued for a few more years; in the meantime, we had two more sons: Cloyd and Bill. Three children and my continuous drinking put a lot of stress on Jan. I was very seldom around to help her with the boys.

My stay in the mag business came to an abrupt end one night when I was out of town working. After being out drinking, I returned to my room; the following morning I awoke in the hospital. I didn't know how I got there till I was told that I had been in a bad car accident. It seemed that for some reason after I had returned to my room that night, I went down and got into my car and was on my way somewhere when I lost control and struck a hydro pole, flipping my car over. When I was found, I was pretty well crushed beneath the car. After a week in the hospital and an operation on my damaged knee, I returned home and was out of work for a few months on account of my injuries.

When I felt better and was able to work, I got into the collection business. As for my marriage ... When Jan learned that the accident was caused by me being drunk, added to the years of my lies and my failure to be faithful, that was pretty well the end—she had had enough and one day she told me that was it, and she left.

As previously mentioned, I went from the collection business into private security. Prior to getting my licence, besides some of the places I have mentioned I worked, I was also employed at the Port of Montreal for the March Ship Lines. This was a dangerous place for security officers. The winter months were a slow time of year for shipping, but the Port was still very active. The Montreal Port had its own policemen patrolling the grounds, but shipping companies such as March Ship Lines hired their own security officers.

In the beginning, my work was rather simple. The first week of employment I spent walking around the huge waterfront storage sheds with the security supervisor. As we walked around, he would point out the things I should be watching out for. The work also involved going onto the huge ships and keeping an eye on the dock workers who were unloading the cargo. A good number of the port workers were involved in thievery, connected with Montreal gangs who specialized in stealing transports loaded with merchandise.

In the sixties, the gangsters were interested in transports loaded with televisions and other electronic equipment, which were highly in demand and easy to get rid of. The criminals weren't interested in just stealing a few items; they would highjack loaded transports after they left the Port and steal the whole cargo. Some of the dock workers, especially the ones who worked in the storage sheds, loading the merchandise on the transports, would inform the gangsters as to what was on those transport trucks. If the cargo was merchandise they wanted to steal, somewhere en route to wherever it was to be delivered, the transport truck would be high-jacked. In some incidents, the transport driver was also involved in the theft. It was prearranged; some transport trucks would be stolen and driven away while the driver stayed overnight at a motel. In some incidents, the thieves had a spare key to the ignition of the truck. They would just drive up to wherever the transport was parked, hop in, start it up, and drive away.

The next morning, when the driver walked out and found his truck missing, he would call the police and report his truck stolen. Later the transport truck would be found somewhere, empty. There were incidents where thieves would drive their own unmarked trailer trucks onto the Port property and hook up quickly to the loaded transport container and haul it away. There were guards at the gates, but somehow they would get through. Those types of theft were usually carried out in the wee hours of the mornings. In the 90s and on into the 2000s, the high-jacking of transports increased greatly, putting the drivers' lives at risk. Some were known to be killed by the thieves for the cargo they carried. In the 60s and 70s, the Port workers were influenced by organized criminals.

While employed at the Port, I didn't wear a security uniform, because part of my job was to mix in with the longshoremen who were responsible for unloading merchandise from the ships. With a steady flow of people always coming and going, the dock workers paid very little attention to who was around them.

After being on that job for approximately six months and learning of certain incidents that had happened to other security officers in the past, I decided that I would leave the job. When I was first hired, I was told that if any of the dock workers learned who I was, the shipping company would have to let me go, because it would be dangerous for me to continue working among them. One night, while on a ship watching the dock workers unload a cargo of expensive Italian boots and shoes, I noticed one of the workers remove a pair of rubber boots from his feet and quickly put on a pair of Italian shoes; then he pulled his rubber boots on over the shoes.

A few minutes later, I saw the same worker come up, and as he left the ship I followed him out into the parking lot to his car. As he was about to remove his boots and place the shoes in his car, I walked over and showed him my ID, telling him that I wanted the shoes he had stolen. As he handed me the shoes, he asked what was going to happen to him. I told him that time, nothing was going to happen, but if he was caught again stealing, he wouldn't get another chance. I would have to take him to the office. It was around 4:00 am. I had three hours left before completing my shift at 7:00 am. I took the shoes to the security office and told the night supervisor that I had taken them from the worker. When I was asked why I didn't bring the worker to the office, I told the supervisor, "When I saw a couple of his co-workers coming off the ship and walking toward us, I just took the shoes and walked away, because there were no other security officers around to help in case I had a problem with him and his co-workers."

At 7:00 am when the security manager came in, I was let go after receiving a lecture from him. He told me that I had no business stopping the worker, and I should have passed on the information to another uniformed security officer, who would have taken care of it. Being that I had blown my cover, he had no other choice than to let me go. That morning as I drove away from the Port, I wasn't upset for being let go, in other words fired, because I had expected it. I was a bit relieved, knowing that I wouldn't have to return.

Working at the water front, I had gained some experience working in another form of security. It was much different than other security work I had been involved with. As mentioned, it was a dangerous place to work. After a while, I didn't feel comfortable working there, especially after hearing stories from other security officers who had run-ins with dockworkers. I was told about one security officer who wanted to make a name for himself by sticking his nose into some dockworkers' affairs, which he shouldn't have. One night, as one dockworker finished his shift and was on his way out to the parking lot, for no apparent reason he was stopped by the security officer and asked what he had in his lunch box. The worker looked at him for a moment and then his fist quickly shot out and struck the security officer in the face. On impact, the officer fell back on his ass, and the worker, with nothing more to be said, got into his car and drove away. A few weeks later, while on the night shift, that officer was nowhere to be found. Other officers walked around looking for him; after searching for a while they found the officer, barely alive, at the rear of one of the storage sheds, pinned up against the wall by a forklift truck. He was rushed to the hospital. The officer would be partly crippled for life from his injuries. It was no accident. The driver of the lift truck, whoever he was, purposely pinned the officer against the wall.

Later, when the police questioned the security officer as to what had occurred, the only information he could provide was that he was walking through the storage shed when he was struck from behind by a man with an object in his hand. He said he only got a glimpse of the man when he was about to turn around after hearing someone rush up behind him. The police said whoever had struck him had then dragged him to another area of the shed. They believed with help from another worker or workers, he held him up while the driver of the lift truck backed up and pinned him to the wall.

The night of the incident, more than a dozen workers were in that section of the shed, but when questioned by police, not one of them had seen anything. It was said that the dockworkers were sending a message to other security officers: back off, or that could happen to you. It was said that on another occasion, a guard who was working at the entrance and exit gate was found lying on the ground, badly beaten. He told the police that he left the guard house to check a transport truck driver who wanted to leave, and as he stepped out he was struck from behind. That morning, a transport truck loaded with over one hundred thousand dollars' worth of merchandise was missing from the dock yard. How true were these stories that the older security officer told? I didn't really know, but they were believable.

We had no protection in those days of working on the water front as security officers for shipping lines; we didn't have two-way radios. The only thing we carried on us were our security IDs. We mostly worked alone, and on many occasions, when we needed assistance other security officers were nowhere to be found. As one officer said, "I'm just putting in my hours and minding my business." Many of the dockworkers unloading merchandise from the ships continuously walked off with concealed stolen merchandise and were never checked by security. It was obvious to security officers that some workers coming off the ships were concealing something under their coats, but they didn't bother to investigate. I would say that most security officers were scared of the dock workers, and the workers were aware of it; so they felt free to do what they wanted. As one dockworker put it, "What was a security officer going to do? If he messed with us, he could end up in the river." The workers were well protected by their union. The same could be said for downtown hotel and restaurant employees who were unionized. And who controlled the unions?

CHAPTER 23
Place Ville-Marie

In October 1970, while employed at with the Place Ville-Marie complex, I was part of a group of six security officers who were given the task of guarding the Canadian National Railway train, which was taken out of service after the FLQ (Front de Libération du Québec) had threatened to bomb the train. It was the fast new CNR Rapido train that carried passengers travelling between Montreal and Toronto. That was a dangerous period, not only in Montreal but all over Quebec. When the news media learned that Prime Minister Trudeau was about to declare the War Measure Act, it came to be known as The October Crisis. A reporter asked the prime minister, "Isn't that a little extreme?" Mr. Trudeau looked him in the eyes and said, "Well, just watch me." Within twenty-four hours, army tanks with soldiers in full battle gear roamed the city streets.

Between 1963 and 1970, the FLQ committed over two hundred violent crimes, including bombings, bank hold-ups, and murders. In 1969, they bombed the home of Mayor Jean Drapeau. Their most drastic actions were in October 1970, when they kidnapped James Cross, the British trade commissioner. Five days later they also kidnapped both the minister of labour and Vice-Premier Pierre LaPorte. Mr. LaPorte was later found murdered, after a FLQ member called a radio station and gave the location where the body could be found. Today, thirty-five years later, I can still picture Prime Minister Trudeau uttering those historic four words to the reporter: "You just watch me."

After the October 1970 crisis and the murder of Pierre LaPorte, the FLQ lost public support due to their criminal actions. In time the ones responsible for the murder of Mr. LaPorte were charged and convicted in court, but they only served a few years in prison for that murder and other crimes. Today, thirty-five years later, certain members of the FLQ are still around, keeping a low profile, waiting for the right time to rise again and fight for their belief in an independent Quebec.

When I was employed with the Place Ville-Marie, sometimes the train was underground on the Place Ville-Marie property, and it was the responsibility of the complex management to have it guarded. When completed in 1962, the Place-Ville-Marie was the largest, most complex office development in the world. It had a forty-two-story office tower; sprawled below ground were multiple levels of shopping, parking, and networks, all linked to buses, subways, and commuter rails, with underground interconnections to much of central Montreal. Shoppers could spend the whole day underground visiting different promenades.

Patrolling that complex as a security officer was at times very tiring. Starting from the bottom floor, by the time I reached the forty-second floor—which could take a few hours—it would be time to start all over again. While patrolling, security officers weren't allowed to use the elevators. It would have been much easier for us if we were allowed to take the elevator up to the forty-second floor and work our way down. It sure would have saved our legs and feet, but it wasn't allowed. We had to start from the bottom floor and work our way up.

CHAPTER 24
Côte-des-Neiges Shopping Mall

Another interesting place where I was employed as a security manager was the Côte-des-Neiges shopping mall. That was a hectic place to work, and stressful. Not only did we have to deal with thieves, we also had to deal with gangs, who would just walk in from the street and roam around the mall, looking for fights and causing problems for shoppers, especially during the cold winter months. Many would just hang around the mall most of the day and night, till closing time.

On some occasions, when the security officers had finished their shift and left the mall, they would be confronted out on the street by some of the gangs, who would threaten the officers with violence. When they were in the mall, an officer would be told that if he called the police to have them removed, they would take care of him, meaning they would beat him up. The thugs didn't operate one-on-one; they were always in gangs, and quite often we would have to deal with more than a dozen of them at a time. They were known to carry knives, brass knuckles, and motorbike chains wrapped around their waists, which they would use whenever in a fight. Prior to being hired as the security manager, I was already aware that the shopping mall was known as a hangout for hoods and trouble makers.

The shopping complex consisted of one hundred and twenty-five stores, a few restaurants, plus a dozen or so business offices, with underground parking for shoppers. Mr. Berube, the manager of the complex, said that he wanted to get rid of the troublemakers who hung around the mall, because he had received many complaints from mall shop owners on account of the hoodlums. When I began working, the security staff consisted of three regular security officers who worked during mall hours, from 8:00 am to 9:00 pm.

One officer worked after the mall closed for the night. His hours were from 11:00 pm till 7:00 am next morning.

For a few days before taking over as security manager, I went into the shopping mall and saw for myself how the security officers were going about dealing with the problems Mr. Berube had mentioned. One of the first things I noticed involved one part-time police officer who also worked at the shopping mall whenever he was needed. Later, I learned from one of the regular security officers that when the police officer worked, which was on Friday nights and Saturdays, he would do very little work besides spending a good deal of his time sitting around in the restaurant, talking with the waitresses and getting free meals, while the regular security officers were patrolling the mall and doing most of the work. I noticed that the policeman wasn't wearing a mall security uniform.

On Monday morning when I reported for work, after meeting with the regular officers, I asked Mr. Berube about the policeman and why he wasn't wearing a security uniform when he was on duty at the mall. Mr. Berube said it was because the policeman preferred wearing his own clothing. When I mentioned that the policeman spent a good deal of his time at the restaurant, Mr. Berube just shrugged if off by saying that when the security officers needed him, they would know where to find him. I didn't like the answers I got regarding the police officer, but for the time being, I didn't say anything more about him. I had the option to wear a uniform or not. I chose not to, because I wanted to mix in with the shoppers to see what was going on with the gangs.

It was in the latter part of October, and the cold spell was coming on; some of the gangs were begging to come in out of the cold and gathered in the mall. The gangs hanging around weren't just teenagers; most were in their twenties. One day, as I was making the rounds and meeting some of the store managers, I came upon one of the gangs gathered below the escalator. As the shoppers came down, they had to make their way around the group. I stood watching them from a distance to see how long they would stay there. After watching for ten minutes, I saw one of the security officers come down the escalator. When he reached the bottom floor where the group was, the officer just stepped around them and continued down the hallway without saying anything to the gang. The officer had seen them but didn't say a word to them.

After my first few days on the job, I felt there had to be a change in the manner in which the security officers performed their duties. It seemed that they were just passing their time and waiting for Friday to pick up their pay cheques. After going over the written reports the officers had filed for the past month, I found the police had been summoned over fifty times to the mall by the security officers. It seemed that any time the security officers encountered a problem, they would call the police instead of taking care of the problem themselves. According to the reports, most of the calls to the police were on account of gangs fighting amongst themselves or because they were bothering some of the shoppers. That Thursday evening, I met with the three regular security officers and explained how we were going to deal with the troublemakers who used the mall as a hangout. The officers were not to let them gather around in groups. When they were seen just standing around, the officers were to approach them and ask them to keep moving. If they refused, the officer was to explain that if they refused to keep moving and continued to gather in groups, they would be asked to leave the mall. More importantly, no security officers were to call the police unless for an emergency.

I could tell by the looks on their faces that they didn't like what they were hearing, especially when I mentioned not phoning the police for help. I told them that as security officers, it was our responsibility to take care of problems within the shopping mall. If they felt that they couldn't do the job, I would get officers who could. I told them that as of that day, the thugs would be no longer allowed to gather in groups and block the passage for shoppers. If they had problems with any of the gangs, I was to be notified.

Security personnel employed at the Place Ville-Marie Complex had to take a course in crowd control. One of the first things we were taught, for the safety of shoppers and office workers, was not to let undesirables such as thugs gather in groups. If they did, they would be ushered out on to the street. At the Côte-des-Neiges Mall, the thugs were in control and not the security officers.

The next day after I explained to the officers what I would expect from them, I made the rounds to see how things were going; it was a Friday afternoon, and the mall was busy with shoppers. The upper section of the mall, which was the main entrance, consisted of a big restaurant called Ben's and a large store, surrounded by a dozen or more smaller shops, and a huge area with benches. As usual, some of the elders were sitting around talking. Quite often shoppers would sit and rest there, and others would sit around chatting. They were harmless and caused no problem. As I took the escalator down to the bottom area, I noticed five or six young fellows whom I had previously seen hanging around the mall standing near the escalator; as I stepped off, I had to walk around them. Ten minutes later I returned, and they were still there. One of the security officers in that area saw me coming, and he walked over and spoke to the group. As he did I stood back and watched; I could hear what was being said. The officer politely asked them to move away from the escalator, as they were interfering with the shoppers as they came off the escalator.

One in the group who looked in his early twenties told the officer that they would move when they were finished talking; the officer said no more and walked over to where I was standing and said, "See, they don't listen. Anytime we talk to them they just tell us to go f*** ourselves." As the officer spoke, I noticed a few of the shop operators in their doorways, watching us. I said to the officer, "Come with me." We walked over the group. I said to them, "Excuse me—you were asked to move away from the escalator. If you want to stay in the mall, you have to move."

The smartass who the officer had previously spoken to said, "Who are you?"

Taking out my ID and showing it to him, I said, "I'm Hudon. I am in charge of security here, and what's your name?" I asked.

"It's none of your f****** business," he smartly answered. The others with him didn't say anything; they just laughed and kept staring at me as of to say, what are you going to do?

As I stood there, I could feel the storekeepers' eyes upon me, waiting to see what I would do. Without further hesitation I said to them, "Come on, all six of you, you're leaving the mall. You were asked twice to move and you refused; so now you're out." With a wave of my hand I pointed toward the exit doors. "Okay, let's go." Seeing that none of them were moving, I took a step toward the smart one who told me that it was none of my "f****** business." He stood back and brought his arms up as if he was ready to fight. I stared directly into his eyes and said to him, "Before you take a swing, I want you to carefully look at my face. I want you to know that the scars you see weren't put there by amateurs."

As he stared at me, I could tell by the look in his eyes that he was having doubts about what he was capable of doing. He dropped his arms by his sides and said to his buddies, "Let's go." As they walked around to take the elevator up, I said, "No," pointing to the lower exit doors. "You're going out that way. Forget about the escalators; they are for shoppers to use." With that said, I walked the six of them to the doors and watched as they left. The smart one hollered out, "We'll be back, you prick." When he had raised his arms I thought he was going to take a swing at me. He was about my size, but as I figured, he was just a loud mouth, and once I stood up to him, he chickened out.

When we walked back, one of the shop operators who had been watching said to us, "That's the way to handle them punks—put them out." At five o'clock that day, I was about to leave when one of the security officers said that they were concerned that the gang would return later. I decided to stay around for a while. At eight o'clock one of the officers came to the office and said that the same gang was back in the mall. They were about a dozen of them. I told the officers to keep an eye on them and if they weren't behaving to come and tell me.

Within a few minutes, he was back, saying that the gang had gathered in front of the Dairy Queen and the woman manager wanted them removed because they were bothering customers. I asked him to go and get the other officer and come back to the office. While he was away I called a friend who had previously worked with me on the waterfront. He was a biker, big and able to handle himself in any situation. Glen was a biker but didn't belong to any gangs; he was a bit like me, a loner. After explaining to him what had taken place earlier and that the gang was back looking for trouble, he said that he would be at the mall within a half hour. I felt better knowing that Glen was coming, because the two officers were in their late forties and didn't seem the type who could handle themselves in a fight.

When they returned to the office, I was told that the smartass whom I had earlier confronted asked if I was around. I told the officers that I was expecting someone, and when he arrived I would go out and talk with the gang. In the meantime, they were to ignore the gang while I waited for Glen. I thought of the options I had in handling the situation with the gang. I could call the police and have them removed from the mall or ignore them. I felt that phoning the police was useless, because they would remove the gang from the mall, but from what I had read in the security reports, the gangs always returned once the police left.

After mulling things over in my mind, I knew what needed to be done. When Glen arrived, I explained how I was going to go about dealing with the gang. Because he wasn't a security officer employed by the mall, I didn't want him to get involved if a fight broke out. He was to stay across the mall with the other officers. If things really got out of control, I would signal him to come over.

As we were about to leave the office, one of the officers returned and said that the gang was getting out of hand, kicking the trash cans placed near the Dairy Queen. I asked the officer if they had asked the gang to move away. He said yes, and they were told to go "f*** themselves." Removing my tie, I asked Glen to go out into the mall with the officers and stand near where the gang was. I would be there shortly. As they walked out, I reminded Glen that he was only to get involved if I needed him.

A few minutes later, I walked out into the mall where the gang had gathered in front of the Dairy Queen; as I approached them, I glanced over to where Glen was standing with the two officers. The gang paid no attention to them. As I approached them, all eyes were upon me. There were twelve of them, and they weren't teenagers. The smartass whom I had previously had words with stood in front of the gang, along with another mean-looking dude with a few scars on his face. He looked in his mid-twenties; he was about my height but much heavier.

I walked up and stood directly in front of the gang and said to the smartass, "You asked for me, here I am. What's your problem?"

The scarred-face one quickly spoke up and said, "You can't put us out of here—it's a public place."

I told him, "The mall is for shoppers and not for troublemakers. Earlier, you were asked by the security officers to move away from that area, but you refused to and continued causing trouble. Now I want you all to leave." I pointed toward the exit doors behind them. I had just gotten the words out of my mouth when the smartass took a swing at me with his fist, saying, "You "f*****—we'll show you." I blocked the punch with my left arm. Within a fraction of a second, my right arm quickly shot out and my fist connected to the side of his face; he crumpled to the floor. As I reached down to get a hold of him, I heard Glen call out, "Fred!" Just then, I saw Scar Face pick up a three-foot metal sign that was near the doorway of the Dairy Queen. He took a swing at me with the sign; I stepped back, and he missed. I laid into him with both fists; first I connected with my left then the right. I dropped him. From the sharp pain I felt in my arm when my right hand made contact with his face, I knew he wasn't about to get up. I reached down and took hold of his coat collar and began dragging him back to the office. As I did, I noticed that the smartass was back up on his feet. He and the rest of the gang took a few steps toward me. I let go of Scar Face and moved toward the gang. With a motion of my hand, I said, "Okay, you guys want to dance, let's go." At that moment, I didn't give a shit if there were two dozen of them. I was angry and pissed off.

It seemed that the gang wasn't about to fight, so I again reached down and took hold of Scar Face's collar. I didn't help him to his feet; I dragged him across the floor toward my office. I sat him in a chair and told one of the officers to call the police. Scar Face sat holding his hands to his face, mumbling that his jaw was broken and he needed to go to the hospital. I told him if necessary, the police could take him there. Seeing that the side of his face was a bit swollen, I felt sorry for him.

While waiting for the police, I got one of the officers to fetch a damp face cloth for him. He asked what was going to happen when the police came. I told him nothing was going to happen; we weren't going to press charges against him, and the police could do whatever they wanted. As he sat there rubbing his face with the cloth, it was easy to see that without his gang, he wasn't so brave; he looked lost. One of the officers I had asked to go out and check on the other members of the gang returned and said that they were still gathered in front of the Dairy Queen. I told the officers to stay with Scar Face.

Glen and I went out to the mall; we walked to where the gang was gathered, and I told them they had to leave. Smartass, with a little blood on his face, was at the rear of the crowd. I pointed to him and said, "Come on out."

He took a few steps toward the exit doors and said, "Where's Mike?"

I told him Mike was in my office and he was okay, adding that the police would deal with him. With that said, the gang slowly moved out the doors and on to the street. I hadn't noticed before, but it seemed that most of the shop operators were out in the mall talking about what had occurred. The manager of the Dairy Queen came out and thanked me. She said, "We've suffered long enough with these bums continuously hanging around causing trouble."

When we returned to the office, the police already had arrived; Scar Face was up on his feet trying to justify his actions to the police. After introducing myself to the four policemen, I explained to them what had taken place. One of the policemen smirked, "It looks like he was the one who got struck with the sign." Another officer asked if I wanted any charge laid. I told him no. As the policemen left with Scar Face, they mentioned he would be driven to the hospital, and they would get in touch with me later.

After the policemen left, the two security officers returned to the mall. I thanked Glen for hollering out when he saw Scar Face reaching for the metal sign.

"Yes," said Glen, "if he had gotten you with that, you would have been the one laid out on the floor." I offered to pay Glen for his assistance, but he refused to take money, saying that I had done all the work. Then Glen and I left the mall; I took him out and treated him to a few drinks. I was still a bit shaken up over the incident and needed to relax. As usual, my form of relaxing was sitting with a drink of rye in front of me. At the time, I seldom drank on weeknights and never drank during work hours, but I sure made up for it on weekends.

Prior to beginning my work at the shopping mall, Jan and I got back together again, after I had made more promises to behave. But each Friday when I finished work, I would head downtown to one of the bars and start drinking rye whiskey. One of my favourite places was the Monterey Restaurant and Bar on Peel Street. The bar was below the restaurant, and a good number of Maritimers would gather there, especially on weekends, to listen to western music and dance. On most occasions, I didn't bother to eat. Sometimes I would think about eating before I began to drink, but usually I would put it off till later. After a few drinks, I would forget about the food till the following morning, when I woke up and realized that I had hardly eaten anything in the previous twenty-four hours. The only thing in my stomach was alcohol. I would then have a solid meal, and later on Saturday evening I would be off again to the bars to repeat the same thing over again. Come the wee hours of Sunday, I would get home and then sleep most of the day so I would be fit to report to work Monday morning. I kept my drinking habits hidden from my employer and the security officers I worked with. The only people aware of my drinking were my wife and sons. I wasn't abusive with her or the children, and at the time she tolerated my weekend drinking, but the day came when she said "Enough is enough." She left again after the incident at the mall with Scar Face.

That Monday morning when I arrived at the mall, Mr. Berube asked what had taken place Friday evening with the gang. He said that earlier he had received a call from the police department saying that the young man they had picked up and taken to the hospital had suffered a fractured jaw. After explaining what had taken place when I had asked the gang to leave the mall and what had occurred that evening regarding the fight, Mr. Berube said, "Was there any other way you could have handled it?"

"No," I said, "not once they took a punch at me. Especially when the one with the metal sign took a swing at me—it was too late for words, sir."

Mr. Tweedie, the marketing manager for the mall, spoke up. "I was in Saturday afternoon and attended a meeting about the store managers' accusations. Some who saw what took place said it was time that someone stood up to these gangs, and they seemed to approve the action that Mr. Hudon took."

Mr. Berube asked, "What about dragging one of them to the office? Couldn't you have picked him up?"

"After what he tried to do with the sign, sir, I wasn't in any mood to pick him up."

"Well, anyway," said Mr. Berube, "we need to be careful because we don't want to get involved with lawsuits."

When everything had been said I left. Within a few minutes Mr. Tweedie came across the hall to the security office. He said, "Mr. Hudon, I want to let you know that I'm totally in agreement with you; if they swing at you, you are in your rights to fight back."

I answered, "It seems that Mr. Berube doesn't approve of my action."

"No," said Mr. Tweedie, "it's not that he doesn't approve of the manner in which you handled the situation; he is concerned, as he mentioned, about lawsuits, if you happen to hurt one of these guys. As a matter of fact, Mr. Berube received a few phone calls this morning from store operators, and

I overheard him say to one of them, 'They are not going to walk over Mr. Hudon—he'll fight back. I told him when he was hired that I wanted a person who was capable of dealing with these gangs.' Before leaving, Mr. Tweedie asked, "Where did you learn how to fight like that? I was told by one of the store managers within seconds after they took a swing at you, you had two of them laid out on the floor."

I grinned and thought for a moment before answering. "I learned at a young age that there was much more pleasure in giving than receiving, especially when it came to fighting."

Mr. Tweedie laughed saying, "Yeah, that could be true."

The week after the incident with the gang, they were seen again in the shopping mall. One evening as I left the mall, I met a few of them, including the smartass they called Louie. They were standing outside next to the entrance; when I noticed them I said "Hi!" and I continued on. Then one of them hollered out, "Sir, are we allowed in the mall?"

I turned around and walked up to them and said, "Yes, you are allowed in, as long as you don't cause any problems and interfere with the shoppers. In other words, you cannot gather around in groups—you must keep moving. If you want to fight among yourselves, you must go outside on the street." Seeing that it was beginning to snow, I added, "And if you don't follow the rules, keep in mind that you will be barred from the mall. Since winter is coming on, you'll find it mighty cold standing outside." While I spoke, Louie didn't say anything, but when I turned to walk away, he said, "Thank you, sir," and they walked in. When I got home, I called the mall security and told them that they were allowed in as along as they weren't causing problems.

During the next three months, seeing that the security officers weren't performing their duties as I asked, especially when it came to the gangs that hung around the mall, I discussed the problem with Mr. Berube. I told him if we were to rid ourselves of the troublemakers, we would need to get another full-time security officer and not bother with the part-timer—the policeman. When I mention not using the police officer, Mr. Berube said that he wanted to keep him because he was a policeman and he was good to have around. That was bullshit, but I didn't say anything except that I would have him come in whenever he was needed.

Within a few days after I spoke with Mr. Berube, he was away for a week; I hired another officer, and within hours after he began patrolling the mall, some of the store operators called the office. Because Mr. Berube was away, they spoke with Mr. Tweedie. He came to the security office and mentioned the phone calls he had received concerning the new security man, because he was black. Mr. Tweedie wasn't aware that I had hired a new officer, especially a black man. I explained to Mr. Tweedie that one of the major problems we had concerning security was that whenever we encountered a problem with some of the black people, the first thing they said to us was that we were prejudiced or racist because of their color. I also mentioned to him that a great numbers of shoppers who came into the mall lived in the Côte-des-Neiges area and were black. Each day, more colored people were moving in. As far as I was concerned it would be helpful to have a black security officer. Mr. Tweedie agreed, saying, "As far as I'm concerned, I have no problem with a black man employed as a security officer; it's just the calls I'm getting."

I said, "Let them talk with Mr. Berube when he returns."

"Is Mr. Berube aware you hired a black man?" he asked.

"No," I answered. "I didn't talk to him about who I would hire, but if it is for the good of the mall, I'm quite sure he'll have no objection."

Mr. Tweedie said, "I agree with you, but when shop owners ask questions, we need to respond; when I received the first phone call, I didn't know what to say, because I didn't know you had hired a black man. Now that you've explained your reasons for having him, I'll go pay a visit to those who called and tell them what you said."

I felt like telling Mr. Tweedie that it was none of their business who we hired, as long as they were able to do their work as security officers; but I kept that to myself and didn't say more to him about it.

When Mr. Berube returned on Monday morning, I was called to his office. Once again, I had to explain my reasons for hiring a black man. At first Mr. Berube didn't seem too enthusiastic, but before I left his office, he said that he believed it was a good idea. Later, I brought Mr. Read, the new man, to the office to meet Mr. Berube. After a few minutes, I got the feeling that Mr. Berube liked Mr. Read. He looked good in his security uniform, and he was a well-spoken man. To me, he didn't seem the type of person who would be easily intimidated by gangs. As I said, the other officers, as far as I was concerned, were useless. Eventually, I would have them replaced and hire Glen, but that would take a little time. Having been there for only a few months, I didn't want to rush and make too many changes regarding security. As days went by, the store operators and shoppers became accustomed to seeing Mr. Read patrolling the mall. At times, even some of the shoppers would make remarks regarding Mr. Read because he was black. I paid no attention to their remarks. He was doing a good job, and to me, that was the important thing.

Thieves continuously walked around the mall, seeing what they could steal, and as usual, some of our office staff would sometimes take items from the office stockroom home with them, especially Mr. Berube. One Saturday afternoon, after stopping by to see how things were going, I happened to walk by the doorway to the underground shipping and receiving area; I noticed Mr. Berube placing a couple of boxes in the trunk of his car. I stepped back a bit so he would not see me through the door window. I watched him return to the stockroom and come out with a box of garbage bags plus a dozen or so bars of soap; after seeing that, I left. The manager of the complex was stealing, and we couldn't do anything about it, because he was the boss. If he, as the manager, was stealing garbage bags, toilet paper, hand towels, and soap; was he also taking more costly items that he had no right to? Probably. As far as I was concerned, Mr. Berube was no different from the thieves walking around the mall. He was a thief, but he got away with it because he was the boss. If I went over his head and reported him to the owners of the shopping mall in Toronto, guess who would loose his job? It would be me.

When spring rolled around, I was glad to see the nice weather coming; we had had a hard winter because of the people who hung around the mall, out of the cold. Now they could spend more time outside. The smartass Louie and some of his friends were often around during the cold spell, but they never caused any problems or overstayed their welcome. Scar Face Mike wasn't seen in the mall all winter.

Shortly after that, Glen began working at the mall and got friendly with Louie. One day Louie mentioned to him that he and Mike were no longer friends because they had gotten into a fight. Louie told Glen that I should watch myself whenever I left the mall at night, because Mike said he was going to get me for fracturing his jaw. When Glen told me that, I told him that I wasn't worried about Mike … at least not till one night when I was on my way home. I stopped at the restaurant across from the mall to have a quick lunch. I was eating, and I happened to look out the window. I noticed Mike and two other fellows staring at me. I ignored them and continued to eat. After a few minutes, one of them tapped on the window next to me and motioned with his hand for me to come outside. He looked much taller and heavier than I was. Again I paid no attention to them, but I knew as soon as I went outside, I would have a problem. There were three of them, and I was alone.

For a moment I thought of phoning Glen, who was at work just across the street, but I decided not to; it was my fight, and I would have to deal with it. I was a bit concerned because I knew that it wasn't going to be a one-on-one situation. After finishing eating, I glanced out and saw they were still out there, waiting for me to leave. I called the waitress over and asked for a double rye with water on the side. When she returned with the rye, I took the glass and drank the shot down. Then I took a sip of water and lit a cigarette. As

I sat waiting for the alcohol to take effect, I noticed the restaurant manager Chris, whom I had previously met when I began at the mall, looking out at Mike and his two friends. Then he looked over at me. I smiled and nodded my head as to say hello. He came over and said, "Are those three fellows waiting for you?"

"I guess so," I answered.

"They are bad news," he replied. "I barred them from here a few weeks ago for fighting. Do you want me to call the police?"

After thinking about it for a moment, I stood up and said, "No, not just yet. Give me a few minutes outside with them, and then you can call the police." Chris agreed. I walked over to the counter and paid my bill.

As I opened the door, Chris said, "Watch the big one, he's dirty."

With a smile I answered, "Don't worry, I will."

As soon as I stepped out the door, the three of them confronted me. The big one who had rapped on the window and motioned for me to come out said, "So you're the tough guy?"

I said as I sized him up, "I didn't say that I was tough. I don't know you, so what is this about being tough?"

"Well," he said, "I heard that you were tough, so let's see how tough you are." He glanced toward Mike and the other fellow.

I said to him, "Just you and me?"

"Yes, just you and me," he answered, bringing up his fist in a fighting stance. He looked in his mid-twenties and was a couple of inches taller than I was, and he out-weighed me by about thirty pounds. Before he took a punch at me, he demonstrated a few hand movements and said, "I am a black belt in karate, so let's see how you'll do with me."

I went to step around him, as if I were going to walk away. "Get lost, you and your karate." Just as I said that; he made a couple of fancy moves with his feet, and then he threw a punch at my forehead. Seeing the blow coming, I moved my head slightly aside, avoiding the full impact of his punch, which only grazed the side of my forehead. Seeing that he wasn't very fast with his hands, I quickly stepped into him and threw a punch with my left, which connected solidly with the bridge of his nose. His legs buckled a bit, and blood began to run from his nostrils. Seeing that he was a bit dazed and not steady on his feet, I threw another punch with my right hand, which got him on the mouth, splitting his lower lip. I stepped back and was about to throw another punch when I saw his hands drop to his sides. By the expression on his face I could tell that the two blows took all the fight out of him. I said to him, "Someone forgot to tell you—if you're a black belt in karate, as you said you were, one of the first thing you should have learned was that if you're going to take a swing at a man, make sure you connect with your first punch, because if you miss, you may not get a second chance." He kept his focus on my hands, maybe thinking that I was going to throw another punch at him. I said, "Maybe you would get away with that, fighting teenagers, but when it comes to fighting a man, it's a different story."

As I spoke, I kept an eye on Mike and his friend—they didn't make a move. They just stood there like two dummies, looking at their friend wiping the blood from his face. Seeing that he had no fight in him, I placed my hands in my pockets and taunted him a bit more, saying, "Here, come on, my hands are in my pocket—take another punch at me, but if you miss, I will split your face open." He didn't move; he just stood there with blood dripping down his chin. I wanted him to take another swing or a kick at me; I wanted to punish him a little more, but I wouldn't if he didn't raise his hands to fight.

As I stepped back, I heard someone who was standing around watching say, "Here come the cops!"

Two police officers jumped out of the cruiser and rushed up to us, asking, "What's going on here?"

I said, "When I came out of the restaurant, that punk took a punch at me, and I defended myself." Pointing to Mike and his friend, I added, "And those two creeps are with him."

One of the officers was the part-time shopping mall officer; his name was Jean. He went over and spoke with the fellow whom I had fought; I would later learn that his name was Jean-Paul. While the other officer asked me what had happened, I thought that seeing Officer Jean at the scene was not good, because when I hadn't called him for work, he stopped by the mall one day and asked me why I wasn't calling him. I told him that we no longer needed a part-time security officer, but when I did need one, I would call him; which I didn't. After that, whenever he came into the mall, he wouldn't say a word to me.

After Officer Jean finished talking with the other three, he came over to me and asked if I had been drinking, I told him yes, I had a drink while I was having lunch, and I added, "Like I said, when I came out of the restaurant, the three of them were waiting for me."

Jean said, "You'll have to come to the station with us."

"Why do I have to go to the station?" I asked.

"You're going to be charged with assault causing bodily harm," said Jean. He took hold of my arm and escorted me to the police car. Again I told him that I was only defending myself after the thug had taken a punch at me. Placing me in the police car, Officer Jean smartly replied, "You can tell it to the judge in the morning,"

"What about the other fellow?" I asked?

"You'll see him in court," said Jean. "He will be testifying against you. He and his two friends said that you punched him for no reason."

"Bullshit!" I answered. "He took the first punch at me."

"Like I said," replied Officer Jean, "you can tell your story to a judge."

At the police station, which was only five blocks away, Officer Jean told the desk sergeant that I was to be charged with fighting and causing bodily harm. The desk sergeant asked Officer Jean, "What do you want him charged with, aggravated assault?"

"Yes," said Officer Jean, "that will do for now, till I make out my report."

Knowing that being charged with aggravated assault was a serious offence, I said to the sergeant that I was the one who was assaulted; I didn't start the fight.

"Who was the other person fighting?" the sergeant asked Officer Jean.

He answered, "Jean-Paul Butler."

"Wasn't he one of the fellows who had caused trouble a few weeks ago at Chris's Restaurant?" said the sergeant.

"Yes," said Officer Jean, "but he wasn't in the restaurant when he was punched by Mr. Hudon; it happened outside."

I said to the sergeant, "I had no reason to punch that man; I don't know him. Matter of fact, Chris warned me about him after he knocked on the window inviting me outside."

The sergeant asked Officer Jean, "Did you talk with Chris regarding what he saw?"

After hesitating for a few moments, Officer Jean answered, "No, because it took place outside of the restaurant."

Seeing that the sergeant wasn't too pleased with Officer Jean's answer, I said, "He also didn't bother to question any of the people who were outside watching the fight."

Looking at Officer Jean, the sergeant said to him, "The inspector is on his way here, and before he arrives, I want you to go back to the restaurant and take a statement from Chris as to what took place. In the meantime, Mr. Hudon will be placed in a cell." As he locked me in, I said to him, "Officer Jean has no reason to charge me; he's just pissed off because since I took over security at the mall, we no longer use him as a part-time security officer."

Hearing that, the Sergeant said, "So you're Mr. Hudon. We heard a lot about you."

"Yeah, and I bet it's all bad," I answered.

"No, not really," said the sergeant, adding, "we'll get to the bottom of this; in the meantime, you relax, and I'll be back later." An hour or so later, the sergeant returned. He opened the cell door and said, "You are free to go; no charges are going to be laid. We got a written statement from Chris saying that you didn't start the fight. He saw the other fellow knocking on the window, and when you went outside he stated that he saw him punch you first."

As I was about to leave, a man dressed in a suit stepped out of the back office, and the sergeant said to him, "Inspector, that is Mr. Hudon."

With a friendly smile, the inspector said, "I hear you are doing a good job down at the mall."

"I am trying to," I answered. The sergeant cut in and said, "It seems that lately the only time we're called there is to take someone to the hospital. At one time, we would be called there three or four times a day."

"We try to take care of the problems ourselves," I replied, "but there are times we need the police, so we call."

"I heard you were from New Brunswick," said the Inspector.

"Yes, I was born there."

"I visit there quite often," said the inspector. "It's a lovely place."

"Yes," I agreed, "especially if you like hunting and fishing."

"Which I do," replied the inspector.

Just then, Officer Jean and his partner walked in and I left. As I walked by Officer Jean, I would have liked to have told him that he was a prick for trying to have me charged with aggravated assault, but I kept my mouth shut and walked out of the station.

As I walked away from the police station, I thought about the other police officer in Toronto, the one who had me falsely charged. He and Officer Jean were two of a kind—pricks. There was one thing I was sure of. If Officer Jean had his way and had me charged, in court, I would have been found guilty, because it would have been my word against the other three fellows, unless I had witnesses to back up my story. If I had been convicted, that would have been the end of ever getting my licence to operate my own security agency, which I was planning on doing in the near future. A person with a criminal record could not be licensed, especially a record of aggravated assault.

CHAPTER 25
Operating my Security Agency

After working at the mall for a year and a half, I applied for and received a licence to operate my own agency. As soon as I did, I left the shopping mall. A few days after I opened my own office, Glen also left the mall and came to work with me. I was fortunate, because when I began my agency, I met with one of the store owners whom I had previously worked for at Canadian Tire and got the contract to supply security for his store. Through him, I also got a few other stores.

I was fortunate also to have Glen with me. He had experience in different aspects of security and was an asset. He had a keen eye for thieves, especially in a crowded store such as Canadian Tire, where shoplifters are continually pocketing items. The more professional thieves try to get out of the store with shopping carts loaded with more expensive merchandise. When I had previously worked at Canadian Tire, my main concern was shoplifters; now it was a bit different. Part of our work also involved checking employees, who would try to leave the store with stolen items. Within a short period of time, I had six other employees besides Glen; at times, I would also use my friend Marc when he was off-duty as a police officer.

I was thirty-four when I began operating my own business, and for the next ten years, besides retail security, I also did investigations for insurance companies and lawyers in Montreal. The insurance company work mainly consisted of investigating fraudulent claims. For lawyers, it could be anything, from following people around to gathering evidence to serving people with subpoenas requiring them to appear in court. That type of work, as well as investigating fraudulent insurance claims, I wasn't too fussy about; but the money was good, and it was good experience.

169

As far as investigating fraudulent insurance claims—that work was tedious, because for about twelve hours a day, you would either be watching the person's residence or following him or her wherever they went. If they went grocery shopping, you would watch to see what they were carrying out to their car, especially if the person claimed that they had very little use of their hands and arms due to some sort of accident at their workplace. In one incident, a man who was off work and drawing compensation forgot about being unable to use his arm.

In his claim the man stated that because of his work accident, he could barely use his right arm; he was unable to lift or pick up anything that weighed more than forty or fifty pounds because of the pain he would suffer. He was a warehouse worker; prior to his accident, his job mainly consisted of loading and unloading delivery trucks; some items were quite heavy. After a month off work, he reported to management that he couldn't return to his regular work due to the continued problem he was having with his arm. In the beginning, it was only his arm that he was having trouble with; later he stated that he was also having trouble with his shoulder. This is when the Compensation Board decided to have him investigated and put under surveillance.

We spent the first few days learning his habits and what types of activities involved the use of his right arm. We knew he was a sportsman, because in his backyard, he had a boat and trailer. We learned that on weekends, he would often take his boat out to a cottage he owned near a lake. He was also a member of a bowling team.

A week went by, and we discovered nothing unusual, until one night, when we followed him to the place where he bowled. About fifteen minutes after he went in, I entered and saw him, along with a few others, getting ready to do some bowling. When he first began throwing the bowling ball down the ally, he used his left hand. After watching him for a half hour or more, I noticed him switch to his right hand. The bowling ball weighs only sixteen pounds, but when people throw a bowling ball, they need to use their hand, arm, and shoulder. As I watched him, he seemed to have no problem. I removed my camera from my pocket and quickly snapped a few pictures of him as he threw the ball down the ally using his right hand. At the time, I didn't think that the pictures were much evidence as to his capability to use his arm and shoulder, but later, when my investigation was completed, those pictures would be helpful.

While observing him in his backyard, I saw him lift the front end of his boat trailer, which was heavy, and hook it up to his truck. Again it showed that he had no problem with using his hand or shoulder. After getting a few pictures I left, knowing that he was getting ready to move his boat somewhere.

Early the following morning, I was back waiting for him to pull out of his driveway with his boat, and when he did I followed him to his cottage. I watched as he backed the boat trailer near the water and unhooked the trailer from his truck. Again I took a few more pictures. The pictures combined with the bowling pictures would show that he had no problem when it came to using his hand or shoulder.

Before beginning the investigation, I was told that the company where he worked had offered to remove him from unloading and loading carrier trucks and give him other less strenuous work. He had refused the offer, saying that he couldn't do it because he was always in pain. The pictures would show otherwise.

After he removed the boat trailer from his truck, I got the pictures I had waited for. After moving his truck away from the trailer, he went into the rear of the truck and proceeded to lift each motor from the truck and placed them on the boat. These were big, heavy motors weighing around ninety pounds each. After he was done placing the motors on the boat, he grabbed hold of the front of the trailer hitch and with brute force moved the trailer sideways about twenty feet, with the boat still on it. He then removed the boat from the trailer, and he struggled to push it into the water.

After the pictures were developed, I phoned the Compensation Board and told them what I had witnessed. A few days later, the man was called to the Compensation Office. When he showed up, I was there with the pictures. After being questioned by the member of the Board who was handling his claim, he continued to insist that he was unable to use his hand and shoulder due to the pain and discomfort. After he repeated that a few times, the pictures I had taken were placed on the desk in front of him, showing that he was very capable of using his hand and shoulder. Besides being cut off from receiving any more compensation, he was sent a notice by the company where he had worked; because of his fraudulent claim of injuries, he was no longer wanted.

Who suffers because of fraudulent claims such as that? Of course when a worker files a legitimate claim of injuries, his family suffers. Often the honest workers have to fight to get compensation to pay their bills and feed their families. Who can we blame? Do we blame the Compensation Board or the insurance companies? I say no; the workers who are filing fraudulent accident claims and are too lazy to work, or the person who gets into an automobile accident and gets a mouthpiece to sue for false injuries—they are to blame. If it wasn't for the fraudulent workers and compensation claims and car accidents that can run into millions and billions of dollars, there would be no need for the Compensation Board and insurance companies to require lengthy investigations. A client would receive money much sooner, which would help to put food on the table to feed their families. The days of the quick payouts by the Compensation Board and insurance companies are gone forever. Who's to blame?

One day I was at one of the Canadian Tire stores assisting Glen, and we were called to go and check two suspicious looking men who were in the music section, where the radios, hi-fi systems, and other electronic items were kept. As we approached, I saw that one of the men was Tommy; the man with him was also a known thief. After watching them from a distance and seeing that they were eyeing the employee who worked in that department, waiting for a chance to slip some items under their coats. Knowing that Tommy was a pro at that type of theft, I decided to go over. Seeing us, Tommy nudged his friend. They both looked at Glen and me. I said, "Hi!" and I picked up an item as if I was interested in it.

"Doing some shopping" Tommy asked?

"No, not really," I answered. After making eye contact with him, I added, "We work here."

"Oh, yeah?" said Tommy. "What are you doing?"

I replied, "We're in security."

Again, "Oh, yeah? You don't have people stealing from here, do you?"

"Yes," I answered, "and mainly in that section. It seems that the thieves in need of drug money find these items easy to get rid of." For a moment, Tommy just stared at me; then his friend spoke up.

"You're not referring to us as thieves, are you?"

"No," I answered, "we don't know who the thieves are, till we see them. Your friend Tommy asked if we had people stealing here, so that was my answer."

After he heard his name, Tommy asked, "Where do I know you from?"

"I have seen you around. I believe the last time I saw you was at Mom's Tavern one night."

"Oh, yeah," said Tommy, "now I remember you; you used to work at Simpson's?"

"Yes, that's me," I replied. I felt like saying, the night I saw you, you were with one of your friend who had spent a few months in jail after getting caught stealing a fur coat; but I decided it would be best left unsaid.

After a few minutes of looking around; Tommy and his buddy left the store. As they walked out, Tommy said, "We'll see you around."

His friend sarcastically echoed, "Yeah, we'll see you around."

I later learned that Tommy's lippy friend had one time stabbed a store security officer in the arm with a screwdriver when the officer stopped him out in the parking lot for shoplifting. I told Glen to remember their faces, because they would be back. Thieves like Tommy don't spend much time in a store; they usually know where the items are that they want to steal. They walk in, and within a few minutes, they are out of the store with the merchandise. They know spending too much time walking around the store looking for items could draw attention to them, so they work fast. That day we were fortunate because there was an employee nearby. They didn't want to take a chance being seen stuffing items under their coats; the next time we might not be as fortunate.

When it comes to shoplifters, an amateur usually draws attention to himself by roaming around the store; a pro is aware of that, so with them it's grab and get out. In one year, over fifty-five thousand dollars' worth of merchandise was stolen from the sports and music department; the worst was the automotive department, with sixty-eight thousand. Between the shoplifters and the corrupt employees, it doesn't take long before amounts run into thousands of dollars.

That location was a large store, with ten cashiers. It was part of a shopping mall, so it was usually busy with shoppers and shoplifters. When I had previously worked there, in one work day, I arrested fourteen shoplifters, seven more than any other officer had previously apprehended.

Working for myself, I concentrated on investigations for lawyers and insurance companies, while Glen and the other officers took care of retail security. Whenever needed, I would go and assist Glen; we had four Canadian Tire stores to take care of, which kept us quite busy. There was never any shortage of thieves, including certain employees.

CHAPTER 26
Wake-up Call

At the age of thirty-six, with two years of operating my own business under my belt, one night after a few drinks at a bar, I was rushed to the hospital with internal bleeding. Sitting at the bar, I felt as if I was going to vomit, so I went into the washroom, but the only thing that came up was blood. Once it began it wouldn't stop. A friend drove me to the hospital. I was examined by a doctor and kept there for two days for more tests. Prior to my release, the doctor asked if I drank much. I answered, "No, not really," which was a lie. He then showed me the X-rays they had taken of my liver and said that my liver was damaged. It resembled a sponge with holes in it. The doctor said that it was caused by excessive drinking, known as cirrhosis of the liver. If I continued drinking, I may not live to see my fortieth birthday. Hearing that was a bit scary. The doctor put me on a strict diet. Among other things, I wasn't to consume any alcohol or coffee, and I was to return in a few months for another check-up.

For a period of two years, I didn't consume any alcohol, but once in a while, I did have a coffee. I wasn't allowed to eat steaks; but as with coffee, every once in a while, I would have a small steak. Within the two years, I had approximately eight check-ups. Then one day after an examination, the doctor said to me, "Mr. Hudon, I have good news for you; your liver has cleared up nicely, and there will be no need for additional regular check-ups." The doctor then added, "If you care to, you may indulge in a bit of alcohol, but you must not overdo it, because if you do, the next time you may not be so fortunate."

In that two-year period, I had no problem refraining from indulging in alcohol, but coffee was a different story. Each morning, the first thing I thought of was stopping at the coffee shop; so that was a hard habit to break.

One might think that, being a drinker, alcohol would be what I had a problem giving up, but no—it was Tim's coffee. It seemed that I was addicted to it.

After leaving the hospital that morning, the first thing I did was stop at the nearest Tim's and have myself an extra large cup. It felt good to have a coffee and not have to worry about the consequences. As for alcohol, I began indulging a bit a month or so after the doctor released me. In the beginning, I would have one or two shots of rye, but as time went on, I figured if I ate some solid food, like a steak, before having some drinks, that would help. In time, I would learn that I was wrong.

Prior to the incident with my liver, I had never been sick and always felt that I was in good health. At 5 foot 11 and weighing 170 pounds, I believed that I was in good shape, and suddenly that occurred. It was scary, especially when the doctor said that if I didn't take care of myself, I might not live to see forty.

CHAPTER 27
Gangs

Tommy and his gang of thieves were a continuous problem. For some reason, it seemed that they preferred shoplifting from the L'Acadie store. I believe it was due to the different exits a person could use; the rear exit from the automobile service area out to the parking lot was a favourite. On one occasion Tommy and his friend kept the security officers busy in one section of the store while two other buddies stole merchandise from another section; that is a diversion often used by experienced thieves. They would do something to attract attention, and while security was keeping an eye on them, other members of the gang would do the stealing. Then they would move on to other stores and pull the same stunt. In the course of a day, thieves could rack up a few thousand dollars in stolen merchandises. Then they'd sell it for booze and drug money—what Tommy referred to as "party money."

Once I learned the tricks he would use to cause a diversion, we sometimes prevented Tommy and his gang from stealing. When he came into the store, one security officer would keep an eye on him while I or Glen would search around the store for his buddies. On one occasion, I was fortunate. As I approached the front entrance, I saw two of Tommy's buddies push a shopping cart among some boxes placed near the exit doors to the mall. When they noticed me coming toward them, they quickly rushed into the mall, leaving the shopping cart hidden between the boxes. Upon retrieving the cart, I found over four hundred dollars' worth of merchandise ready to be stolen. After taking the merchandise over to the front counter, I walked around looking for Tommy. I found him over in the sports department, with the nearby security officer watching him. When he noticed me, he and his friend headed toward the front exit and out into the mall. A few minutes later, we watched as the four of them left the shopping mall empty-handed. I had one thing going for me; whenever dealing with Tommy and his gang, I knew who they were. The unfortunate thing for me was they also knew who I was.

Late one night a month or so after the incident with the shopping cart, I had stopped in at the Parkview Lounge. While having a drink at the bar, I noticed Tommy and a few of his gang walk in. When Tommy saw me at the bar, he and his buddies sat at a table directly behind me. I couldn't pretend that I didn't notice them, because there was a huge mirror on the wall directly in front of me. After Tommy had ordered a round of drinks for his friends, he hollered to me, "Hey, Fred! Come join us and have a drink."

"No, thanks," I answered. "I have one, and I'm waiting for a friend." I wasn't waiting for a friend, but I let them think so. The smart one who had left the store with Tommy a few months earlier who was called Lenny, came up to the bar, and after mumbling something, he walked away and rejoined Tommy and the others at the table. I didn't feel comfortable sitting just a few feet from their table, especially with my back to them. I knew that Tommy and his gang were dangerous, especially when they were on drugs, which was most of the time.

The Parkview Lounge was located in the Park Extension, a section of Montreal where Tommy and his gang usually hung out, and I was aware of that; it was pure stupidity on my part to stop in at the Parkview. As I sat sipping on my drink, through the mirror I noticed Lenny leave the table a few times and go to use the pay phone, which was located near the entrance. Later he received a phone call at the bar; when the barman yelled out that Joe wanted him on the phone, Lenny said to tell him that he would call him back shortly. Lenny then got up and went to use the pay phone once again. I had heard of Joe; he was a drug friend of Tommy who used to do some of his dirty work. When I heard Joe's name mentioned, I sensed I had to get out of there.

I finished my drink, and as I got up to leave, Lenny said with a smirk on his face, "There goes the big security man." I didn't answer; I just smiled and walked away. When I got outside, I expected to be followed by Tommy or his friends, but they didn't come out. I walked around the corner to where I had parked my car. As I walked past a van parked at the curb, two men quickly jumped out of the rear of the van. As I turned to face them, I was struck on the forehead with an object. The next thing I remember was falling to the sidewalk and feeling a sharp pain in my hand. I don't know how long I was lying on the sidewalk; I only remembered being helped up by a man and a woman, whom I later learned had witnessed the two men kicking me as I lay on the ground. One had a baseball bat in his hand. After the couple yelled at them they jumped in the van and sped away. I was bleeding badly from a cut over my eye, and my right hand bled profusely. I also felt a good deal of pain in my rib area. I removed my tie and had the man tighten it above my wrist to help stop the bleeding. A cab driver who had stopped to help then drove me to the nearby hospital. I found out that I had been stabbed in the hand just below the thumb, which sliced into part of my wrist. It took the doctors three hours to operate on my hand. The cut above my eye needed ten stitches to close the wound. I also had some abrasions where I had been kicked in my ribs, but the X-rays showed no fractures.

For the next month or so, I mostly stayed around the house waiting for my wounds to heal. I wasn't too concerned about the cut over my eye, but my hand was a different story. The doctor said that I might not regain full use of my thumb because of damaged nerves. I was concerned about that.

When I returned to the hospital to have the stitches removed, the doctor said that the cut over my eye had healed nicely and there wouldn't be much of a scar. As for my thumb, I could move it a bit. The doctor said that I wasn't to force my thumb to move till it was well healed, because the cut had been deep.

The night I was taken to the hospital, I was questioned by the police about what happened and whether I knew the two men who had attacked me. I told them that everything happened too fast, and I didn't get a good look at their faces. When one of the officers asked if I had any known enemies, I told him that I was sure I had, but I didn't know any of them by name. When the officer asked why I was sure that I had, I told him that I was a private investigator and also worked in retail security apprehending thieves. Hearing that, the officer said, "Yes, I'm sure you do have a few enemies."

Within a few months, I had full use of my thumb; the only reminder of the incident was the three-inch scar that remained. While at home recuperating, I kept thinking of Tommy and his buddies, especially Lenny. I felt that he had something to do with my beating. I believed he had set it up. I realized if I went around asking questions about who may have been involved, I wouldn't get anywhere.

I contacted a person who owed me a favour. I wanted to know who was responsible and felt that the man could help. I was quite sure that it was Tommy and his gang, but I wasn't positive. Bobby, who I turned to for help, had once been stopped for shoplifting at a clothing store within the mall. I had nothing to do with security for that particular store, but at times I would stop by and talk with the manager, as I did at other stores within the mall. That day, as I walked by, I noticed the store manager arguing with a man near the doorway. Seeing me, the manager called out, "Fred, will you come here for a moment?"

"Yes, what's the problem?" I asked

"This man tried to leave the store with a pair of children's jeans concealed under his coat, and I want him to pay for them."

Glancing at the man, whom I had previously seen a few times around the mall, I asked the manager, "Did you call the police?"

"No, not yet," he replied, "but if he doesn't pay for the jeans, I will call them and have him arrested."

"I didn't try to steal the jeans," said the man, who I would get to know as Bobby.

"Well, if you didn't want to steal the jeans, pay for them."

For a moment, he just stared at me with a stupid grin on his face; then he said, "I just realized I forgot my wallet at home."

"That's bull, and you know it," I said to him. "Why did you want these jeans?" I asked.

With that grin of his, he answered, "For my daughter. My wife gave me the money for the jeans, but I had to use it to repair a flat tire I had on the way here."

"So, with no money," I said, "you decided to steal the jeans?"

"Well, sir," he answered, "to be honest, yes, I tried."

I thought for a moment, and then I asked the shop manager, "Where was he when you stopped him with the jeans?"

"He was about to leave the store," said the manager.

"So he wasn't out the door yet?" I asked.

"No," he replied.

"Well," I said, "if you want my advice, just let him go. I don't think calling the cops will help. They will tell you that because he was still inside your store when you stopped him, he didn't commit an act of theft, but they could charge him with intent. You would need to go to court and testify, and that could take up a lot of your time."

Hearing that, the manager said to the man, "You get the hell out of here, and don't come back."

I walked away. As I approached the mall entrance, I looked back and saw the man coming. As I was about to walk out, he said, "Thank you for your help."

I looked at him and said, "Just don't steal again, because the next time you may not be so lucky."

He hesitated for a moment and then said, "I don't know what I'm going to do now. The wife wanted them jeans for the girls to wear to school; they start tomorrow," he added.

"Don't you work?" I asked.

"Not right now," he replied. "I was laid off a month ago."

"I suppose you will go somewhere else and steal jeans," I said.

"No shit! I learned my lesson!" Then he added, "You may not believe me, but I am not a thief."

For some reason, I believed him, and I said, "How much did those jeans cost?"

"I think around eight dollars," he answered. I reached in my pocket and handed him ten dollars. I said to him, "Here. Go back and buy those jeans for your girls. You can pay me back later, when you find work." For a moment, he didn't know what to say; he just stood there with his mouth open.

"You mean you are going to lend me the money?" he said as he reached for the ten dollars.

"Yes," I answered, "but like I said, you'll pay me back later."

"Gee, thanks, sir! I will come and pay you back."

"You know where I work?" I asked him

"Yes," he answered. "Right there at Canadian Tire; you work in security."

"How do you know that," I asked

"I saw you and the other fellow stop someone in the parking lot one day." Bobby looked like the type of person who had had some fights. He had a few scars on his face. He reminded me a bit of Al Capone, the American mobster, and was built a bit like him, short and heavy. Later on, I would get to know more about Bobby; the ten dollars that I loaned him was a good investment.

One of the employees who worked in automotive services at Canadian Tire was known to pocket a few tools now and then, but we couldn't catch him at it. We learned from another employee that he would sell the tools he stole to friends at a tavern. Late one Friday night, after the store had closed, Glen and I were parked at the rear of the store, talking, when we noticed the employee walk out. Glen noticed that he seemed to have something under his coat and asked me if he should check him. I said "No, let's follow him and see if he stops at the tavern." We followed him. He didn't stop at the tavern; he continued on. I told Glen to pull into the tavern parking area, and we'd go in for a beer. I hadn't been there before, but I knew it was the same place that the employees went to. I wanted to see what type of place it was. It was a Friday night, and the tavern was very busy. After finding a table and ordering a drink, I heard a familiar voice holler, "Hey, Mr. Hudon! Come over and join us." I turned around, and there was Bobby with four or five other men.

I said, "Thanks, but we're only having a fast beer and then leaving." Bobby got up and walked over to where we sat.

"Funny seeing you here," he said. "We were just driving by, so we thought we'd stop in for a minute. Why don't you come over and meet my friends?" said Bobby.

I repeated, "We're just here for a few minutes."

"Okay," he said with that twisted grin of his. "We'll see you later." I wanted to talk with Bobby regarding the beating I had received, but since he was with friends, I would call him at home later.

Bobby wasn't back at his table for more than a few seconds when Glen said, "One of his friends is coming over, and he's big."

Picking up my glass, I said to Glen, "Let's finish our drinks and get the hell out of here."

Before we had time to stand up, the man reached our table and struck out his hand. He said, "Hey, you guys, Bobby tells us you're from New Brunswick. I am also from there."

"Yes," I answered, shaking his hand. He seemed friendly, so we talked a bit, and suddenly Bobby and the others came over with their drinks and sat. Glen looked at me as if to say *What now?* I didn't feel comfortable, but I didn't just want to get up and leave, so I said to Glen, "Okay, we'll have another beer." The words weren't out of my mouth when Bobby hollered over to the waiter, "Bring us a round of drinks." When the waiter came over and placed the drinks on the table, I reached for my wallet and offered to pay. "No," said Bobby, "we're paying."

As we drank, I noticed that Bobby seemed to be very popular among the other men at the bar; each time one would pass our table, he would stop and say hi to him. I had noticed some people in the club shopping at the store. As we spoke, I learned that most of the people there were employed at the nearby Canadair plant. They all seemed like a nice bunch of fellows, as did some of the women with them. It was a Friday night and they were out to enjoy themselves. One extra beer led to a few others; Glen was enjoying himself talking with the men, especially when he learned that most of them were bikers, including Bobby. I mostly listened while they exchanged biking stories. I was enjoying myself, till one of them asked Glen what he did for a living. Glen answered, "I'm in security." The one who asked then looked over at me and said, "Now I know where I've seen you. You are a dick at Canadian Tire."

"Yes," I answered. "That's one of the places where we work." He continued asking about our work, and I said to him, "We don't usually talk about our job when we're out relaxing and having a drink." The fellow wasn't being sassy; he was only asking questions because he was curious. Still, it made me feel uncomfortable talking about our work in a bar. He didn't take the hint when I told him that we didn't usually talk about our work, so I said to Glen, "I need to leave. I have other things to do."

"Okay," said Glen, "I'll finish my beer and we'll go."

Bobby quickly spoke up and said, "Have another before you go."

"No thanks," I said to him. "Like I said, I have to leave."

When Glen had finished his drink, we stood up. I told Bobby I would give him a call at home, because I wanted to talk to him. We were on our way out, when the big fellow who had first came over to our table walked over to us and said, "By the way, Fred, that was nice what you did for Bobby when he had a problem at the mall. He told us about it. We all like Bobby, so we appreciate what you did."

"That's okay," I answered.

Reaching out to shake my hand, he said, "Well, if ever you need us, we'll be there for you," With a smile, I said I'd keep that in mind. It wasn't hard to tell that he was from the Maritimes, because usually when he spoke, he added "eh?" to whatever he said. Canadians had a habit of doing that, but especially people from the Maritimes. When you met one, he'd say, "Boy, it's a nice day, eh?" It was like a question that needed to be answered.

The following day, which was Saturday, I called Bobby and asked him if he knew any of the guys who hung out in Park Extension. "Oh, yes, many of them," he answered. When I mentioned Tommy and Lenny's names, Bobby said, "Oh shit, don't tell me you're having problems with them two."

"You know them?" I said.

"Yes," he answered, "very well; I had a run-in with them a few times."

"Are they friends of yours?" I asked.

"No way," said Bobby. "They are bad news. They'll knife you quicker than looking at you." Hearing that, I asked him if we could meet. I wanted to discuss something with him; he said that I could come over to his home, because his wife was out shopping so we could talk.

When I got there and explained what had happened to me, Bobby said, "So it was you who got beaten up?" He went on to say that he had heard about someone getting knifed at the Extension by a couple of Tommy's friends. When I asked him if he knew the two persons who used the bat and knife on me, he said no. "But it won't take me long to find out. As a matter of fact," he added, "I'll be going over to that area tonight, and I will see what I can find out."

I mentioned that prior to me leaving the club that night, Lenny, who had made some smart remarks to me, had made a few phone calls and received a call from a guy named Joe; as Lenny spoke with him on the phone; Lenny kept glancing over toward where I was sitting at the bar. Bobby said that he knew Joe and that he was part of Tommy's gang.

Before I left Bobby's home, he showed me a double-barrel .12-gauge shotgun that he had modified by cutting off the barrel and part of the stock, so it could be easily concealed under a coat. Such a gun as that modified .12-gauge was illegal to own. At the time, I didn't ask Bobby why he would want such a gun; later I would learn why.

A few days after meeting with Bobby, I received a call from him; he said that he had found out from one of the gang that Joe and one of his buddies had put a hammering to me and that Lenny had it set up. The cut to my hand was caused by a knife, which Joe was known to carry. After I thanked Bobby for the information, he asked if I wanted him to take care of the problem. I told him no; when the time came I would handle it myself.

I got a bit more information about Joe, and I told Bobby I would get in touch with him later. I asked him to keep it between him and me. I was told that Joe wasn't a regular member of Tommy's gang, but Lenny often used him when he wanted some dirty work done; Joe was paid with drugs. Bobby mentioned that Tommy didn't like him around, because he was a boisterous and loud person, especially when he was on booze and drugs.

For the next few months, I stayed away from the Park Extension area. I wanted things to quiet down before I made a move to settle things with Joe and let Tommy and his gang think that as far as I was concerned, the matter was forgotten. Soon enough, they would learn that I was not the type of person who would easily forget that type of beating. If I had been beaten in fair fight, it would have been a different story. I would forget about it after a fair fight, where it was either take a beating or give one; but when it came to someone using a bat and a knife on me, that was a different matter.

CHAPTER 28
A Hometown Visit

Some years earlier, while visiting my hometown for a week, I experienced a similar incident two days before I was to return to Montreal. It was a Thursday, and I was to leave on Saturday. Just up the street from the hotel was a club called the Air Force Wing. That Thursday evening, I left the hotel and walked up to the club. My intention was to have a few drinks and then return to the hotel and rest up a bit. On the previous few days I visited family members and friends, and I had done quite a bit of partying and got little sleep.

Arriving at the club, I met a few people I hadn't seen in years. As mentioned, my intention was to have a few drinks and return to the hotel; but a few drinks led to others, and I stayed at the club till closing time. I don't recall leaving the club or how I got back to the hotel. When I woke up the following morning, I could barely move my body because of the pain in my ribs. I got out of bed and saw the bruises on my body, and I quickly realized that someone had put the boots to me. For a while, I sat there trying to remember what had taken place. I could only recall sitting with a bunch of people at the club exchanging stories and having a good laugh. What occurred after that was a total blank till I awoke the next morning at the hotel. There were no bruises on my face; it was all in the stomach area. I knew I had damaged ribs and I needed to go to the hospital, but first I needed to put some food in my stomach.

After cleaning up, I went down to the hotel lobby and sat reading the newspaper; I wanted to see if anyone would make a remark about what had happened. I found it very embarrassing to sit there, not knowing how I got back to the hotel or what had taken place. The desk clerk greeted me with a smile as he usually did and asked, "How are you this morning?" Others in the lobby didn't mention anything, and I was too embarrassed to ask questions. In the restaurant, it was the same; no one was talking. It seemed that no one had heard anything. I was quite sure that if any of them were aware of what had happened, they would have made some remarks about it. After eating I drove to the hospital and found out that I had three fractured ribs. After the doctor taped up my rib area, I returned to the hotel, knowing I would be leaving the next day. I tried to rest up a bit and mostly stayed in my room for the remainder of the day. At times I went down to the lobby to see if anyone would make a remark, but again, no one said a word or asked any questions. I was baffled about what had taken place; no matter how hard I tried, I still couldn't remember anything,

The following day, around noon, as I was checking out of the hotel, the desk clerk mentioned that a man had stopped by and asked if I was still registered. The clerk told him yes, but that I was out; he left saying that he would be back. As I was placing my luggage in the car, a man walked up to me. I remembered seeing him at the club the night of the incident. He said, "Freddie, I'm sorry about Keith putting the boots to you the other night. When I went out and saw him kicking you when you were lying on the ground, I stopped him."

As soon as he mentioned the name Keith, I recalled seeing him at the club earlier that night, when one of the fellows with whom I was seated mentioned my brother's name, Wild Bill. Keith, who was seated a few tables from us, made a comment regarding my brother. I recall looking over at him and saying, "You should tell that to him."

One of the men at our table said, "Don't pay any attention to him. He's just a troublemaker."

When I asked the man why Keith attacked me, he said that he didn't really know, other than Keith had mentioned earlier something about Wild Bill and his brother having a fight; his brother ended up getting the worst of it. I thanked him and asked if he knew where I could find Keith. He said that he usually hung out over on Main Street near the five-and-ten-cent store. Before he left, he warned me to be careful because Keith was a mean person. I returned to my room.

Now that I knew who had put the boots to me, I sat there for a while, thinking about what I was going to do about it. I knew before I left town that I needed to confront Keith. With my damaged ribs, I didn't really know what I was going to do about it; but I knew I had to do something. After sitting around for an hour or more, I decided what to do.

I went down to the lobby and checked out. I got into my car and drove away, and I noticed a police car behind me. Thinking nothing of it, I drove over to Main Street. When I saw Keith standing with a few other fellows near the five-and-ten-cent store, I pulled over to the curb and got out. Just as I did, the police car pulled in behind me. I was walking up to confront Keith when I heard someone holler out, "Don't do it, Freddie. If you do, I'll have to take you in."

I turned and saw Police Chief O'Neil walking toward me. I continued walking up to Keith and then stood directly in front of him. I said to him, "You prick, you put the boots to me the other night, and there was no need of it, because the condition I was in, you could have easily beaten me with your hands." By now the chief was standing near us. Keith didn't say a word; he just stood there with a smirk on his face. I turned and said to the chief, "This prick put the boots to me, and there was no need of it."

"Well," said the chief, "you can come to the police station and lay a charge against him."

I turned to Keith and said, "I am not going to bother laying any charge against you, but I will tell you one thing—take a good look at me, Keith, because one day I will be back looking for you."

As I walked back with the chief to my car, he said, "Freddie, are you leaving town?"

"Yes," I answered, "but like I said, one day, I will be back."

With a grin, the chief said, "I know you will. In the meantime, have a safe trip back."

That afternoon I left and drove back to Montreal. Over the next two years, I often thought of Keith and what he had done. Finally, one Friday night, I decided to return to Bathurst as I said I would. Before leaving Montreal, I made a phone call to a so-called friend of Keith's I knew, and I offered him a bit of money to have Keith at the Union Hall around noon the next day. He assured me that he would.

I got a few hours' sleep, and at 3:00 am Saturday morning I was on my way to New Brunswick. It would take me around eight hours to get to Bathurst. As I drove, I thought about how I was going to go about dealing with Keith. I knew that because it was Saturday, the Union Hall would be packed with union men. That was precisely what I wanted when I confronted Keith—a lot of people around. I wanted them to see just the kind of man he was.

Since that incident, I had learned a lot about him. He was well-known around town as a bully who would wait till a man had a bit too much to drink, as with me. Then like a snake, he would viciously attack. Once he got the person down, he would use his feet on them. He was also known to bully and beat up teenage boys, as well as his own wife. The more I learned about him, the more I detested him, not only for what he did to me, but also for the beating he put on others.

I arrived near Bathurst just around noon. Before I drove into town, I stopped along the highway and thought about how I was going to approach

Keith in front of all those union men. I knew that whatever happened, I would have to quickly leave town before the police arrived.

Arriving outside Union Hall, I parked near the entrance and went in. I walked down a dozen or more steps, and when I reached the bottom I stopped and looked around for Keith. Standing there, it seemed that all eyes were upon me. Seeing Keith seated with a few other men, I walked over to his table and said, "Hi, Keith, can I see you for a moment?"

I could tell by the look on his face that he was surprised to see me. He slowly got up and followed me outside. When I got out the door, I turned and faced him and said, "Keith, remember two years ago? I told you that I would come back." With that said my left hand quickly shot out and got him on the jaw, and he dropped to the ground. I stepped back and told him, "Get up, you prick, and try to use your feet on me now." I waited till he slowly picked himself up from the ground and got to his feet. Thinking that he was going to fight, I was ready to step into him, but to my surprise, instead of coming at me he turned around and rushed downstairs. As he did, I gave him a kick in the ass, and he fell to the bottom of the steps. As he got up, I said in a loud voice, so all could hear: "This prick, when I was here two years ago, put the boots to me when I had too many drinks and couldn't defend myself. I told him then that one day I would return." As I spoke, I took my eyes off Keith, who was standing to the side of me rubbing blood from his mouth. Seeing his opportunity to strike out at me, he threw a punch at my face, but I was ready for him. I avoided the blow and threw a punch at him, which got him in the face and knocked him back against a table. Everyone in the club was now on their feet watching Keith and I.

Suddenly someone grabbed a hold of me from behind. Thinking it was one of Keith's friends, I quickly grabbed hold of the man's arm and threw him over my shoulder. I looked at him as he hit the floor; to my surprise, it was my brother Wild Bill. For a fraction of a second, I just stared down at him. Then I heard someone say, "Freddie, the barman called the police, get out." When I heard the word *police*, I headed for the stairway and quickly got into my car and drove away. Knowing that they would be driving around looking for me, I headed back out of town. As I drove I kept watching in my rearview mirror for a police car.

I drove a good ways out of town before I stopped at a pay phone and called the police station. The chief answered; I said to him, "Sir, it's Freddie Hudon."

"Where are you?" the chief asked.

"First, sir," I said, "I just asked Keith to go outside to talk, and he took a swing at me. I defended myself, and the men at the hall can tell you he also took a punch at me down in the club. Again, I only defended myself."

"What about your brother?" he asked

"I didn't punch him. When he grabbed a hold of me from the back, I flipped him over my shoulder, and it was only then that I realized it was my brother."

Again the chief asked, "Where are you now?"

"I am on my way back to Montreal."

Hesitating for a few moments, the chief said, "Well, Freddie, we'll investigate that, and if there's any charges to be laid you'll need to return."

"That's okay with me, sir. If necessary I'll return. You know yourself, sir, that Keith has been going around for years putting the boots to people and getting away with it."

After a bit of hesitation, the chief said, "Freddie, the next time you come to Bathurst, I want you to give me a call before you get here."

After I spoke with the chief, I continued on my way. I felt good about taking care of Keith. Two years was a long wait. As for my brother, Wild Bill, I was baffled as to why he grabbed me from behind; that was the only part I felt sorry about. Later, I would learn that he grabbed hold of me because after I punched Keith in the club, he thought that I was going to continue punching him. To prevent that, he decided to grab hold of me. My answer to that was, "Why didn't you just talk to me instead of grabbing me from the back?" I knew that Bill had a lot of pride; me flipping him in front of all his union friends might affect his feelings toward me. In later years when we met again, I would learn that I was right.

CHAPTER 29
Montreal Mobsters

As for Joe and Lenny—I waited a few more months. For a couple of nights, I drove around the bar zones in the Extension, looking mainly for Joe. I didn't go into any of the clubs. At closing time, I would drive up and down the streets to see if I could spot Joe. After a few nights without success, I gave Bobby a call and went over to see him. I mentioned what I had been doing for the past few nights, and Bobby said "Shit, Freddie, you should have called me. I know the bars he hangs out at."

"Okay," I said, "I'll tell you what I want you to do. When you're out and you see Joe at a club, I want you to give me a call." He said that he would.

A week went by, and I didn't hear from Bobby. Then he called one Sunday night around 11:00 pm and told me that Joe was at the Parkview; neither Tommy nor Lenny were around. Then I went into one of my sons' bedrooms and picked up a device which he used in martial arts, a metal chain with a five-inch piece of steel pipe attached at each end. I had watched my son use it when he was practicing martial arts. I stuck the device in my pocket, picked up a roll of dimes that was lying on the table, and went looking for Joe. When I got to the Parkview, I parked across the street and watched as customers left. Bobby mentioned that Joe was wearing a hat and a light-color jacket. It was around 11:30, and the bar closed at 1:00 am.

Because it was Sunday night, not many people were walking the street. It was a good time to get Joe. Bobby said that Joe lived nearby, so he believed he would be walking. An hour went by—no Joe. Then shortly before one, I spotted him coming out of the club. I watched as he staggered up the street and disappeared along one of the side streets. I drove around the block and parked at the end of the street, facing him. I pulled the hat I was wearing down slightly and held the roll of dimes firmly in my right hand. When I

189

was a few feet from him, I said, "Joe!" and pointed behind him. "Someone is calling you." As he turned his head to look back, I took a swing at him, holding the roll of coins in my hand, and connected with the side of his face. Instantly he dropped to the sidewalk. I knew he wouldn't be getting up soon. I stuffed the roll of coins in my pocket and pulled out the steel pipes. Holding one in my hand, I pulled him up a bit by his hair and gave him six or seven solid blows to the rib area. The pipe extended from my hand about a quarter of an inch, and each time it made contact with his ribs, I could feel the pipe dig in. Putting the device back in my pocket, I again held the roll of coins in my right hand and punched him a few times over each eye, till I split his eyebrows open. Then I landed the final two blows to the bridge of his nose. I quickly rushed to my car and drove toward home, leaving him moaning and groaning on the sidewalk.

I don't believe he had time to recognize me with the hat pulled down over my eyes. I don't usually wear a hat, and the street was dark and he was drunk. I felt there was a slim chance he knew who attacked him. I would just have to wait and see. I could have walked away after I worked his ribs over with the pipe, but I wanted to mess up his face, and there's no better way of doing it than busting a man's eyebrows open and slamming his nose. With the bridge of his nose busted, his face would swell up in no time, and he'd have two black eyes. One thing I was sure of—he would remember that beating for a while. Each time he looked at himself in the mirror, he would see the busted eyebrows to remind him.

Early the next morning, which was a Monday, I called Glen and told him that I would be out of town for a few days; I would meet with him when I returned. As I drove out of town that morning, I thought about Joe and what I had done to him. I didn't feel too good about myself; I had never before used an object or even my feet on a man as I had with Joe. It wasn't a good feeling, but as I said before, with Joe it was a different matter.

After completing my work in Ottawa, on Wednesday evening I returned and gave Glen a call. He said that Bobby had stopped by the store asking for me. When he learned that I was out of town, he asked Glen to tell me to give him a call when I returned. I was anxious to hear what Bobby had to say, so I called him and was told that Joe had been seen lying on the sidewalk by a passer-by, who called the police. He was taken to the hospital. Joe was kept there for two days because of broken ribs and the surgery needed to repair the bridge of his nose. Bobby went on to say that Joe reported to the police that he had been attacked by two men. I said to Bobby, "Do you think that anyone around the Extension thinks that it was me?"

"Hell, no," said Bobby. "Joe believes that it was members of a gang he had previously fought. He was told that one night they'd come looking for him. Anyway," said Bobby, "last night at the bar, Joe's friend, who picked him up at the hospital and drove him home, said that his face was a hell of a mess, and he could barely move because of his broken ribs." I asked Bobby if he had mentioned to any of his friends that it was me who worked Joe over. He assured me that he hadn't and he wouldn't.

Months went by. I hadn't seen Tommy and Lenny around the mall or any of the stores we took care of. Then one Friday afternoon, as I walked by the grocery store in the mall, I noticed one of Tommy's gang inside the store. Another stood near the doorway, eyeing people as they shopped. I knew what they were up to. I returned to Canadian Tire and called the grocery store and told the store manager that I believed they were in there to steal steaks. After I described them to the manager, he thanked me and said he would check them out.

Tommy and his gang were known to go into different grocery stores, especially on Fridays, and steal a bunch of steaks for barbecuing over the weekends. Tommy and his gang were high-livers but did very little spending; anything they needed, they stole. Some, like Lenny, walked around dressed to kill, wearing nothing but the best, all stolen. They'd rip off store after store; what they didn't need they would sell. In the run of a day, they might steal thousands of dollars' worth of merchandise.

Shortly after I called the store manager, I noticed two police officers enter the mall and head toward the grocery store. I went in the mall and watched from a distance to see what was happening. The grocery manager and another man had Tommy's two buddies pinned up against the wall just outside of the doorway to the store; sprawled on the floor next to their feet were about two dozen steaks. The police officer handcuffed them and walked them toward the exit. As the manager and the other man picked up the steaks; I walked over to the manager and said, "Well, you got them."

"Yes, we did," said the manager, "and lucky for me, this police officer was doing some shopping in the mall. We watched as they left the store with the steaks, and then they stopped them."

Because he mentioned that the man with him was a police officer, I said to him, "I bet if you went out to search their car, you might find a lot more stolen merchandise." The officer dropped the steaks he had in his hands and headed out to the parking lot.

The policemen were just about to drive away when the officer rushed up to the car. A few minutes later, the two officers got out, leaving the two thieves locked in the rear. I watched the three officers walk around, checking various parked cars. Because it was a Friday; the parking lot was full of cars.

After ten or fifteen minutes of walking around, looking into cars and seeing nothing, they returned to their police cruiser. The off-duty officer walked back toward the store. Then I noticed an empty car parked next to the grocery pick-up service. I walked over and looked in the back; sure enough, on the floor among other merchandise were several steaks. I called out to the off-duty officer, "Their car is here." He motioned to the officers who were in the police car, and they moved their cruiser to where we were and got out. They looked into the car and checked to see if the doors were unlocked. They weren't, so one of the officers went back to the police car and spoke with the two fellows. Within a few minutes, the officer returned with the car keys and opened the car doors. Not only was the rear loaded with stolen merchandise, including steaks, but the trunk was also full of merchandise. As I walked by the police car on my way back into the mall, I heard one of the thieves holler, "You prick, you!" I just looked at them and smiled and continued on.

The following week, I heard that the police recovered over eighteen hundred dollars' worth of stolen merchandise from the car, including over three hundred dollars' worth of steaks from the mall grocery store and another four hundred dollars' worth of steaks from other grocery stores in the area. Come Monday morning, those two would stand in front of a judge to face theft charges. After a lecture from the judge regarding theft, they would be out on the street doing the same thing again.

A week or so after the incident at the grocery store, Bobby told me that Tommy and Lenny had heard about my involvement in having his guys arrested and that they were really pissed off. Bobby warned me to be careful.

One night as I was driving home, I noticed a car with two men in it following me. I didn't go directly to my residence; instead I drove a few streets away and stopped at a corner store. When I got out, I saw the car that was following me stop and park up the street. I returned from the store and got into my car, and as I pulled away from the curb, they continued to follow. I drove around, thinking about what I was going to do, because I didn't want to drive to my home; I didn't want them to know where I lived. When I came upon a police car that was stopped along the street, I got an idea and pulled in behind the police car. I got out and walked up to the officer seated at the wheel and asked him directions to a certain street. As the officer explained where the street was, I pointed back toward the car that had been following me, letting them think that I was telling the police about them following me around. The car started up and drove past as I stood there talking with the police officer. I got a look at the driver. It was Tommy, with Lenny sitting in the passenger side. After they were out of sight, I thanked the officer and got back in my car and drove away, making sure that I wasn't still being followed.

I didn't know what Tommy and Lenny were up to. At the time, Jan and the boys were still living with me, and I didn't want to put them in danger. There was no telling what Tommy and Lenny were capable of, especially when they were under the influence of drugs. Jan was unaware of the ongoing problems I was having with Tommy and his gang, especially Lenny, when Joe and his buddy had worked me over and put me in the hospital. I told her that I had been beaten when I went to the aid of a friend. Jan knew very little about my work, other than I was an investigator involved in private security. As far as the likes of Tommy and Lenny, I was sure of one thing—if they ever went near Jan and the boys, I would think nothing of having them taken care of.

There were other professional gangs like Tommy's we had to deal with, but none as dangerous. About a month after I was followed by Tommy and Lenny, early one morning, as I was about to get in my car and drive to work, I heard someone call my name from across the street. Tommy and Lenny were parked. Without showing any fear I walked over to their car and said, "Yes? What do you want?"

I stood on the passenger side where Lenny sat, and Tommy said, "Freddie, we are only here to talk with you."

"What about?" I asked

"Well, Freddie, as you know, you and your fellows have been giving us a hard time for a few years, and it's now getting to the point where we need to do something about it."

Before he could say more, I said, "What do you intend to do?" I felt fearful, but I didn't want them to see it.

"Here's the deal," said Tommy. "You have your guys lay off when we go shopping, and you will be well rewarded."

Leaning over a bit so I could look at him directly in the eyes, I said, "Tommy, if we don't do our job, they will hire someone else to do it. So my answer is no. If you and your gang come in and you are caught, you will be treated just like anyone else."

After saying that, I happened to look down, and that's when I noticed Lenny had a gun in his lap. Looking over toward the apartment building where I lived, Lenny said, "So that's where you live with your wife and boys?"

I believe if I had a gun, I would have shot them both right there. Staring down at Lenny, I said to him, "You better be careful, Lenny. Some kids may take that gun away from you and shoot you in the ass." As he glared at me, I could see the hate he felt for me, and the feeling was mutual. I watched as they drove down the street. I then returned to my car and sat there, nervous, for about fifteen or twenty minutes, thinking about what I was going to do.

When I first noticed the gun, I didn't think that Lenny would shoot me, because there were too many people out on the street leaving for work. After I called Lenny a little prick, I thought for a moment he might shoot me. I was about to reach in and try and grab his gun, when Tommy spoke up and said, "We'll talk again." As I sat there trying to compose myself, I thought, *Now the bastards know where I live. What will they be up to next?*

A few days after the encounter with Tommy and Lenny, my youngest son, Bill, came home and told Jan that he believed he was shot at as he drove through the park after school. When I got home, he showed me where something had hit his bike. I looked at the bike; I could tell by the mark on the rear fork that he really had been shot at. I could plainly see where the bullet had struck and bounced off. My son said as he drove through the park, he heard a pop, and then something hit his bike. When he got off to check, he saw a car pull away. I told Jan that it was no use calling the police; it was someone just trying to be smart. But I knew the difference. Tommy and Lenny had something to do with it; I felt that they weren't aiming to hit my son, though he could have been seriously hurt or killed if the bullet had bounced up and struck him. I believed that they wanted to put a little fear in me and prove that they weren't fooling.

After that incident, I quickly realized that something needed to be done about Tommy and Lenny. I wasn't concerned about the rest of his gang. I owned two handguns, a .38 Special and a .25-calibre automatic with a shoulder holster, which was easier to conceal. I had no permit to carry a gun, but I felt that if those hoodlums could go around carrying guns and threatening people, I would also carry one. I knew that if I were ever caught packing a gun, that would be the end of my security and private investigator's business; at the time, I didn't really care. The only time I didn't carry the gun on me was when I stopped by a club for a few drinks. Then I would leave it under the front seat of my car. Otherwise, I always had it on me.

The only person besides Jan and the boys who knew that I had guns was Marc the policeman, who, as I said before, at one time worked part-time for me. But one night over a few drinks he had told me that he was involved with certain people, and I never hired him again. That night I had found out that Marc had his own personal problems that also involved a gang; but a much more dangerous gang than Tommy's—the Montreal Mafia. When Marc had first mentioned that to me, because he was a policeman, I thought he was joking, just to see my reaction. As he continued, I realized he was serious.

He said that one night he was in a bar that he frequently went to where he knew the manager quite well, He believed at the time that the manager was also the owner. That night as they sat together, Marc mentioned that he was having financial problems, and the manager offered to help by lending him some money. Marc could work it off a few nights a week as a spare doorman for the club. Marc said he was given five hundred dollars. As agreed, he would go to the club and work on the nights he was off-duty, especially on weekends. As time went on, he kept borrowing more money from the manager.

Then, for some reason, he didn't show up at the club for a couple of weeks. One night, he received a phone call from the manager, who said that he needed to talk with Marc. That night he went to the club and was asked into the office. To his surprise there sat two other men. One he recognized as Frank Cotroni, the Montreal Mafia boss, who quickly spoke up and said to Marc, "I see that you are into us for a good deal of money."

Marc said, "What do you mean, *us?*"

"Well, I own this place," said Frank, "so the money you owe the club belongs to me." Marc didn't know what to say, and for a few moments he just stood there looking at the manager.

Finally the manager spoke up and said to Marc, "Yes, Mr. Cotroni is the owner, and you need to deal with him regarding the money you owe." Marc was then told to sit down, and Mr. Cotroni told him what he expected from him. Frank didn't ask Marc if he would do what he was asked or repay the money; he *told* him what he wanted him to do. Marc said it began with Marc using the police data base to get information regarding certain people Mr. Cotroni wanted to locate. Whenever he was given a licence plate number or the name and birth date of a certain individual, he would get the information and pass it on to them. Each time he did it, a bit of the money he was loaned would be deducted from what he owed.

Marc said that he had been set up by the club manager; that was why he kept offering to loan him more money, till it got to the point where he was unable to pay it back, and that's when Frank stepped in.

CHAPTER 30
Underworld Activities

Later, I would learn how the Mafia recruited other policemen to work in their crime organization. They would gather information regarding some illegal activities that the police officer was involved in and then use that information against the officer to persuade him to work for the crime family. After that meeting with Marc and hearing his story, we began seeing less of each other, but once in a while I would give him a call and ask how he was making out, because I didn't want to lose contact with him; he was a good source of information.

After the incident with my son and his bike, I began planning how I was going to go about dealing with Tommy and Lenny. First I needed to wait till school ended for the summer, which was just a couple of weeks away. Jan planned to leave for New Brunswick and visit her family with the boys.

After she and the boys left, I was bothered because I worried that Jan and the boys might not be returning soon, if ever; I felt it was the end for Jan and I. Before she left, we were at a point that we were barely communicating. It seemed that I was always out doing one thing or other, and my continuous drinking had a good deal to do with our problems. One of my worst mistakes, as I would realize later, was that my work was always my first priority, and my family came second.

After Jan left, I got in touch with Bobby and arranged to meet with him. I told Bobby that Tommy wanted to make a deal and about Lenny having a gun. I also mentioned that my son had been shot at. When Bobby heard that, he said, "I can't believe they went after your son." When I assured him that they had, Bobby again offered to take care of the problem for me, and again I told him no; I would take care of things.

I was aware that each weekend Tommy and Lenny would leave the city and go up north to party. Exactly where, I wasn't sure; so I asked Bobby. He said as far as he knew, they spent a lot of their time in Sainte-Agathe, but he had overheard them mention the Old Pine Inn near Rawden. I asked him if he knew the type of place the Old Pine Inn was. He said yes, that he had been there on weekends. It was mostly a party place where people gathered to indulge in booze and drugs.

A long weekend was coming up and because Monday was a holiday, I was sure that Tommy would be heading out of town to party. So I asked Bobby if he would find out for me where Tommy would be going. After assuring me that he would, he asked what I was intending to do. I told him that my family was away, and I wanted to see Tommy and find out why he and Lenny had a gun when they came over to see me and about my son being shot at. Bobby said that Tommy and Lenny were always together, so I would have the two of them to deal with. He then asked if I wanted him to come along. I told him no and explained how I was going to deal with Tommy.

After I discovered which room he was staying in, I would wait around outside till the club closed. When Tommy returned to his room, I would walk in on him.

"Then what?" Bobby asked.

"Right now, I don't really know, but I do know one thing. I will be prepared for whatever happens."

"You have a gun?" he asked Yes I told him. "What kind?"

I said, "I'll be taking my .25, because it is small and easy to conceal."

Bobby laughed. "What damage do you think you will do with that pea shooter?"

"Don't worry," I answered. "Up close, it can do a lot of damage, especially with the type of bullets I use."

"Look," said Bobby, "you can use one of my guns. I'll loan you my .45, which has no serial number and can't be traced, in case you need to get rid of it. But make sure if you use it, you don't leave any prints on it."

I told him that I would borrow his gun, but I had no intention of using it, because it would make too much noise.

I drove with Bobby to his home and waited outside till he returned with the gun. He handed it to me, saying, "You're sure you don't want to take the .12-gauge? You can always blow their kneecaps off with it."

"Forget about that," I answered. I took the .45 and placed it under the seat and left. As I drove away, I thought of what Bobby had said about using the .12-gauge to blow their kneecaps off.

After I got to know Bobby a bit, I had asked Marc to check to see if he had a criminal record. I was told that he did have a police record and had served time in jail for aggravated assault. Marc said that at one time Bobby was known to be an enforcer for a union he was involved with. After getting in a fight with a strike breaker, he was knifed in the face. A few weeks later, the man who had used a knife on Bobby had part of his kneecap blown away by a shotgun. Marc added that Bobby had been under investigation for the shooting, but because the man didn't see who shot him, nothing came out of it, and the investigation was dropped.

Friday afternoon, I received a call from Bobby. He told me that he had heard that Tommy and Lenny were going to the Old Pine Inn that weekend. Usually on Fridays after work, I would have a few drinks, but that Friday, I didn't; I did not want to be drinking if I was going to confront Tommy and Lenny. That night around nine, I left in a rented car and reached the Inn shortly after ten. As I sat in the parking lot of the Inn watching who was coming and going, I figured it was going to be a long night of waiting. I didn't actually know if Tommy and Lenny were in there.

Around midnight, I noticed a car drive in with three men. They parked a few rows down from where I was. I thought nothing of it when they didn't get out of the car, but as time passed and they stayed in the car, I thought to myself, *Maybe they are undercover police officers.* I believed that they hadn't noticed me, so I just sat and waited for them to leave, which they didn't.

A half hour or so later, I saw Tommy and Lenny stagger out of the Inn. They got in their own car and drove away. I was about to follow them, when I saw the car with the three men pull out behind Tommy and Lenny. For a moment or two, I didn't know what to do; then I decided to follow to see what was going on.

I stayed back far enough just so I could see the rear tail lights of the car following Tommy. At that hour, there was very little traffic. When Tommy's car headed out of the village, the other car continued to follow. When both cars reached a wooded area, I saw the car following pull up alongside Tommy's car. From what I could make out, it seemed that his car was forced to stop on the side of the road, and the other car pulled up and stopped in front of him. I stopped and hesitated for a moment, and then I heard some yelling and cursing. I could see by the dim light of Tommy's car that his doors were open. I heard more commotion, so I moved my car closer. In my headlights, I saw Tommy and Lenny being viciously beaten.

I should have just sat there and enjoyed watching as they were savagely punched and kicked. Instead, without thinking about why I had come to Rawden, I stopped my car and reached for Bobby's .45, which I had under the seat. I stepped out of the car and hollered, "What in the hell is going on here?" The men paid no attention to me and repeatedly kicked at Tommy and Lenny on the ground. Not certain that they weren't policemen, I brought the .45

up and fired two quick shots over their heads. At the same time, I yelled out "Police!" Instantly, the men rushed to their car and took off down the road.

I walked up to Tommy and Lenny as they managed to get on their feet. Seeing it was me with the gun in my hand, Tommy said, "Fuck, Freddie! What are you doing here?"

I looked at both bloodied faces and their torn clothing and said, "You two are lucky that I happened to come along when I did."

As they leaned up against their car for support, Tommy again said, "Freddie, what are you doing here?" Seeing a car approaching from a distance and thinking that it might be the police, I headed to my car.

"I'll tell you about it later. You two get your asses back to the Inn before someone comes along and shoots you." Noticing the car lights getting closer, I jumped in and headed back toward Montreal.

The next morning, I called Bobby. When he stopped by to pick up his gun, I told him that I had used two bullets. With that stupid grin of his, he said, "You shot them?"

"No," I answered. "As a matter of fact, I helped them."

After hearing the story, Bobby laughed, especially when he heard about Tommy seeing the gun in my hand. He said, "You are quite a guy! You go out after someone, then you end up helping them." Before he left, Bobby said, "It's going to be interesting to see what's going to happen now with Tommy and Lenny, after you helped when they were getting the shit beaten out of them."

"Yes," I answered, "but we'll just have to wait and see."

The following day was Sunday, and I called Jan just to say hello. I mentioned that although they only had been gone for a few days, I already missed her and the boys. Her reply was, "It's strange. When we're there, you are very seldom around; as soon as we are gone a few days, you call and say that you miss us."

I told her, "Yeah, I guess you are right." After talking with Jan, I thought to myself, *It's going to be a long lonely road ahead for me.* It's strange but true. You may not fully realize what you have till it slowly begins to drift away from you. Then the realization sets in, and you ask yourself, *What am I going to do now?* When I was working, being alone didn't bother me, because I had other matters on my mind; whenever I returned to the empty apartment, then it would bother me. So the way I kept from loneliness was to keep always busy.

At the time, I had found myself a hobby: putting together electronic gadgets. Back then, we didn't have such electronic devices as we have today, like surveillance cameras, two-way radios, and home computers. The first time that I saw a computer was at Radio Shack. They just came out with a small one. After the clerk showed me how it worked, I purchased one, thinking that it would be a good toy. Out of curiosity, I learned how to use it. I soon had it apart and added another device to it that enabled me to send data over the phone line without the use of a modem; which at the time was unheard of. I was always working on some kind of electronic gadget that wasn't yet on the market. Years later, I would receive a great amount of publicity from the news media about my tinkering with these gadgets, especially a device I had put together that some said could replace the computer modem.

At the time, besides investigations and security work, I was also involved in a bit of collecting money owed to business people I knew; the regulations that governed private investigators clearly stated that as a private investigator, I wasn't allowed to be involved in collecting bills. One day while my car was being serviced down the street from where I lived, the owner, who knew me very well, said, "Freddie, were you once in the collection business?" I said yes, he then asked, "How can I go about finding a guy who owes me money?" He proceeded to tell me about a close friend of his who he had co-signed a bank loan for. Shortly after, the friend left the city. Now he was stuck with paying the loan.

After getting a bit of information from him regarding his friend, I told him that I would see what I could do to trace him. A week or so went by; I had forgotten about it, till one morning I stopped at the gas pump, and he asked how I was making out in finding his friend. I told him that I didn't have time right then to check into it. He told me, "Freddie, I'll tell you what I'll do. If you find that person and collect the money, I am willing to pay you half of whatever you collect from him. If you get the full amount, which is thirty-two thousand, you keep sixteen thousand of it, plus your expenses." I found that very interesting; that day, I started trying to locate the person.

First, I visited his last known address and got very little information other than he had left town over a year ago. Shortly after, he began seeing a woman who lived outside of the city and ran some sort of business. After a couple of weeks, I learned that the person whom I was looking for had relatives named Lemieux living in Quebec City. I had no first name to work with; when I checked the Quebec City phone book for Lemieuxs, there were more than a dozen listed. One night, I began calling each listed phone number. Whenever someone answered, I would introduce myself as a friend of Pierre, the first name of the person I was searching for. Finally, after many calls, a woman answered. When I told her that I was a school friend of Pierre's, she said that yes, she was a relative of his, but she hadn't head from him for the past six months. I said that the last time we spoke, he told me to call him whenever I was in town, but I had called his phone number and was told by the operator that the number had been disconnected. She said, "Just wait—I'll get his phone number for you."

The following day I called Pierre's number, which was in a small town near Cornwall, Ontario; when a woman answered, I said in a friendly manner, "Is Pierre around?"

"No," she answered, "he's at work."

"Oh, is he still working at the same place?"

"Yes," she replied, "he's still with the oil company."

I said, "The last time we spoke, he gave me his work number and asked me to call whenever I got in town, but I misplaced it."

"Are you in town now?" she asked.

"No, but I'll be there tomorrow for a few days. I'd like to meet him for lunch." Believing I was a friend of his, she gave me his office number.

After a few days, I dialled the number she gave me. A woman answered, and I asked for Pierre. When he got on the line, I said to him; "Hi, Pierre, my name is Bruno. We've been looking for you for quite a while."

After hesitating, he asked, "Why?"

"It seems that you left Montreal rather quickly, and before you left, you forgot to take care of certain business."

Again after hesitating, he asked, "What was that?"

I quickly answered, "You ripped off your friend for money"

He paused for a few seconds and then said, "Who are you?"

I said, "I am the one you are going to have to deal with regarding that money you owe. Remember your friend Michel, the service station operator? When he talked to you about the thirty-two thousand, you told him that the ball game was over? He was the one who had to repay the bank loan. Well, Pierre, it's now a new ball game, and we are in control. I am now the pitcher, and my boss is the umpire who calls the shots, and your only way out is to repay the money, and the matter will be forgotten."

"Are you the one who called my home and spoke with my wife the other day?" He seemed very nervous. I confirmed. "Did you mention anything to her about the money?"

"No," I answered, adding, "not yet."

"Please don't call my home."

I said to him, "I can assure you we won't, as long as you repay the money. You have a week to come up with the money, and I don't care how you get it. Next Friday, I will be calling you to make arrangements to have someone pick it up." Before he had time to say anything more, I hung up. I knew I had him and that he was scared.

I chose the name Bruno because it was Italian and also said "we" instead of "I." I wanted him to think that I wasn't alone: a bit of psychology I used on him. He may have thought that I belonged to a criminal organization such as the Mafia. That always helped to get money from people like Pierre. When I had been in the collection business, most of the time I'd listen to people's sob stories, but when it came to that type of collection, I came right to the point and ignored all sob stories.

When the following Friday came, I phoned Pierre; he said that he could only come up with twenty thousand. I was elated but said that I was disappointed, because I had told the "boss" that he would be repaying the full thirty-two thousand. Pierre said that he would need a month or so to come up with the other twelve thousand. When I asked him where to meet him, he said in the parking lot of the shopping mall. After getting the description of the car he would be driving, I asked if he would be alone. He confirmed. I told him that we would meet at a certain time. Before hanging up, I said, "Pierre, if you are thinking of pulling anything on us, they will find parts of your body all over town."

"No," he said, "I just want to get this over with."

I had made arrangement to have another fellow come with me to Cornwall, and he was big. He didn't know my reason for going; I told him that I needed to pick something up for a friend.

After we arrived and saw Pierre's car in the parking lot of the mall, we parked away from the area and sat for a while; I watched Pierre's car. He was seated in it. After ten minutes, I pulled up alongside his car, got out, and walked over to the driver's side. Staring up at me, he said, "Bruno?" I nodded. Picking up an envelope from the seat, he said, "Here's the money," and he handed me the envelope, which I quickly stuffed in my pocket, without counting it. I said, "This isn't personal, Pierre, it's just part of my job."

"I know," he nervously answered. "Please don't call my home again; my wife knows nothing of this." Again, I assured him that we wouldn't, as long as he came up with the balance within a month, as he said he would.

Pierre was unaware of it, but I was just as nervous as he was. And after getting the money, I just wanted to get the hell out of there, so I said as I walked toward my car, "I'll call you in a month."

Before leaving Cornwall, I stopped at a service station, went in the washroom, and counted the twenty thousand. Back in Montreal, after dropping my friend off, I removed twelve thousand from the envelope and then drove to see Michel. When I handed him the envelope with the eight thousand, Michel seemed surprised. He said, "Don't tell me you found him and got some money from him?" I told him that I had gotten twenty thousand, but I kept an extra two thousand because of the trouble I had finding him and that I had to go to Ontario to meet him. I told him that I would have to go back in a month to pick up the other twelve thousand. Michel said, "I don't know how you managed to get that money from him." The last time he had seen him and mentioned the money, Pierre had told Michel to go fuck himself and that he would never get a cent. I said to Michel, "Once he understood that he needed to pay the money back, I had no problem with him."

A month later, I called Pierre. Rather than driving to Cornwall, I had him make a bank transfer to my bank account in Montreal. Before the end of the day, I phoned my bank and was told that the twelve thousand had been transferred.

On that deal, I made a quick eighteen thousand. That was my favourite type of collection. Later, I learned from an employee that Michel and Pierre were queers who at one time lived together, till Pierre came home one night and found Michel in bed with another lover. Back in those days, gay men were referred to as queers, but today people like them are referred to as gays in a much more respectful manner.

As for Tommy and Lenny, after coming to their aid, for a while I hadn't heard anything about why they had been beaten up or what happened after. A few weeks later, as I sat in the mall having lunch, I noticed Tommy walk in the restaurant. He was alone. He looked around and, seeing me, he came over to my table and asked if he could sit for a minute. I agreed. He said that he had stopped by the store; Glen had told him I was at the restaurant. Because he wasn't with Lenny, before he had a chance to say anything else, I said, "Where's your other half, Lenny?

He said, making eye contact, "You may not believe this, but the night you were beaten up, I had nothing to do with that, and I didn't know about it till a few days later.

I said, "Is that what you came here to tell me, Tommy?"

"No, not really," he answered. "I wanted to thank you for what you did up in Rawden that night. I still don't know why you helped us."

"Well, Tommy," I said, "to be quite honest with you, I had no intention of helping you and Lenny. I did go up there to see you two, but those men got to you first."

"Now I know why you had that gun," said Tommy.

I looked at him for a few moments, and I said, "It's one thing to have someone work me over"—Tommy quickly said, "I had nothing to do with that"—"but when someone begins to mess around with my sons, that I will not accept."

When I mentioned my sons, he looked at me as if he were surprised and said, "What about your sons?"

"I suppose now you're going to tell me that you had nothing to do with my youngest boy being shot at?"

For a moment, he just looked at me, dumbfounded, and said, "Freddie, I have sons of my own. I wouldn't do anything to hurt your son."

"Well, Tommy, maybe you should talk to your buddy Lenny, because my son was shot at. No one would have a reason except you and Lenny." Just thinking of my son and what happened was beginning to piss me off; so I said, "Tommy, what do you want?"

As he stood up from the table he said, "I just came here to thank you for what you did and to tell you that from now on there will be no more trouble from us; as a matter of fact, I have already told the guys to stay away from the stores you secure."

I answered, "Yeah, if they want to steal, let them go rip off some other stores."

About to leave, Tommy said, "I just wanted you to know I am indebted to you, Freddie, for what you did, and if I can ever be of help to you, just let me know."

I watched Tommy walk away and felt a bit sorry for him. He looked like a very sick person; even his face had a yellowish colour to it. I guess the combination of drugs and alcohol were taking a toll on him. When I returned to the store, I told Glen that I didn't think that we would have any more problems with Tommy and his gang. Glen said, "What did you do? Threaten to shoot them?"

"No, not really," I answered. "They just got tired of you following them around the stores, so Tommy said from now on, he and his buddies will do their shopping at other places."

"I believe there's a little more to it than that," said Glen

"Yes, Glen," I answered, "there is, and one day over a few beers we'll talk about it."

A month or so after the meeting with Tommy, as I was on my way to work early one morning, a car pulled up beside me and honked its horn. The lone driver showed me a police badge and pointed for me to pull over, which I did. He parked in front of me. I noticed another unmarked car with another lone driver stop directly behind me. I thought to myself, *What the hell is this?* The two drivers approached my car and asked if I was Fred Hudon; I said "Yes, I am Mr. Hudon." They showed me their Quebec provincial police IDs, and I was asked to get out. As I did, I said, "What is this about?" They proceeded to search my car. One said, "We got a report that you were seen carrying a gun."

I replied, "No, sir, I don't carry guns." After they searched the car and found nothing, I was then searched. Lucky for me that I stopped carrying my .25 after talking with Tommy. After the search, the officers, without any further conversation, got in their cars and left. As I continued on my way, I thought, *Who would have reason to report that I was packing a gun?* Then I thought of what Lenny had said at a bar one night after the incident up in Rawden; Bobby mentioned to me that while they were having a drink and talking about what had taken place, Lenny had said, "I thought a private eye wasn't permitted to carry guns?" I now felt that it was Lenny who had reported me, maybe thinking that that was one way to get me out of the business and get rid of me. It was fortunate for Lenny that I wasn't packing a gun when I was stopped; because if I had my gun with me and had been charged, later I would have gone after Lenny. That time the outcome would have been much different.

One day while I was at Canadian Tire talking with Glen, Mr. Claude walked by and asked me to his office. When we got there, he said, "Fred, how would you like to have the job as personnel manager?"

That surprised me. I said "Personnel manager?"

Mr. Claude confirmed and then added, "For a while."

"But what about Jerry?" I asked. "Besides being the store manager, isn't he also the personnel manager?"

"Yes," he answered. "But like I mentioned, your position as personnel manager will be temporary." Mr. Claude went on to explain that he wanted to get rid of certain employees but had a problem doing so because some of them were relatives. Some were related to him, and others were related to Jerry.

"In other words," I said to Claude, "you want to give me the job to get rid of them?" He confirmed.

One night shortly after I accepted the position, after the store closed and the employees had left, Mr Claude and Jerry and I sat around and discussed how we would go about handling the problem with the relatives. I was given a list of fourteen employees they wanted out. After discussing how I was going to go about handling the situation, Mr. Claude said that in the morning, he would put a notice on the bulletin board notifying the employees that I was now the new personnel manager.

One of the main employees they wanted to get rid of was the sports manager. He was related to Mr. Claude's wife. The day after the notice was put on the bulletin board, as planned, I began visiting each department and talking with the section manager or supervisor regarding employees who were taking too many breaks during work hours; some were overstaying their lunch hours at the mall restaurant while customers were in the store waiting around to be served. As expected, none were too happy and showed their dislike, especially the sports manager, Daniel, and his cousin Leonard.

Occasionally when I stopped by the sports department to talk with them,

I was told that they were too busy to talk, even though at the time there were no customers around. Seeing that they were making excuses to avoid talking with me, I changed the manner in which I would go about dealing with them. I had them come to the office instead. I began with Daniel; I called down to the service counter and asked them to page Daniel and tell him that Mr. Hudon would like to see him in his office.

After waiting for half an hour, I went down to the sports department. He was talking with Leonard. I said, "Daniel, I had you paged to come to the office—didn't you hear it?

"Yes," he answered, "but I was busy."

Giving him a stern look, I replied, "Seeing that you're not too busy now, come to the office. I want to talk to you." As I said that, I turned to walk away, expecting him to follow; he didn't. He continued talking with Leonard. I said, "Are you coming?" He answered sharply, "Like I told you, we are busy."

Seeing that there were no customers to be served, I stepped directly in front of him and said, "Daniel, I had you paged, and you refused to come to the office. Now I ask you again and still you refuse. You have a choice. Either you come to the office or you can take the door and leave." Daniel didn't reply.

Leonard took a step toward me and said, "You can't order us around and tell us what to do. You are not the owner or the boss."

"No, I am not," I answered, "but I am the personnel manager. I do the hiring and the firing, and if you're not careful, you'll be gone." I turned to Daniel and told him if he wasn't in my office in fifteen minutes, I would give him notice that he was finished working at Canadian Tire. Without saying more, I walked away and waited to see what Daniel would do. Fifteen minutes passed and then an hour. Still Daniel didn't come to the office. Because it was then lunchtime, I didn't do anything further regarding Daniel.

Later I was told that he had gone home for lunch and wouldn't be returning till the morning. I wanted to talk with Mr. Claude concerning Daniel. But he wasn't in and wasn't expected back for a few days, so I spoke with Jerry. After telling him what had occurred with Daniel, Jerry said, "He chose to go home rather than meet with you. Well, let him stay home."

Early the following morning, I was at the counter waiting when Daniel came in. As he was about to walk by, I said to him, "Daniel, you chose to go home yesterday rather than come to the office, so you're finished; you no longer work for Canadian Tire." Daniel looked around and then said to the counter girl, "Page Mr. Claude and ask him to come here." When she told him that he wasn't in, Daniel said, "Then get Jerry."

Jerry came to the front, and Daniel said to him, "This guy tells me I'm finished working here." Jerry threw up his hands and said, "Daniel, there's nothing I can do about that; come back in a few days when Claude gets back and speak to him." Then Jerry walked away, leaving Daniel standing there, dumbfounded.

Leonard walked in, and seeing that Daniel was upset, he said to him, "What's going on?"

"I was told to go home, that I no longer have a job here." As he and Leonard stood there talking, I went to the information counter. When the doors opened for business and customers began entering, seeing that Leonard was still over talking with Daniel, I walked over to him and said, "Leonard, if you are here to work, it's time to get started." After whispering something to Daniel, he walked toward the sports section, and Daniel left the store. As he did, he looked over toward me and said, "I'll be back, you'll see." It didn't take long for the news regarding Daniel's dismissal to get around to other store employees; many were quite upset.

As I walked around later, I could feel all eyes upon me. I previously had had problems with certain employees who referred to me as the Englishman, even though I had a very well-known French name. I speak the language, but some still called me the Englishman. At the time the language issue was brewing in Quebec. A good number of separatists who didn't like the English and showed it were employed at the store. Glen, who was English but spoke French, also had problems with some employees, especially whenever he checked some of them for merchandise as they left the store at closing time. Employees weren't always checked for stolen items, maybe twice a week. Some were checked, just to keep them honest.

A few days after I had told Daniel that he was no longer wanted, Mr. Claude returned and told me Daniel had called him at home and told him that I had let him go. Claude said that he was already aware of it because before he received the call from Daniel, he had spoken with Jerry about it. When I asked Claude what was going to happen now, he replied, "He is gone; I told him to come and see me in a few weeks, because when my wife learns of it, she'll kick up a fuss, but he will not be rehired."

In the meantime, things were tense among the employees. The following day, Friday, matters got much worse. Usually Friday nights after work, employees would meet at the bar that was part of the mall restaurant and have a few drinks. Sometimes Glen and I would go and sit around for a while and have a beer. That Friday night, without thinking, I went over to the bar after I left the store to have a quick one. As soon as I walked in I could feel the tension in the place. When I sat at the bar, Leonard, who was seated there with two other employees, gave me a dirty look and said to the others,

"Mr. Big is here. Let's move to a table." I paid no attention to his remark and ordered a drink.

About a dozen store employees were in the bar, and none sat at the bar as some usually did. As I sat there, I could hear remarks Leonard was making to the other employees about me. Leonard was a muscular person who was into weight lifting and known around the store to be very strong. I ignored his remarks, until I was about to leave and heard him refer to me as the "fucking Englishman." I turned around and said to him, "Are you referring to me?"

He answered, "Yes, so what are you going to do about it?" I looked at the barman, who had also heard him refer to me as the fucking Englishman. Then Leonard added, "You're not in the store here, and we don't have to put up with your shit."

On the way out, as I passed his table I said to him, "Leonard, your mouth is just about as big as your muscles, and as for the limited brains you have, you're sitting on them." He quickly shot up from his chair and said, "I'll show you what I can do with my muscles." When he rushed at me, I was just outside of the doorway into the mall. As I turned to face him, he reached out to grab me; that's when I let him have it. I threw a right punch at him that connected to his mouth. The force of the blow drove him back a few feet; he landed on his ass. As he slowly picked himself up, I was about to unleash another punch at him when I heard the barman holler, as he walked over to help Leonard to his feet, "Mr. Hudon, that's enough." I turned to Leonard's two other buddies, who were standing near the doorway, and said, "Now your friends know what the Englishman can do, eh? Look at him with all his useless muscles."

As I spoke, the barman stood between Leonard and me. Seeing the blood running down Leonard's chin and the fear in his eyes, I said to him, "You asked me what I was going to do about you calling me a fucking Englishman? Well now, you know." As I turned to walk away, I added, "By the way, I will be talking to you tomorrow when I see you at work. Remember what you said about not having to put up with my shit."

To me, Leonard was like most muscle-bound weight lifters; to cause any damage to a person, they would need to grab him, and if they couldn't, they would suddenly realize that they had a problem, especially if the other person knew how to use his hands. It was only when I walked out of the mall that I noticed that I had bruised a knuckle and was bleeding a bit.

I had planned to go to work Saturday morning, but when I woke, I decided not to. When I got to the store first thing Monday morning, I was told that Mr. Claude wanted to see me. When I got to his office, he said to me, "Fred, what the hell happened between you and Leonard at the bar Friday?"

I said, "After insulting me and calling me a fucking Englishman, he came after me. As I left the bar, he tried to grab hold of me, so I let him have it."

"Well, now," said Claude, "he called this morning saying that he wouldn't be in and that he would be suing you for damages to his mouth. He lost two teeth and has a split lip."

"Let him sue," I replied, "he's the one who came after me."

Claude said, "This morning while I was at the restaurant having a coffee, I spoke to Peter the barman, and he said that you hit Leonard an awful blow, and you would have punched him again if Peter hadn't stepped in."

"Yes," I answered, "I would have, and he wouldn't have gotten up from the floor."

"We need to be careful," Claude replied, "because you are part of management, and I could also be held responsible. So in the future, try and keep your hands in your pockets. As for Leonard, I don't believe he'll try to sue, because Peter said that he started it all by insulting you. Then he went after you as you were leaving the bar. I also spoke to one of the employees who was with Leonard, and he did say that Leonard went out in the mall after you."

As I got up to leave, I said, "Anyway, I don't mind having to pay for his teeth—to me, it was worth it. By the way, what's going to happen now in regards to his job, seeing that he is one of the employees you want to get rid of?"

After thinking for a moment, Mr. Claude said, "Did you find a reason to let him go?"

"Like you said," I answered, "because I am part of management, as an employee, Leonard had no business insulting and trying to degrade me by calling me a fucking Englishman in a public place."

"I don't believe you need to worry too much about Leonard, because I have a feeling that after what you did to him in front of other employees, he will not want to return. He will be too embarrassed, given that he was the strong man around here."

Just as Mr. Claude had guessed, a few days later Leonard phoned and said that he wasn't returning to work, but he did ask to be paid for his damaged teeth. Mr. Claude said he would pay just to get rid of him.

It's strange how quickly things change. Before the incident with Leonard, whenever I walked around the store, employees seldom looked at me or said hello. Afterward, when they saw me, it was a big "Hello, Mr. Hudon!" accompanied by a smile. Everyone was now so nice and friendly. What a difference a punch can make, eh?

After two months as the personnel manager, I got rid of half a dozen unwanted employees. Then I told Mr. Claude that I was finished, because it had taken too much out of me. Also, it was taking time away from my investigation work. If it wasn't for Glen, I wouldn't have been able to perform both functions.

As for Glen, he told me that he had applied with the CN Railway for work as a CN police officer. The money he was paid to work for me wasn't the issue. He wanted to better himself, and he couldn't see any future in retail security. He was right. But when the time came for him to leave, I did miss Glen. He was a good security man, and he would be hard to replace.

I had no trouble recruiting security officers; the problem was hiring good ones who performed well in the retail business. Retail security was just like any business; if you did your work well, you stayed. If not, you are gone. As far as I was concerned, there were two types of security officers: the ones I referred to as security guards, whose work only involved protecting property, such as a night watchman; the second type of security officer not only protects property but can function in many aspects of security, as officers in the retail business need to do. Most of all, the officer needs to have the capability to make good decisions on his own without continuously being supervised. An officer who works in the retail industry and doesn't use good judgment, especially when it comes to arresting thieves, let it be a shoplifter or an employee, it could end up costing the company a good bit of money if he or she makes a bad judgment call.

A month or so after Glen told me that he had applied for work at the CN, he got the job and left. A few days later, while at the store training a replacement for Glen, I happened to notice a man pocketing an item; he was well dressed and looked like a businessman. From a distance, we watched him as he walked around the store looking at different items. I said to the young man who had just began work that morning, "You see him looking around with his shifty eyes, checking to see if anyone is paying any attention to him?" As I spoke we noticed him pocketing another item. After looking around again, the man headed up front to one of the counters and paid for an item.

We followed as he walked out of the store. It was lunch hour, and a good number of mall workers were out near the entrance relaxing and getting a bit of fresh air. To avoid a commotion in front of the mall workers, I let the man walk toward the parking lot. As I approached him, I said, "Sir, you forgot to pay for an item in your pocket." The man, who was a head taller than I and looked to be in his forties, glanced back at me and then continued on into the parking lot. Because he didn't stop, I approached him and touched his arm again, saying, "Sir, you have something in your pocket that you didn't pay for." He quickly pulled his arm away and took off, running through the parking lot with me and the new man in pursuit. When he reached the end of the lot, he continued running to the rear of a service building, which was about two hundred yards away. Seeing an open door, he ran inside, with me directly behind him.

A group of men sat at a table having lunch; when they saw us rush in, one yelled out, "What the hell is going on?" Paying no attention to them, I grabbed hold of the man's arm and swung him around. As I did, he reached inside his coat and pulled out an eight-inch kitchen knife, which I would learn later he had stolen. I quickly reached out to grab hold of the man; as I did, I felt the tip of the knife go into my arm, and instantly blood gushed out from the wound.

The man dropped the knife. As he did, I threw a punch that connected to the side of his face and dropped him to the floor. As I reached down to pick him up, I said to the workers, "I am a security officer, and that man has stolen merchandise on him." I then asked if they knew him/ They said no, and no one had seen him before. Seeing the blood run down my arm, one of the men came over and handed me a cloth. Meanwhile, the man kept repeating in broken English, "I am sorry, I am sorry, I didn't mean to cut you, I was only handing you the knife." After I told the young man with me to pick up the knife, I practically dragged the man back to the store, up to the security office, not realizing the extent of my wound. After one of the office employees bandaged it, I asked the man, who was in tears, why he pulled out the knife. He said that's what he thought I was after him for, so he took it out of his coat to hand it to me. I believed him, because he hadn't reached out with the knife as if to stab me.

After searching him, I found that besides the knife, he had three other small items. He said that he came to the store on his lunch break to buy the knife for his wife. When no one came over to serve him, he decided to steal it, along with the other items. I watched as he tried to explain in broken English and felt kind of sorry for him, especially when I noticed the side of his face was a bit bruised and beginning to swell. Thinking that I was going to call the police and he would be taken to jail, he begged me to let him go, which I did, because I had no intention of calling the police.

Before he left, I told him to call his work and tell them that he was involved in some kind of accident and wouldn't be returning that day. He said that's what he would do. Seeing that he had money on him, I told the new security officer to go down and get a knife just like the one he had stolen. When he returned with it, I said to the man, "You said that you came here to buy a knife for your wife?"

"Yes," he answered, "that's why I came here."

"Here," I said handing him the knife. "You go downstairs and pay for it. I'll watch from the window."

He went up to the cash and paid for the knife and then walked out.

The young man I had hired that morning sat down and said, "Mr. Hudon, I decided that this type of work isn't for me." I didn't try to change his mind. I told him it was okay, I understood, and he left.

I knew that I needed to go to the hospital and have the cut taken care of. When I arrived at the emergency room, the doctor who took care of me asked how I got the cut. I told him that I was accidentally stabbed with a knife; he said that he needed to summon the police. I told him okay. He was stitching my arm up when two police officers walked in; when they asked me about the stab wound, I told the officers what had happened and that the man had no intention of stabbing me. One officer asked, "Did you have him charged for stealing?"

I answered, "No, I gave him a break and let him go."

"I sure would have charged him," said the other officer. Thinking about a few policemen to whom I had given breaks when I had stopped them for shoplifting, I replied, "Over the years that I have been in retail security, I have given a break to many people, some deserving, others not so much, especially a few who were professionally well aware that shoplifting was a crime." By the look on the officer's face, I believed that he got the drift of my comment. After the police officers had left and the doctor had finished stitching up my wound, I was told that I was very fortunate that the knife had entered just below the muscle of my arm. The doctor said that if it had cut into my muscle, my arm might have sustained permanent damage.

CHAPTER 31
My Brother's Friend in Montreal

Over the years, I have experienced a few strange incidents outside of my work. One such incident began one evening when I went to visit my brother Romeo at his place of work. He had moved to Montreal from Ontario; he was employed at the Julius Richardson Rehabilitation Hospital in Côte-St-Luc as the maintenance supervisor. At the time, I very seldom saw him. That night, I decided to stop by and see how he was doing. I arrived at the hospital and didn't see him around. I asked a man who wore a white uniform and was about to get on the elevator if he had seen Romeo. I thought he was one of the doctors. He answered yes and said that Romeo was down in the boiler room. When I went to the boiler room, I mentioned to Romeo that one of the doctors had told me where to find him. He said that he wasn't a doctor; he was Charles the maintenance man, who just helped Romeo take a stiff down from the upper floor. Later I would learn that a "stiff" meant a dead person. I told Romeo that Charles didn't look like a maintenance man; he looked more like a doctor or a businessman.

I spent some time with Romeo. As I was about to leave, Charles appeared and asked Romeo if there was anything else he wanted done. I eyed Charles as he spoke with Romeo and found it hard to believe that he was a maintenance man. He was very good-looking and well-spoken. When Romeo finished talking with Charles about work, he said to him, "Charles, I want you to meet my brother, Freddie."

I stood up and shook hands, saying that I was pleased to meet him. After he left, I said to Romeo, "I find it hard to believe that he's your maintenance man."

"Yes," said Romeo, "he goes around scrubbing floors. He's been with me for about a year now and is a very good worker."

I again met Charles as I was on my way out. He was standing near the doorway having a cigarette. I had a brief conversation with him, and I detected a foreign accent. Later, Romeo mentioned that he was Polish.

Later, I kept thinking of Charles. Something didn't seem right. He was a handsome, well-groomed man who seemed very intelligent and well-educated and there he was, working at the hospital, scrubbing floors. Something about Charles bothered me; for some reason, I couldn't picture him going around the hospital scrubbing floors. Not that there weren't any good-looking and intelligent maintenance men going around scrubbing floors, but for some reason Charles stood out. Later, I would learn why. Even Romeo was in for a surprise.

A month or so after I first met Charles, I returned to the hospital and asked Romeo how he had hired Charles. He said that one day Charles just walked in off the street and asked if they had any work for him. Because the hospital needed another maintenance man, Romeo said that after interviewing Charles, he hired him. I asked Romeo if Charles had any other work references; he said that he didn't ask for any. He liked him, so he hired him.

Romeo and his young son Shawn lived on the premises, as did Charles. They each had their own living quarters. Romeo had an apartment-type set-up with a few rooms. Charles had a single room located down the hall from Romeo. I didn't want to ask Romeo too many questions regarding Charles, because I didn't want to look too inquisitive, but before leaving, I said to him, "Charles sure looks in good shape."

"Yes," said Romeo, "he's in good condition because four or five nights a week, he runs about five miles downtown to see his girlfriend and then runs back again. He also has some workout equipment in his room." Romeo also mentioned that Charles never took a bus or taxi; he either walked or ran, and when he left to see his girlfriend, it was always later at night, after dark. When Romeo mentioned that Charles only left after dark, I asked him why that was. Romeo answered, "I don't know. Even in the daytime, he doesn't go out. He'll only go as far as the corner store and back."

That night, after talking with Romeo and learning more about Charles activities, I was a bit more confused as to why he would only go out after dark, and during the day he'd go no farther than the corner store. Besides going to see his girlfriend, he'd go nowhere; he kept pretty well to himself. Romeo had mentioned that when Charles didn't go visit his girlfriend, he would pass his nights in his room painting. He said that Charles was a good artist and had sold some of his paintings to employees of the hospital. The more I learned about Charles, the more interested I became.

Over the years, I had gotten pretty good at reading people; body language and the manner in which they expressed themselves could reveal a lot. With

Charles, I would need to get to know him a bit more before I could form an opinion. When I first met him, I only spent ten or fifteen minutes talking with him. Because of my interest, I needed to find a way to spend a little more time with him. One night, I phoned Romeo and told him that I might be interested in buying one of Charles' paintings, if I could see some of his work. Romeo said that he would speak to Charles and get back to me. My brother wasn't surprised, because he knew that my son Cloyd was an artist—a very good one.

One weekend, I received a call from Romeo; he said Charles would be glad to show me some of his paintings. That night, I drove over to the hospital and brought a bottle of rum with me; Romeo had mentioned that sometimes he and Charles would sit around and have a few drinks. Knowing that alcohol sometimes helped loosen tongues, I felt it might assist in having Charles talk a little more about himself. When I arrived, Charles was with Romeo. It was a Saturday evening, and they were sitting at the table having a beer. I placed the bottle of rum on the table, and within minutes, Romeo poured us each a drink. We sat around for a while listening to Romeo telling a few stories about when we were young; we laughed and had more drinks.

At one point Charles said to me, "Romeo mentioned that you were a private investigator?"

"Yes," I answered.

"That must be interesting work," said Charles.

"Not really," I replied. "When I first got into the business, I found it interesting, but later on, I found it boring." To change the subject, I said, "Romeo tells me you're quite an artist. I am interested in seeing some of your work."

"Okay," said Charles as he stood. "I'll go get a few." I would have liked to go to his room with him, but he didn't ask me to go with him, so I stayed with Romeo. A few minutes later, he returned with an armful of paintings and laid them on the floor for me to see. I found one that I liked and asked how much he wanted for it. He said two hundred. I felt that it wasn't worth two hundred, but I agreed to buy it. I told Charles that I would have to come back because I didn't have two hundred on me.

Charles said, "That's okay. Because you are Romeo's brother you can take the painting with you and pay me later."

I agreed, because it would give me a reason to see him again.

After discussing the paintings, Charles asked more questions regarding my work. He was interested in how one would go about finding a person, especially if the person didn't want to be found. I told him that if a person didn't want to be found, then the work got a bit more complicated. People might never be found, because they could have changed their name and their usual habits. Usually, they would have no contact with past friends or even close family members.

"So that would make it more difficult to locate the person?" said Charles.

"Yes, but we have our ways and means," I replied. "If we keep digging, sometimes the unexpected turns up."

"Very interesting," said Charles. "Someday, I may like to get into that type of work."

To get away from the subject of my work, I said to Charles, "I see that you keep yourself in good physical condition."

"Yes," he answered. "I run and exercise a lot."

Romeo spoke up. "Yeah, Charles, you like to arm wrestle. Why don't you try Freddie? He's got a good arm."

Charles quickly placed his arm in front of me. "Okay! Come on, Freddie, let's see how good you are." On the first attempt, after a bit of struggle, I managed to lay his wrist over. He tried again. This time, he laid my wrist down.

I laughed, saying, "I had to let you lay me or you would have broken my arm."

"For a small fellow," said Charles, "you have a strong arm."

When I had first arrived, Charles didn't do too much talking, but now that he had a few drinks in him he seemed to relax a bit more, but he didn't say much about himself. Because he had asked about my occupation, I asked, "How about you, Charles? What did you do before coming here?"

"Not much," he answered. "I travelled around the country, seeing a bit of the world, and I worked at different jobs till it was time to move on."

That was the only information I got out of Charles that night, that he had travelled and done odd jobs. Romeo had said that Charles was in his mid-forties, and he knew little about him other than that he had mention at one time that he had a brother living somewhere in Ontario. For the next few months, I visited Romeo a couple of times, and each time I saw Charles, I would think to myself, *What is he hiding from?* Something about him kept bothering me. He seemed well-educated and yet he was at the hospital, working for my brother, scrubbing floors.

Over the next year or so, I didn't see much of Romeo, except for the odd times when I would stop by and spend a few minutes with him and Shawn. Shawn was twelve years old, a big boy—very tall for his age. Sometimes, I would say something to him just to bug him, especially when he was eating; he would give me a dirty look and leave the room. At one time, Romeo said to me, "You be careful. If you keep bugging him, he's going to punch you."

I looked at Shawn and said, "You wouldn't punch your uncle Freddie, would you, Shawn?"

"I sure would," he answered. "You keep bugging me and you'll soon find out."

After Romeo told me that it bothered Shawn when I would say something to bug him, I stopped making remarks to him about his eating habits.

As for Charles, one night I received a call from Romeo saying that Charles had left, and he asked me to drop by to see what Charles had left him as a souvenir. At the hospital, Romeo took me to his workshop and pointed to a motor vehicle licence plate he had on the wall. It was a German licence plate with the Waffen-SS emblem on it.

"Look at this," said Romeo, reaching down and retrieving a paper box from under his workbench. "This is what Shawn found in the dumpster, along with the licence plate."

"So he didn't give you the licence plate?"

"No," said Romeo. "It was in the box with other items." Romeo emptied the contents of the box on the counter. It contained many pictures of German SS officers, including Hitler, with Charles standing next to him in uniform.

Looking at the many pictures of Charles and other officers, I said to Romeo, "I knew there was something about Charles that didn't seem right."

Romeo didn't say much; he seemed a bit disgusted. He said that Shawn had noticed Charles placing a few boxes out in the dumpster just before he left and that Shawn went out to see what was in the boxes.

In one of the photos, Charles was standing directly in front of a car beside Hitler, and I noticed that the licence plate numbers matched the plate Romeo now had on the wall. I didn't mention that to Romeo, but I did ask what he was going to do with the licence plate. He said that he might sell it to a collector. I told Romeo that if he was going to sell it, I would be interested in buying it. He said that he would wait and see before he decided what he was going to do with it.

Among the many pictures were a few of Charles that were taken in the past few years. I was interested in one of Charles in a suit, standing under a wall emblem of the Unites States Presidential Seal. It looked as if it had been taken in the last few years, because Charles looked the same as when I met him. I asked Romeo if I could have that picture of Charles. He agreed.

Some time later, I returned and again asked Romeo about the licence plate. He said that he wanted to keep it; if he decided to sell it, he would let me know. I mentioned that I was also interested in the pictures. He said that he had destroyed all the pictures. I didn't ask why, but later I learned from Shawn that when Romeo took the pictures to show to the hospital management, he was told to destroy all of them, which he did. It was understandable why the hospital didn't want those pictures around—the hospital was a Jewish

Rehabilitation organization. It wouldn't look too good for them if word got out that they had employed an ex-German Waffen-SS officer, especially if he was wanted for war crimes. That had to be hushed up, so the pictures needed to be destroyed, and no more was said around the hospital about Charles.

After a year, I managed to buy the licence plate from Romeo. Some years later, I would be sorry that I hadn't also got the pictures. A lot was being reported by the news media regarding the Simon Wiesenthal Centre, the Jewish rights group, and the Holocaust, when millions of Jewish children, women, and men were put to death by the Germans because they were Jewish. The Simon Wiesenthal rights group had centres all over the world and searched for German officers to bring before the courts for their involvement in vicious hate crimes against humanity. It was said that many of the Waffen-SS officers were hiding in Canada. When I heard of that, I thought of Charles and the picture I had of him.

I made a phone call to the Simon Wiesenthal Centre in Toronto and gave them the information I had about Charles. When I mentioned the pictures I had seen of Charles taken with Hitler and other SS officers, I was asked if I still had the pictures. When I said that they were destroyed by my brother at the request of the hospital, the person whom I spoke with said it was too bad they were destroyed. Besides Charles, they could have identified other officers that they may have been interested in. When I mentioned that I did have a picture of Charles, I was asked if they could have the picture. I said yes, I would mail it to them, along with other information I had about Charles. They said they would also get in touch with the Julius Richardson Rehabilitation Hospital, so I mentioned that I was quite sure because they requested that the pictures be destroyed that any other information they had on Charles might also have been destroyed. The man said that because the Rehabilitation Hospital was Jewish, he didn't believe that they would have any problem getting additional information that the hospital may have regarding Charles.

Within a few days, I mailed the picture of Charles that I had kept over the years to the Simon Wiesenthal Centre. I included a brief letter about what I knew about him and also wrote that Charles had at one time mentioned that he had a brother living on a farm somewhere in Ontario. I wrote that I also had the Waffen-SS licence plate, he asked if they could have it. I said no, that I wanted to keep it. I kept the licence plate and a copy of Charles' picture, which I had made prior to sending the original to the Simon Wiesenthal Centre.

Twenty years later, when a friend who was a RCMP officer stopped by the office, I showed him the German licence plate and told him about Charles. The officer said that if I was ever to sell the licence plate, he would be interested in getting it for his father. He had told me that over the years his father had collected war memorabilia; it would be nice if he had a German licence plate for his collection. I handed my friend the plate, along with the picture of Charles, and told him to give it to his father.

I learned from Romeo that a few years after Charles left the hospital, he had suddenly returned for a brief visit. Charles had asked Romeo about me and said that he would like to see me. Romeo said that he had tried to call me, but he was told that I was out of town. Over the years, I would often wonder about why Charles wanted to see me. Romeo said that Charles only stayed for half an hour or so. I asked Romeo if he had mentioned to Charles anything about the pictures that he had left behind in the dumpster. He said no, he hadn't, and the only thing Charles had said about himself was that he was with his brother in Ontario. If I had seen Charles, I sure would have asked him about his past as a German SS officer.

Some forty years later, I sometimes think of Charles and wonder if he was one of the Waffen-SS Germans hiding out in Canada and hunted by the Wiesenthal Centre for war crimes against humanity. If not, why was he hiding out at the hospital, scrubbing floors? Later in my travels, when I met men with Polish or German accents, I would think to myself, *Could he be one of the Germans the Wiesenthal Centre is searching for?* The question was always there, but as with Charles, I believed that I would never have the answer.

In regards to searching for a certain person, I'd always ask questions as to why someone wanted the person found. If I felt that their reason wasn't satisfactory, I would refuse to get involved. In one incident concerning a man who wanted me to help find his sister; he said that they were both adopted by different families at a young age when their parents separated, and their mother couldn't raise them by herself. The man was in his mid-thirties and said that he hadn't seen his sister since they were parted twenty-eight years earlier.

As he was giving me the information concerning his sister, for some reason I got the impression that he wasn't being honest. When he began explaining how she might look like today and gave me her name, I knew he was lying. Before he gave me more information about his sister, I had asked him if he knew the name of the family that had adopted her; he said no. But later he gave me her name and described what she looked like twenty-eight years after he had last seen her. I cut in as he spoke and said to him, "Look, for some reason, you are not being honest with me. First you tell me that you didn't know the adopted family name; now you're telling me her name and what she looks like now. If you haven't seen her for twenty-eight years, how do you know what she looks like today? And you know the name she is using now."

After a long pause, he said, "Okay, I am lying. She is not my sister, she's my wife. She took off a few months ago with our three children after we had an argument, and I want to find her."

"Did you try asking her relatives? I am sure they know where she is."

"Yes," he said. "I called them, but they would not talk to me." When he mentioned that the relatives didn't want to speak to him, I felt that they may have had good reasons not to. So I said to him, "Right now, I am very busy working on other matters, so I won't have time to help you at the moment."

My reason for refusing to help that man was because his wife and children might have been abused by him. I can't see a wife taking off with the children over an argument and staying away for three months, but I could visualize a wife who's in an abusive relationship taking off and not returning. If that was the case, there was no way that man could get me to help him locate his wife and children. As far as I was concerned, if he was abusive, they were better off without him. It might have taken the woman years to finally get up enough nerve to leave. Many wives who continue to live with an abusive husband stay in their relationship because of fear of what might happen if they left. A good number of women who continue to live in an abusive relationship do so mainly because they lack the confidence in themselves to do something about it. They feel lost and don't know whom to turn to; their self-esteem has been ripped away from them. Abuse could be physical or mental. Personally, I feel without self-confidence and self-esteem, one is lost. I compare it to living the life of a zombie. To regain self-confidence and self-esteem in oneself, the women who continue to live in abusive relationships need to reach out for help. If they gather the courage to ask for help, they will be helped. First, they must ask. Today there are so many women in fear of raising their voice because of fear of retaliation by their abuser.

Such women must raise their voices and convince themselves that they will not continue to let themselves be abused. Once they make up their mind, the next step is to reach out and ask for help. They can be assured that someone will be there to help. There are people waiting to help. They do not know who is in need of help because women are not asking for it, perhaps on account of fear or shame. They'd be ashamed if their relatives, friends, or neighbours knew that they were being battered by their husband or live-in boyfriend, so they try to hide it by making up excuses about why they have scars on their face or body.

There are people out there who are capable of helping, but they need to know who you are. Exercise your voice, like you haven't used it for years. Holler out, "I'm just not taking it anymore," and pick up the phone and dial that number. They are waiting for your call. They want to help. Once an abusive relationship begins, it doesn't usually end. Some women and children come to a drastic ends when their abuser becomes their killer.

CHAPTER 32
Who's to Blame for Abuse?

Speaking of abusers, consider some of the special care homes that have sprouted up all over the country. If you think that some people who live in these residences are not abused in some form or another, you would be wrong. Abusers work in many professions. Abusers are a bit like thieves; they come in many forms. They steal the innocence from people, as well as their willpower to do anything about their situation. I consider some grown-ups to be a bit like children who, at a young age, were continually told by their parents that they couldn't do a thing correctly. No matter how hard the child tried to satisfy the parent, it was never good enough. Instead of helping to build their confidence, parents continuously degraded the child's efforts. Typically, the child grows up with very little confidence because of the manner in which he was brought up.

Thousands of young people walk around staring at their feet; they avoid making eye contact with anyone. Too often, that behaviour is because of the drugs they are continuously given by doctors. Eventually, a young person becomes dependent on the drugs and continues using them. Doctors find so many reasons to feed them drugs. If a child is a bit hyper, he or she is given some form of drug; if children have low self-esteem, they are given another drug to help them cope with their everyday activities. Doctors are not always to blame. If teachers and parents have a problem coping with the children, often the first thing they think of is to take him or her to a doctor. Over the years, I have met a few psychiatrists who I felt were a bit weird themselves and might themselves have been in need of some form of help.

I find it very sad when senior citizens who are unable to fend for themselves and younger people who have some form of disabilities end up living in such places and are mistreated. I'm very bothered by the fact that many seniors are forced to live in such homes by family members. As children grew up to be adults, their parents were always there for them, but when the parent got older and needed their help and understanding, it was a different story. Many seniors who want to live out their last years in their own homes, which they had known all their lives, are forced to live out their remaining years in these institutions.

I believe some were actually better off living in these senior homes, because they had someone taking care of them who cared about their well-being, which had to be better than living alone, in a situation where no one cared. I wonder what would happen to all the elderly and younger people in need of special care if there weren't such senior and special care homes.

It would be wrong for me to say that workers at most of the seniors and special care places are abusive—I know that it isn't the case. But people in management sometimes take their personal problems to work with them and take their frustration out on employees. What if a special care worker did the same; who would he or she take out their frustration upon?

Some elders and special needs people are afraid to tell someone that they are being abused. Perhaps they just don't know how to go about getting help, so they say nothing, even to family members. A good number who may have been abused forget about it within minutes, because they haven't the ability to remember things. Take the woman who asked for my help in finding out if her elderly mother who lived in a senior home was being mistreated. She said that on a few occasions when she went to visit her mother, she noticed that during each visit, a certain care worker came into her room; her mother would stop talking and keep her eyes on the worker till she left the room. She seemed afraid of her, but when another worker came into her room, the daughter noticed that her mother seemed more relaxed and talkative. On one visit, the mother said to her daughter after the problematic care worker had left her room, "She hurts me." That's when the daughter began to wonder if that care worker was actually mistreating her mother. She decided to hire a private investigator to check it out. I told the daughter that there wasn't much that I could do and asked her if she had talked to the management. She said no; before she did so, she wanted to know if her mother was actually being mistreated. I asked if she had seen any bruises on her mother's body, such as the arm or shoulder areas. She answered no, she hadn't noticed any. I mentioned that even if she had seen bruising, it would be hard to blame it on the worker, because elderly people tend to bruise easily. It doesn't take much pressure to leave a bruise on an arm. It could be also that the mother didn't like that certain worker; maybe she wasn't as gentle with her as the other care workers. Maybe that's why she complained that she was being hurt by her.

I told the daughter to do a bit of checking on her own, to see if her mother had bruises on any part of her body and to try to get information from the mother as to why she had said that she was being hurt. After some checking on her own, if she felt that she still needed help, then she should get in touch with me. I never heard from the daughter again. Maybe she found that the mother was just acting up, because of her dislike for the care worker. Yes, some care workers abuse seniors and special needs people, but the question is which ones take their frustrations out on those who are in need of special care?

If a concerned member of the family questions the management regarding abuse, the first thing they will be told is, "Oh, not here! We don't tolerate care workers being rough with clients." My answer to that is, "Oh, yeah?"

Another fact we must keep in mind is that many of the elders who reside in such homes are continuously being fed drugs to keep them from being too hyper. After a while they become zombie-like, passing time, just waiting to die. Whenever I see young people walking around the streets continuously staring down at their feet, I wonder what kind of drugs they are on—and I am not referring to illegal drugs. I am referring to drugs prescribed by doctors.

In 1978, a year after Jan left, she applied for and was granted a divorce. At the time, our oldest son, Brad, rather than going to college, chose to join the armed forces and was selected to go to military college. Our two younger sons, Cloyd and Bill, stayed with their mother and continued on in school. I recall the day that Brad phoned me at work and told me that he had joined the army. At the time, I was a bit disappointed because I thought he was going to go to college. When I asked him why he chose to join the army instead of going to college, his answer was, "Right now, I don't know what I want to do with my life, but I know that the army will make a man of me." Later, I would see that he was right, especially when he was chosen to go to military college for five years.

Shortly after the divorce, I met with my sons and told them that it wasn't their mother's fault that things didn't work out between us and that I was to blame. Years later, I would be glad that I did tell them that I was to blame and not their mother, because they always remembered what I had said. As for Jan being their mother, the best words that I could use to describe her parenting are: "Her life was our boys." Without her love and guidance, our sons wouldn't be what they are today, loving and caring. After the divorce Jan and I continued being friends.

CHAPTER 33
Life After Jan: The Mafia's Offer

It wasn't long after the divorce that things began changing for the worse. As previously mentioned, I would often have a drink to help forget my problems. Late one night, while I sat at a bar I hadn't been in before, a man came up to me and said that Mr. Cotroni wanted to see me at his table. When he said Mr. Cotroni, I knew it was Frank, now the head of the Montreal Mafia. I hadn't noticed him because the lights in the rear of the club weren't bright. From the bar, I couldn't make out who were seated at the tables. When I approached Frank's table, he said to me, "You're Fred? I said yes. "Sit," he replied, "I want to talk with you." I sat, and he asked if I wanted a drink. He said that he owned the club. He then said, "Fred, were you once in the collection business with Chuck?" I agreed. "Well," said Frank, "I am interested in getting into the collection business." Hearing him say that, I could have laughed, because he was already involved in collecting money, but not legally.

"I want to open up a collection agency, and I want you to come in with me as a partner and operate it for me. I'll put up the money to get it going."

As soon as he said he wanted to get into the collection business with me, I knew that I wasn't interested. So I quickly answered, "I now operate my own security agency, and I am doing well."

"Look, Fred," he said, "with me, you'll make a lot of money—you'll be the boss and take care of things."

I felt like saying, "Oh yeah? It may begin that way, but I am sure it will not end that way." Instead, I said, "Yeah, it sounds good, but I'll need a little more time to think about it. I just can't up and leave my business."

"That's okay," said Frank. "Once you get the collection agency up and going, we can include your security business with it."

When he mentioned that, I acted a bit excited and said, "Yeah! That will be real good, having the collection and the security agency together."

"We are talking big money," said Frank.

One thing I was sure of was that I wanted to get out of there. I couldn't just suddenly get up and leave, so I said to him, "That is very interesting, but like I said, I'll need a little time."

"No problem," said Frank, handing me his phone number. "You give me a call in a couple of weeks and we'll meet to set things up." Frank spoke as if I had already said yes, which I hadn't.

I said, "I will be in touch with you in a couple of weeks," then I left the club, very glad to walk away from there. If there was anyone that I didn't want to get involved in with any manner, it was Frank Cotroni, the crime boss. If I did, I was sure that it would eventually mean death for me. I could end up at the bottom of the St. Lawrence with cement shoes on.

For the next few days, I thought about how I was going to go about telling Frank that I wasn't interested in his offer. One would think that was simple—just give him a phone call and tell him no. But it wasn't that simple, because when you get an offer from the likes of Frank, especially when he wants you to go in business with him, if you refuse, that could be an insult to him. I thought of the movie *The Godfather*. In one scene the Godfather, played by Marlon Brando, is asked to help a person find a part in a movie that he had previously been refused. When Brando agrees to take care of it, the man who asked for help says, "What if he says no?" The Godfather looks at him and says, "I'll make him an offer that he can't refuse." Thinking back to that scene made Frank's offer a bit scary for me.

Not knowing how I was going to handle the situation with Frank, I called Marc. When I told him about Frank's offer, he didn't hesitate over his answer. "Fred, once you get involved with Frank, you will never get out."

I asked, "How do you think he will take it when I tell him no, that I'm not interested in his offer?"

Marc said, "If you don't want to tell him no, the best thing to do is to call Frank and tell him that you need a few months, because you have other work commitments. Wait to see what happens. In the meantime, he may just forget about it. But stay away from that club. It's being used as a front; you'll have nothing but trouble there." I replied that if I had known that Frank operated the club, I wouldn't have gone in.

When it came time to call Frank and give him my answer, I phoned. When I asked for him, I was told that he wasn't there. I asked the person to give Mr. Cotroni the message that Fred had called and said that he would need a few months because of other commitments before he makes up his mind regarding his offer.

After I hung up, I was glad that Frank wasn't there. I said that I would call him, and I had. I felt that I had a few months to decide about what I was going to do regarding his offer. I already knew my answer would be no. I was sorry that I hadn't told him that I wasn't interested in his offer at the time, instead of letting him believe that I might be.

People like Mr. Cotroni and others who are involved in organized crime try to get in other legal businesses to use as fronts for their illegal activities. If they tried to get a licence from the justice department to operate a collection or security agency, they would be refused. That is why people like Frank Cotroni try to get someone like me to apply and register the business under their name; they hide their involvement by being a silent partner. As with Chuck, in the beginning they may be silent, but they soon end up being the voice of the business. When you think of if, what better type of business is there to get into, if you are a mobster, than the private security and collection business?

A year before my meeting with Frank Cotroni that night at his club, he and other members of his crime family were under investigation for the murder of a fellow crime member, Paolo Violi, who was invited to a friendly card game at a bar he once owned. As he sat with his back to the rear of the club, two masked men entered the back door and shot Violi. The men who did the shooting were later arrested for the killing; it was determined that the Cotroni family had no direct link to the killing.

Back in the mid 70s, the Quebec Government had set up a Commission of Inquiry on organized crime activities in Montreal. When Vincent Cotroni was summoned before the crime probe, he, along with others, said that they didn't know the meaning of *Mafia*. When Mr. Cotroni was asked to explain about his business activities, he told the Commission that he was in the cheese business, and he wasn't involved with any Montreal criminal organization. The cheese company which Mr. Cotroni mentioned was well known and did business in the Maritime provinces with most of the restaurants and pizza outlets.

The Quebec Commission of Inquiry proved to be fatal for some members of crime families, such as Paolo Violi and others who had fallen into disgrace within the criminal organization. As with Violi and others, they were killed.

In the 80s, crime families like Frank's made fortunes by shipping tons of illegal drugs from other countries, using the Maritime provinces as a drop off and then arranging to have the drugs shipped to other parts of Canada and the United States. In the early 80s, I noticed many delivery trucks travelling through New Brunswick and other parts of the Atlantic East Coast from

Montreal delivering restaurant products belonging to the cheese company Mr. Cotroni told the Crime Commission he was involved with. I thought to myself, *That would be an easy way for drug dealers to get their drugs out of the Maritimes, using delivery trucks back and forth from Montreal.*

Years later, as many as thirty men were arrested in a massive Montreal drug bust; among those reported in the news was none other than alleged Mafia boss Frank Cotroni, whom the police described as one of the most powerful drug smugglers in the world. I wonder what happened to the cheese and restaurant supply business?

In those days, ordinary people like me didn't really understand how the Mafia operated, besides knowing that they were a powerful criminal organization. Years earlier, in Italia, the Sicilian Mafia made a good deal of their money from shaking down Italian businesses for protection. In the 20s when some Sicilians began emigrating to other countries, including the United States and Canada, they began to use the same extortion tactics as they had back home. If businesses, including restaurants or constructions companies, refused to pay them for protection, they would be threatened with bodily harm or have their business destroyed. As time went on, the Mafia became involved as administrators in many aspects of construction, such as the public works contracts and road building programs that boomed after the war. They also controlled the powerful unions; if any contractor refused their services, strikers would bring any project they were working on to a standstill.

Eventually the Mafia was making millions, if not billions, of dollars from their involvement with the construction business. Besides that, they were in many other rackets, including prostitution, gambling, loan sharking, rum running, and murder. Eventually, they got into the drug business, especially cocaine. At one time, their main source of income was extortion and the protection racket; once they were into drugs and arms trafficking, they needed outlets in the legal economy to launder their illegally earned money. When the Mafia got involved in drug trafficking, suddenly pizzerias, which were being used as fronts for the Mafia, sprouted up all over the United States and Canada. The same was true for restaurants and night clubs they owned all over Montreal; that is where the heads of crime families would meet to plan their criminal activities.

In the United States, criminal organizations were in a fierce struggle for control over the illegal drug business, which lead to the killing of certain crime bosses and even members of their families, including women and children. This fierce struggle for power between the crime families continued for decades, till a wise Jewish Mafia leader named Meyer Lansky stepped in and gathered the Italian crime bosses and other powerful crime leaders from around the country together. Instead of killing each other off for control of the drug business, Lansky suggested that they form a national syndicate and share equally in the earnings of the drug trafficking business.

Meyer Lansky's group was known as the Kosher Mafia, because they were Jews. After Lansky laid out the plan for how the drug money could be equally shared among the crime families, it was agreed by the leaders that murdering for control would stop, and each crime family would share equally. Lansky, who was known as the Brain, pulled strings, and then the National Crime Syndicate was formed. Some groups, such as the Sicilians, didn't like being involved and hated gangsters of other ethnicities, such as the Jews, and were looking forward to the day when they could get rid of them.

The Sicilian bosses didn't like sharing with the Jewish Mafia. Shortly after the crime syndicate was formed, Lansky plotted with another crime boss to get rid of two older members who showed bigotry. Lansky felt they were counter-productive and that there was no room in the underworld for such leaders. Later Joe the Boss Masserea and Salvatore Maranzano would be gunned down, along with other members who the syndicate felt were no longer needed.

While murders, drug trafficking, and other illegal activists were being carried out by the crime bosses, FBI Director Hoover was continually glorified by the news media for his actions against public enemies like Dillinger, who was gunned down by the FBI, and others, like Ma Barker and Pretty Boy Floyd, who were active gangsters. Each time one of them was killed by the FBI, Hoover was glorified, but he avoided fighting organized crime and the Mafia. He went after targets that were more easily hit than the Mafia, and each time the news media would write about him as if he were some kind of hero.

It was said that Hoover paid so little attention to organized crime that he could be accused of dereliction of duty. Hoover thought that organized crime was a bit exaggerated and constituted no immediate danger to Americans. So he devoted his efforts to lesser criminals while the news media continued to glorify him. But history would show that Hoover wasn't as good an FBI Director as he was made out to be by the news media. Hoover's devotion to duty within the FBI has always been a bit exaggerated. While his men were out searching for less dangerous crime people than the Mafia, Hoover would often be seen out at the race track placing sure bets on races after getting solid tips from a Mafia boss that the race was fixed.

When Robert Kennedy was appointed attorney general in 1961, he pushed Hoover off his ass to go after crime organizations such as the Mafia. Up until then, Hoover denied the existence of organized crime. Robert Kennedy got the FBI to go after the Cosa Nostra, a Mafia organization with what was known as a Capo Di Capi—Boss of Bosses. Until he resigned as attorney general,

Kennedy kept the pressure on Hoover to go after these known criminal organizations. Once he resigned, Hoover eased up on the bosses of criminal organizations like the Mafia and the Cosa Nostra. After Hoover's death in 1972, the true facts regarding his friendship with certain crime bosses were reported by the news media. Why weren't these facts regarding Hoover's connection with the crime bosses reported earlier while he ran the FBI and directed other FBI members to go after less known criminals? I believe the answer to that question was that even the news reporters feared Hoover's power. If not, why were activities such as his meetings and lunches with crime bosses not brought to the attention of the public by news reporters till after his death? I believe it was fear of Hoover's retribution. When you think of it, back then, what news reporter in his right mind would want to make known to the public anything negative regarding the two most powerful organizations in the world—namely the FBI and the Mafia? It wasn't until later years, when new technology became available to crime fighters, that they seriously went after such criminal organizations.

At the time, listening bugs that they had placed on their phones were the sources of information that the FBI was gathering to use against the organized criminals. They hid other bugging devices in places like flower pots, lamp shades, and under tables. When the crime bosses learned of the electronic bugs that the FBI were using to gather evidence to use against them in courts, they became more careful about where they met to discuss business. Often their business meetings would be held out on sidewalks, where there was a lot of noise from the traffic going by. If there was a bug planted nearby, the FBI would then have trouble hearing precisely what was being said. They would also meet in open areas like beaches, places where it would be hard for anyone to hear their conversation. The FBI went as far as using lip readers, who spied through binoculars.

After years of gathering evidence on the crime families, the big break came for the FBI when they managed to get one of the crime leaders to talk about the criminal activities within the Mafia. That was when different Mafia criminal organizations began to crumble. After the first crime boss began spilling his guts to the FBI, others did the same. That allowed them to make special deals with the FBI so they could get lighter sentences when they were brought up in front of a judge to answer for their crimes. The same took place in Canada. Today, a good number of past Mafia criminals all over the country are now running legitimate businesses. One of your neighbours who keeps a low profile and is always in church may be one of those past Mafia criminals.

With so many leaders of crime families brought to justice and convicted, one might think that the Mafia has been wiped out, but that isn't so. The crime families are still around and very active; the big difference is that the leaders who are now involved haven't got the brains that the older generation of Mafia leaders had. They are still earning big money in drug trafficking and other illegal activities, but that can't compare to the billions that the Mafia earned with their crime syndicate in earlier years.

After the death of the Philippines' ousted president and dictator Ferdinand Marcos in 1989, his wife Imelda was denounced by the U.S. president for appearing on different TV talk shows and boasting about her wealth and her exclusive collection of over three thousand pairs of shoes. In 1993, four years later, two Montreal Mafia members were trying to liquidate three billion dollars' worth of gold that belonged to her late husband. If the money rightfully belonged to the Marcos' and was legally earned, why were members of the Montreal Mafia involved in trying to liquidate it? The three billion that the Montreal Mafia was trying to get rid of was nothing compared to what the Marcos family had taken out of the Philippines when they went into exile in 1986, receiving safe passage to Hawaii from President Regan's administration. The custom agents discovered twenty-four suitcases of gold bricks and certificates for gold bullion valued in the billions of dollars. It was reported that while in power in the Philippines, Marcos had embezzled more than thirty billion dollars. The Marcos' had property investments in various cities in the United States worth hundreds of millions. And some in law enforcement say that crime doesn't pay—who are they kidding? Crime pays big time—just don't get caught.

Over the years, Canada has had its own thieves in various agencies of the federal government who pocketed millions, along with their business cronies. In Quebec alone, businessmen who had connections within the federal government fraudulently obtained millions of dollars of the taxpayers' money without doing a bit of work. Contracts were handed out by the government, and falsified invoices were sent in and paid. When that scandal was brought to the attention of the public, our government leaders suddenly set up a commission to investigate the accusations of wrongdoing by certain members within the government. The investigation cost the taxpayers millions of dollars. And when the commission had completed its lengthy investigation, what actually happened to those crooks who had bilked the government out of millions with their illegal acts? When they were charged and brought before the courts, one government agency leader, who had invested his embezzled money in a huge ranch in the United States, stated that he couldn't afford a lawyer to defend himself. Out of all the crooks involved, only a couple served any time in jail.

Let's say that I was an employee of the government and had the opportunity to embezzle a great deal of money from government funds. If I knew that if I were caught and brought before the courts for my crime and convicted, I would only have to serve a year or less in jail—would I commit the crime? Yes, I would. After all, I am not killing anyone. I am just stealing some of the taxpayers' money. If I have to serve a year in jail, so what? In the end, I will still have my millions. Who in their right mind wouldn't opt to serve a year or less in jail in exchange for a couple million?

Corrupt politicians, federally and provincially, pocket a good deal of the taxpayers' money. What has the taxpayer to say regarding these forms of theft within our government agencies? Nothing, really. Some of the lesser corrupt politicians are later re-elected back into power. Could it be that the voters who help re-elect these crooks had a memory lapse when it came to voting? Did they forget about their illegal deeds?

I hear politicians continuously boast that "I am for the people." A politician might be 10 percent for the people and 90 percent for himself. Some people seem to forget that our government and its agencies are businesses, like any large corporation. The only difference between them is the government is funded by the taxpayers' money, and who's in charge of all that money? Our government leaders, who are the "people," and as long as we have people deciding where our money goes, you can be assured that somehow a good number of dollars will find their way into their own pockets. This is done in many devious ways. Again, we must bear in mind that if you take something that doesn't rightfully belong to you, you are committing an act of theft, and many within our government agencies are doing just that. They can all be described by one simple word: *thief.*

At the time, Montreal was considered the key centre of organized crime activities in Canada, including the Dubois brothers and groups of French Canadian mobsters, the West End gang, the Irish gangs, the Hell's Angels, the Asian groups, and the Colombians. But the most dominant and influential of all crime groups, in every aspect, were the Italians.

After hearing so much about these crime families, especially the Mafia, I decided to learn a bit more about the word itself. What I found was rather interesting. In the dictionary *Mafia* is defined as an international criminal organization, but it didn't start out that way. I traced the word to when it was first used by the Sicilians in Palermo, Italy, back in 1552. A struggle for power and territory took place between France and Italy, as well as other major states of Western Europe. One night as a young Sicilian girl was walking home from a chapel where she was to be married a week later, she was raped and murdered by a French army sergeant. Sicilians got together to avenge her death; the plan was to kill as many French army men as they could. They roamed around after dark. Whenever they met a Frenchman, they would slit his throat. They discovered that they had mistakenly killed one of their own, so they made up a password to use whenever they met up with someone in the dark of the night. The password they made up was *Mafia*; each letter had a meaning. *M* was *Mortie*; *A* was *All*; *F* was *Frenchmen*; *I* was *Italian*; and *A* represented the name of the girl who was raped and murdered, Anila. As the men roamed the village searching for French army men to kill, instead of saying "Hello," they would say "Mafia." If the person they met repeated the word back, they would then know that the person was one of their own and not a Frenchman.

After the many wars of that era, especially between Italy and other European countries, were over and the killings had stopped; the word *Mafia* was forgotten. Years later local hoods began to threaten shopkeepers with extortion. If the shopkeepers refused to pay protection money, the criminals would damage their stores. Seeing what was happening in their community, a group of Sicilian men got together to help those shop owners. When the group was formed, they referred to themselves as the Mafia. Whenever the hoods went after shop owners for protection money, the group now known as the Mafia would step in to help, and they didn't charge the shop owners for their services.

So in the beginning, the Mafia was an asset to the community, not the murderous criminal organization we now know. After generations of family had passed on, some of the younger generation of Sicilians came up with the idea to charge shop owners for their protection service. Eventually, the groups of Sicilian men known as the Mafia branched out into other illegal activities. Besides extortion, they got involved in thievery and prostitution. Centuries later, after getting into drug trafficking, they would come to be known as the most powerful and dangerous crime organization in the world. As time went on, many other criminal groups, such as the Jewish and French, would be formed and would also be referred to as the Mafia, but none was known to be more dangerous than the Italian Mafia. They had the power and capability to buy off police chiefs and bribe city officials and judges, as well as people who held high positions in private corporations. If their "hit men" were charged with murder, if a lone judge decided on their guilt, not a selected jury, often the verdict was not guilty, because the judge had been paid off. In one well-publicized case, a hit man was found not guilty for killing a person and was set free. The lawyer who acted on behalf of the Mafia later confessed to authorities that he had paid the judge $10,000 to find the killer not guilty. Once that was made public, the killer was retried and found guilty for the crime. The judge who took the bribe committed suicide. No one was beyond their reach. The Italian Mafia became the untouchables.

Getting back to Frank Cotroni and his offer regarding the collection business—I stayed away from his club and avoided any contact with him. Four months passed, and I didn't call him again, as I said I would. He hadn't tried to get in touch with me, and I figured that he had forgotten or found someone else to go into the collection business with.

One night, more than a year later, a friend and I happened to stop in at the Métropole Café on Ste Catherine Street for a few drinks. We arrived at the club around nine; a couple of hours later, while we were sitting at the bar, I noticed a group of men come in. One was Frank Cotroni. As soon as I recognized him, a bit of fear came over me, and I said to my friend, "Drink up—we're leaving." Before we could leave, Frank noticed me at the bar. He stopped directly behind me. Touching my shoulder, he said, "You didn't call me like you said you would."

I turned around and said, "Yes, I did call, and I left a message for you."

"Bullshit!" he answered. "That was a year ago."

He stood there with a couple of his men, and I didn't know what to say to him. The others who had come in with him had gone over and sat at a table.

"So what's happening?" he asked.

I said to him, "I told you when we spoke that I was operating my own business and was busy."

"Look, Fred, when I tell someone I am going to do something, I do it. You told me that in a couple of weeks you were going to get back to me, and you didn't. Right now, I am here for a meeting, and I haven't got time to listen to bullshit and excuses, so you give me a call." One of his men was arguing with a couple of other men seated next to them, so he quickly left and walked over to their table.

I didn't hesitate; we left our drinks on the bar and walked out.

I would learn that later the same night, Frank and about thirty of his goons walked into the Chezparee Club and smashed up the place, causing thirty thousand dollars' worth of damage. Over the years, I have often said that I fear no man, but I did fear Frank Cotroni—I would have been crazy not to. Many referred to Frank as the Big Guy, and they had good reasons. He was not only big in size, he was also big in the Montreal crime racket. After hearing what he had done to the Chezparee Club, I made up my mind to call him and get it over with. I decided to tell him that I couldn't accept his offer because I would soon be leaving Montreal and returning to New Brunswick.

At the time, I had no intention of leaving Montreal. I made up the excuse because I hoped it was an easy way to get rid of him. When I mentioned that

I was leaving Montreal, he asked, "What about your security business?" I told him I was selling it. "Okay," he said, "I'll buy it."

For a few moments, I didn't know what to say. He added, "I'll buy it on the condition that you leave it registered under your name."

Finally I got the nerve to tell him, "When it's sold, I will be removing my name as an operator." I could tell by his voice that he didn't like what he heard.

He said, "You didn't sell it yet?"

"No," I answered, "but someone wants to take it over." The conversation with Frank ended when he told me that he was having a meeting; he would get back to me later.

I knew I would be crazy to sell him the business and leave my name as owner and operator, but I did consider it, knowing how eager he was to get into the security business. I was tempted, because I believed I could get a good deal of money from him if I did what he wanted. But just talking with Frank made me think of death, and that put fear in me. Months went by. I didn't hear from him.

Then late one night, I received a phone call from Paul, a friend who owned a bar and restaurant in Park Extension. He asked if I could come over because he was having trouble with a couple of drunks he had previously barred from the place. I didn't feel like going, and I was a bit tired after a hard day. I wasn't in a good mood. I told Paul that I would stop by.

Paul and I were close friends; he was a Greek in his sixties. He wasn't well and had heart problems, so one night over a few drinks, I told him that if he ever needed me to give me a call. Later, I would be sorry that I said that. Over the years I had become a close friend with many Greeks and Italians who operated legitimate businesses. Most of these friends operated restaurants and pizzerias and were honest, hard workers. Some would work seventeen to eighteen hours a day to keep their businesses in operation, and I knew some were paying for protection.

Arriving at Paul's place, I sat at the bar and ordered a drink from the waitress, who was also serving tables in the restaurant section. I told her to tell Paul, who was back in the kitchen, that I was there. When he came out, he nodded toward a table where two men, who looked in their early thirties, sat. I said to Paul, "What's the problem?"

He said, "These same guys came in a couple of weeks ago and threatened the waitress if she didn't serve them free food and drinks. Eventually they walked out without paying, and when they returned a few nights ago, I asked them to leave or I would call the cops. They left, saying they would be back." Paul mentioned that whenever he had trouble, he would try and handle it himself rather than call the police. Seeing that they had drinks on the table,

I asked Paul if they paid for their drinks. Paul said, "Yes, but only when the waitress refused to serve them if they didn't pay right away."

I sat at the bar for fifteen or twenty minutes observing them. They began to get loud and bothered other customers. It seemed that they were trying to stir up trouble. It was a Friday night, so there were many people in the place. I asked Paul, "If you barred the pair, why are they being served?" He said that when they came in, the waitress was busy and had forgotten that they were barred. So she served them. By the time he had noticed them drinking at the table, it was too late, because they had already been served.

Because the two were trying to stir up trouble, I told Paul to tell the waitress not to serve them anymore drinks. Through the mirror at the bar, I watched their reactions as they ordered another round of drinks and were refused. One kicked a chair and stood up, demanding that they be served. I got up from the bar, walked over to their table, and said to the one who had kicked the chair, "You are not going to be served—you have to leave."

The one who was still seated quickly stood, kicked his chair back, said, "Who the f*** are you?" and grabbed for my throat. As he did I swung at him and got him on the chin, which drove him back onto his chair. The other fellow grabbed hold of me. As we struggled, we both fell to the floor. Just as I reached up with my right hand to grab hold of the table to pull myself up, the other one, whom I had punched, picked up a chair and brought it down heavily on my hand on top of the table. I felt the pain quickly shoot up my arm. I managed to pull myself up and step back from the two. With my damaged right hand, I knew that I had to act quickly. The one advantage I had was that they weren't very steady on their feet because of their drinking. Seeing that their backs were to the doorway, to distract them I said, "Here come the police!"

When they heard the word *police*, they turned around to face the door, which gave me the opportunity to quickly punch at both of them. I dropped one to the floor with a punch to the side of his face. As for the fellow who struck my hand with the chair, I managed to grab his long hair, and I smashed his face heavily down on the table a few times. Blood gushing from his face, he slowly slid to the floor. I stood over them; when they tried to get up, I continued pounding them with my fist. When I realized that I had no feeling in my right hand, I kneed one in the face as he tried to get up. The one whose face I had smashed on the table was bleeding badly. I reached down and grabbed hold of him and forced him out the door to the street. I did the same to the other one, but him I dragged him across the floor and out onto the sidewalk.

I was still furious about being struck with the chair, and I wasn't finished with them yet. Seeing a garbage container attached to a nearby hydro pole, I took hold of one of them and tried to shove him head first into the garbage container. As I was trying to force him in, I noticed an approaching police car. Dropping him, I returned to the restaurant, sat at the bar, and gulped down the shot of rye I had left here. From where I sat, I could see the police through the window helping the fellow that I had tried to stuff in the garbage can. The other guy took off down the street. When Paul served me another drink, I said, "If the police ask what happened, tell them that the two were causing trouble and for no reason punched me in the face." I could see in the mirror that I had a few light bruises on my face. I was more concerned about my hand. I had no feeling in it, and it was swelling up.

One of the police officers stayed outside; the other came in and spoke with customers seated in the restaurant section. I sat there, quietly sipping my drink. Paul went over and spoke to the officer. A few minutes later the policeman walked over with Paul to where I sat. Laughing, the officer said to me, "Did you think you could get him in the garbage can?"

I looked at him and said, "Well, I tried."

The officer said, "Paul and the other customers told me what happened. You had a right to defend yourself." Before he left, the cop said, "Be careful of those guys. Tonight you may have been lucky; the next time, you may not be so fortunate."

After the police had driven away, taking the fellow with them, I said to Paul, "I need to go to the hospital. I believe he broke my hand with the chair." Paul drove me to the hospital and X-rays were taken. I was told that I had a badly damaged hand. One of my knuckles was shattered, and smaller bones and ligaments in the back of my hand were also severely damaged. The doctor said that my hand needed surgery and for me to return to the hospital in the morning. In the meantime, I was to take the pain killers he had given me and keep an ice pack on my hand to try and get some swelling down before the surgery.

I had no business going over to help Paul. When he called I should have told him to get the police to take care of the problem. But as always, I was trying to help someone and really didn't know why, besides the fact that I didn't like elderly people like Paul being pushed around by these hoods.

The following morning, after little sleep due to the pain, I returned to the hospital to have the surgery. When it was over, I was told that a part of one of my knuckles had to be removed and that I had some damaged nerve tissue in the back of my hand, along with a few small bone fractures. The doctor said that I might not have the full use of my hand again, but he would have to wait for the hand to heal a bit before he could tell the full extent of the damage.

I was devastated to think that I might not have the full use of my hand; being right-handed, I couldn't visualize being able to function without it. Pain

I could endure, but constantly thinking about not being able to fully use my hand bothered me greatly. In four weeks, I would return to the hospital to have the cast removed. While my hand was healing, I would touch the tips of my fingers—I could feel a bit with my fourth finger and thumb, but as for the other fingers, there was barely any feeling.

While at home recuperating, I received some more disturbing news. I got a call from Paul saying that he had been told by one of the customers the night of the fight at his restaurant that the two goons were part of a group that went around causing trouble to get the owners to pay for protection. I asked Paul if they had tried to get money from him. He said no, only free drinks and food. Then he added that around the time these guys began to come in to his place, he had received a phone call from a man who had asked if he was having any problems with rowdy customers. When Paul asked why he was asking, he was told if he did have trouble, they would take care of things for him. Paul said he realized then that the man was looking for protection money. After he told the caller that he wasn't interested, the two started to show up, causing trouble. I asked Paul if they had come around again since that night. He said no, but the next night he did receive a phone call from the man who had previously called. The man told Paul that it wasn't over with and hung up without saying more. That was the way those guys operated. They would send punks to try to instigate fights with customers and then smash up the place, as Frank and his men did at the Chezparee Club.

I was concerned about my hand. When the time came to return to the hospital and have the cast removed, I was very discouraged, and more so after the cast was taken off. The doctor asked me to try and close my hand, which I could barely do; he then had me try and hold a pen that he placed in my hand. I couldn't; it dropped out of my hand—I didn't have the power to hold my hand closed. As the doctor had mentioned, I might have incurred permanent damage. It seemed that some tiny bones in the back of my hand hadn't healed together correctly. As for the damaged nerve tissue, the doctor said that once I began having therapy involving exercise of the hand, I might get some power and feeling back in my fingers.

After returning to the hospital a few times for therapy, where I did little besides hold a soft rubber ball in my hand and squeeze it, I told the therapist that I could do that at home without having to go to the hospital. Each day for a couple of hours I would use the rubber ball. After a few weeks without any success, I was very discouraged. One day as I was reading the newspaper, I got an idea. I folded the newspaper and laid it on the table and tried to tear the folded paper using both hands. Each time, the paper slid out of my right hand because I couldn't close my hand firmly enough to grasp the paper. Over and over again, I continued trying to tear the paper and failed.

Chapter 34
Going Within

I sat there looking at my hand, not believing that I wouldn't have the full use of it again. I thought of my mother and something she had always said: if you want something to happen, pray. She strongly believed in the power of prayers. I wasn't a religious person, but I strongly believed in God, and thinking of my dead mother, I began praying. I continuously repeated the prayer "Our father whom art in heaven" as I attempted to rip the newspaper. Finding that prayer a bit too long, I made one up, which was short and simple. As I repeatedly tried, I would pray, "Holy Mary, mother of God, please help heal my hand." I repeated that simple prayer over and over again, asking for her help. For some reason—I didn't know why—I strongly felt that she would help. At night before I fell asleep, I repeated that prayer.

One night a week or so after I began asking Mary for help, I suddenly awoke in the middle of the night. Something in my mind was telling me to go downstairs and tear the newspaper. After a few moments, I got out of bed and went downstairs and picked up the paper that was lying on the table. When I first tried to tear it, I couldn't, but on my second attempt, I managed to tear the newspaper. Then I sat and cried, thanking Holy Mary for what she had done. For the rest of the night, I sat there tearing papers and repeating the prayer. After I got some sleep, I went out and bought a few newspapers and continued tearing them up in small pieces.

When I ran out of newspapers to tear, I began using pages from the phone book. By that time, I was only able to tear about ten pages at a time. As days became weeks, my hand got stronger, and feeling was slowly returning to my fingers. I gradually regained enough power in my hand to tear twenty or more pages. Maybe to someone else that may not have seemed like much, but to me, it was amazing. When I had no more phone books to use, I went out looking for some. One day as I was on my way to a nearby store, I noticed a parked Bell Telephone truck. I went over and asked the driver if he had a couple of spare phone books. He said no and asked why I wanted them. I lifted my hand up and said I used them to exercise my damaged hand. He asked, "How does a phone book help your hand?" I told him I tore the pages to help strengthen my hand. Again looking at my hand, he said, "I can't give you new phone books to tear." I thanked him and began to walk away. He called out and asked where I lived. I told him just down the street. "Okay," he said, "give me your address, and I see if I can get you a few." A few hours later, I heard a knock on my door. I opened it and there stood the phone man with an armful of phone books. "Here," he said, "these are old ones we don't need. That should do you for a while." I thanked him and offered him a few dollars, but he wouldn't take the money. As he left, he smiled and said, "When you are able to tear one, let me know." I laughed and said I would. I didn't know at the time that with continuous prayers and a positive attitude, the day would come when I would not only be able to tear a Montreal phone book in half, but also in three parts.

In the process of healing, I made many promises to the Virgin Mary; one was that if she helped me, some day I would help others. Even when I was driving my car, I would exercise my hand by gripping on the steering wheel and closing it as hard as I was able to. Each time, I would repeat the prayer, asking the Holy Mother to help.

I received a call from Paul telling me to be careful because a couple of men had been in asking questions about me. I moved out of the area where I had been living and kept busy travelling to different areas of the province, investigating fraudulent insurance claims. My hand healed quite nicely, but the damage would always be noticeable.

I stayed away from Paul's bar and restaurant and the Park Extension area. When I stopped by one of the stores where I had security officers working, I spent very little time there. At one Canadian Tire store, which was located up near the Extension, I was told that a man who was in shopping had asked the security officer if I was around. The officer described the man, saying that he had a long knife scar on his face. I knew it was Bobby.

A few days later, I called Bobby. Like Paul, he told me to be careful. Bobby said that there was talk around the clubs in the Extension that the two guys I had fought with worked for the Cotroni family. I didn't know the extent of their damages until Bobby mentioned that he had heard that one of them needed surgery because of a shattered nose. He also said that Lenny had asked him if he knew where I lived; because Lenny had no reason to ask, he felt that Lenny wanted to know so he could pass the information on. When he asked about my hand, I didn't go into details other than to tell him that it was okay. Bobby said that I shouldn't have gotten involved with these guys. "You may have beaten them, but in the end, you'll not come out a winner." I told Bobby that it had happened nine months before, so they might have forgotten about it by now. "Don't fool yourself," he answered. "Nine months or nine years, it doesn't matter; these guys don't forget. So far," he said, "you have been lucky that you haven't run into them. When you do, you better be prepared." I agreed with him. "Yeah," said Bobby, "you better, because if you thought that Tommy and his friend Lenny were dangerous, they are just amateurs compared with these guys." When I asked him if he was sure that the two fellows were associated with the Cotroni's, he said they were, but not directly with Frank; they were part of Frank's sons' gang, which was just as bad. Bobby said, "Fred, I should know because it was one of them who slashed my face with a knife."

I may have been a bit concerned when Paul had said that those guys were dangerous, but hearing it from Bobby, I knew that I had a much more serious problem than I had anticipated. I thought about what he had said about those guys not forgetting and that I should be prepared for what could happen when I met them again.

Over the years, I have managed to talk myself out of many situations, but knowing who I'd be dealing with, I felt that I wouldn't have a chance to do much talking, especially after what took place at Paul's restaurant. Different ideas entered my mind as to how I could go about dealing with the problem. One thought was to get it over with. I considered just going about my work; when I did meet up with them, I would have to suffer the consequences, and then it would be over with. After remembering what Bobby had said about them using a knife on him, I quickly forgot about that option. During the couple of weeks after I talked to Bobby, wherever I went, I carried a gun. If I ran into them and they pulled a knife on me, I would use the gun and kill them if I had to. With the type of gun I carried, I could empty a nine-shot magazine within a few seconds.

After two weeks of just going to work and returning home each night, staying away from clubs, I came to realize that I needed to do something else. Even though my sons weren't living with me, I thought back to when my youngest was shot at, when he was returning from school. I knew what I needed to do—leave Montreal. I felt that eventually I would kill or be killed.

I called Claude at Canadian Tire because he had once mentioned that if I ever wanted to get out of doing security work, he'd be interested in buying my business. After meeting with Claude and haggling, we finally settled on a price, and within two days, the security agency was transferred over to

Claude. But before selling it to him, because I had decided to move back to New Brunswick where I was originally from, I contacted the New Brunswick Justice Department in regard to licensing requirements. I was told by Chief Inspector Daley, who was with the New Brunswick Licensing Commission, that I would have no problem being licensed because I was already in the security business and licensed by the Quebec Justice Department.

Shortly after applying for and receiving licensing and work permits, I moved to New Brunswick, to the town in which I was born and had lived till the age of seventeen. I still had family ties there. I could have chosen other places in New Brunswick to work from, but I decided on that town after carefully checking into where it would be most feasible to start up a private investigating and security business. Shortly after arriving, I would learn that starting up a business in that town would not be as easy as I had anticipated. Previously, I was told by the Licensing Commission that there were no private investigators or security officers' licensed to operate in the town. As far as I knew, I was the only one legally licensed, but I soon learned from a local lawyer that other people around town were doing private security work.

The people involved were members of the town police force. It was said that some police officers were making more money on the side, tax free, moonlighting as private investigators and security officers, than they were earning as police officers. Besides moonlighting, it was rumoured that some were involved in other matters around town that were unbecoming to a police officer who had taken an oath to serve and protect.

The town had a population around thirteen thousand. Besides the police chief, there were twelve police officers. It was said that half of them were moonlighting as security guards and private detectives, directly in conflict of the New Brunswick Police and Private Investigators and Security Acts. The Security Service Act clearly stated that to perform private security work, one must be licensed and bonded and also have liability insurance, which those police officers had none of. Even though they were police officers, that did not give them the right to moonlight as security officers or private investigators.

Certain police officers were hiding behind their badges to carry on their illegal affairs. In the beginning, I had no interest in what certain members of the town police were involved in other than their involvement in performing private security work. How I went about dealing with that problem would eventually lead to a seventeen-year struggle between myself and the unscrupulous police officers, a struggle that would have long-lasting mental and emotional effects on all who were involved, plus a few scars here and there.